ORNAMENTAL & FIGURAL

NUTCRACKERS

AN IDENTIFICATION & VALUE GUIDE

Judith A. Rittenhouse

COLLECTOR BOOKS
A Division of Schroeder Publishing Co., Inc.

The current values in this book should be used only as a guide. They are not intended to set prices, which vary from one section of the country to another. Auction prices as well as dealer prices vary greatly and are affected by condition as well as demand. Neither the Author nor the Publisher assumes responsibility for any losses that might be incurred as a result of consulting this guide.

Searching For A Publisher?

We are always looking for knowledgeable people considered to be experts within their fields. If you feel that there is a real need for a book on your collectible subject and have a large comprehensive collection, contact us.

COLLECTOR BOOKS
P.O. Box 3009
Paducah, Kentucky 42002–3009

Printed by IMAGE GRAPHICS, INC., Paducah, Kentucky

DEDICATION

To the most wonderful people I know,
My Parents

On The Cover

Soldier with paper label on bottom of stand, ca. 1989. Label marked "Erzgebirgische Volkskunst" and "Made in German Democratic Republic, Expertic" 16" high, 5¼" across, 4" deep. $85.00 – 90.00.

Brass double-faced jester nutcracker. Probably English, early 1900s. Approximately $85.00.

Brass squirrel nutcracker with paper label on bottom marked "Made in Taiwan." Reproduction of earlier design. 4¼" high, 5¾" long, 2" across. Late 20th century. $15.00 – 25.00.

Wooden man nutcracker with separate stand. Painted and lacquered, probably Swiss or Tyrolean. Nutcracker - 8⅜" tall, 1½" across, 2" deep. Base - 5" long, 1⅝" across, ⅜" high. c. 1930s-1940s. $45.00 – 55.00.

Wooden jackdaw nutcracker with glass eyes. Stained and painted, 8⅝" high, 2⅛" across, 4½" deep including tail. English, c. 1860. $525.00 – 600.00.

Illustrations by: Renaissance Studios, Inc. of Parlin, NJ
Photography by: Tartaglia Photographic of Bloomfield, NJ
Book design: Karen Geary
Cover design: Beth Summers

ACKNOWLEDGMENTS

I wish to recognize those individuals who contributed greatly to this project by providing information, assistance and much-appreciated encouragement.

FAMILY AND FRIENDS for being supportive and caring during the writing of this book and for accompanying me on so many antiquing excursions to find new additions for my collection.

TYPISTS who worked on various stages of the manuscript: Amy Mehring, Kathy Liva, Joyce Vertun, and most notably Kathy Freestone who worked with me continuously for two years.

ILLUSTRATORS from Renaissance Studios, Inc. of Parlin, New Jersey, namely, Lisa Nocks and Brian Regal for their enthusiasm and artistry.

PHOTOGRAPHERS from Tartaglia Photographic of Bloomfield, New Jersey, namely, Victor Tartaglia, Joanne L. Tuchrello and Deborah L. Turi for their imaginative approach to photography.

BOB CAHN The Primitive Man, from Carmel, New York, who over the years found so many special nutcrackers for me.

EDWARD F. GALLENSTEIN Editor of *Chip Chats* magazine for his interest in this project.

BOB WARDLE Owner of The Straw Star Christmas Shop in New Hope, Pennsylvania, for sharing his knowledge of German nutcrackers.

MICHAEL GESCHLECHT Owner of the Boro Art Center in Metuchen, New Jersey, for his expertise on a wide array of antiques topics.

GLENN McANDREWS Writer of the column "Patent Penning" in *Antique Week* for guidance on patent research.

MANFRED SCHUBACH Of Clearwater, Florida, for information on contemporary German nutcrackers.

KEN ALTHOFF Chairman of Midwest Importers of Cannon Falls, Minnesota, for information on the history of German nutcrackers.

OTHER PROFESSIONALS Various reference librarians, in particular Chris McKee and Tony Pizzuto from the New York Patent Library, museum curators and antiques dealers who assisted me along the way.

AND LAST, BUT NOT LEAST all of the individuals who over the years utilized their time, energy and creative and mechanical talent to produce the many fascinating and beautiful nutcrackers which exist today.

TABLE OF CONTENTS

INTRODUCTION

Nutcracker: *Then as now, sturdy tongs or pliers for breaking the shells of nuts.*

This definition from *The Collector's Complete Dictionary of American Antiques* by Frances Phipps is accurate as far as it goes, and understandably concise for a dictionary entry. It is also the description which most likely comes to mind when most of us think about nutcrackers. This definition, however, only captures the intended function of these implements and the design of some of the most basic models. It hardly prepares us for the story which will unfold, tracing the development of nutcrackers from the earliest times to the present day.

By providing a little background information on how I became involved in nutcracker collecting, I will, hopefully, give some insight into the creativity and diversity which drew me to this field. This information should also help to set the stage for the more detailed discussions on nutcrackers which follow.

My first nutcracker was purchased quite innocently, about ten years ago, because it was in the shape of a dog (Plate 1). Being an ardent dog-lover, it was the form rather than the utilitarian purpose of this black cast iron nutcracker that intrigued me. In fact, I had to ask the dealer from whom it was purchased to explain its function. Shortly thereafter, I spotted a similar black cast iron squirrel (Plate 1). At least this time I knew what it was, and was sure at once that the squirrel would look very good next to the dog. Squirrels, as it turns out, are a very popular subject for nutcrackers because of their obvious real-life fondness for nuts. This is confirmed in Plate 2 which pictures a selection of squirrels made in a variety of styles

PLATE 1
Left: Black cast iron dog nutcracker – 4½" high, 10½" long, 1½" across. Base – 4½" wide, 7¼" long, ½" high. Marked "24H" on handle. Early 20th century.
Right: Black cast iron squirrel nutcracker – 4½" high, 5½" long, 2" across. Reproduction of earlier model. American, c. 1970 (original c. 1900).

from several different compositions. (A number of squirrel designs either appear or are referred to later in the book. Most of them crack nuts in their jaws or between their chins and front paws.)

After deciding it would be fun to see how many black cast iron animal nutcrackers I could find, I came upon a delightful wooden one in the shape of a bear (Plate 3). It completely shattered my attempt to limit my collection to the black cast iron variety. My determination to collect only animal figures was also short-lived. My many trips to flea markets, antique shows and shops soon brought me face-to-face with several human-shaped nutcrackers which were too beautiful and interesting to pass up.

Initially, I did not dream of the almost infinite variety of figural nutcrackers nor of the high cost of the more unusual and rare examples. Needless to say, by the time of that realization, I was already hooked. To this day, I continue to be amazed by the manner in which the makers of these pieces have combined beauty and utility in such fascinating ways.

One advantage I have found in collecting figural nutcrackers is the challenging search. Although there are many varieties out there, they are not so easy to find. As time has gone on, I have learned that looking in some rather unlikely places will increase the chances of success. Antiques dealers who specialize in tools will sometimes also deal in nutcrackers. Antique toy dealers, especially those who handle iron banks, frequently will have one or two choice iron figural nutcrackers on hand. Occasionally, it is possible to become associated with a dealer who handles a large variety of collectibles. This person may have access to a nutcracker collection which is being liquidated. Several fine examples may be acquired this way.

Nutcrackers can also be classified as folk art in that they often have been the product of rural artisans and, at times, reflect designs and motifs of a particular ethnic group or geographic region. Consequently, antiques dealers who specifically handle folk art will sometimes have one or two interesting nutcrackers in their stock.

PLATE 2

Background: Wooden squirrel with reddish stain – 6½" high, 9½" long, 2" across. Most likely Swiss, German, or Austrian, mid-20th century. Black cast iron squirrel on base – 5¼" high, 7¼" long, 2" across. Base – 4⅝" long, 3" wide, 1" high. Marked "1370 EMIG" and "4" on bottom of base. Mid-20th century.

Center: Gold-painted cast iron squirrel – 6¼" high, 8½" long, 2¼" across. Log-shaped base – 5" long, 2¾" wide, ½" high. (Similar model is made in combination with a nut bowl.) c. 1900. Brown painted cast iron squirrel – 4½" high, 5½" long, 2" across. American, early 20th century. Brass-plated cast iron squirrel with glass eyes – 7½" high, 5½" long, 2⅜" across. Handle/lever concealed within, but not part of tail. Bottom paws encircle nut which serves as part of base. Late 19th to early 20th century.

Foreground: Brass squirrel seated on branch – 5½" long, 2¼" high, 1¼" across. Late 19th to early 20th century. Brass squirrel on branch – 5" long, 2" high, ¾" across. Early 20th century.

PLATE 3
Wooden sitting bear – 8¾" high, 4½" deep, 3¾" across. Has glass eyes. Probably German, late 19th century.

A truly excellent way to acquire difficult to find nutcrackers is through other collectors. Dealing with them can be very rewarding as most collectors will have a few duplicates that they are willing to part with, sometimes in exchange for another nutcracker rather than for money.

There are no absolutes in nutcracker collecting. I have found wonderful examples from many different sources. Dealers, who sell primarily furniture, porcelain, textiles, etc., occasionally come across a nutcracker of interest. I have also had success through newspapers like the *Antique Trader* and the *Maine Antique Digest*. One thing is certain – a great deal of the fun is in the searching and the looking, as well as in the finding.

Once I began finding nutcrackers, I became curious as to their ages and origins. Some of this information was available from the dealers from whom the nutcrackers were purchased, but more often than not, their knowledge was limited. And unlike many other areas of interest in the antiques field, I could find little written information dealing specifically with this topic. It became necessary to begin "digging" to uncover the answers I desired. My search has culminated in the completion of this book which is a patchwork of information pieced together from numerous sources.

Conducting this research was particularly difficult because the subject area is so broad. It includes nutcrackers of various international origins made over a period of several hundreds of years, encompassing a wide selection of mediums and including both mass produced and individually made specimens. Also, the written material available on this subject is not plentiful. Often times, the indices of antique books would contain references to the extremely popular "nutmeg grater," but no listing for my personal favorite, the "nutcracker." Equally disappointing was the lack of information available through some of our nation's most prestigious museums. Many curators, although enthusiastic about the idea of my exploring this little known topic, were themselves unfamiliar with the subject of nutcrackers, primarily because their museums' collections usually contained not a single example.

Even the hundreds of plates selected by Erwin O. Christensen for publication in his book, the *Index of American Design,* and by Clarence P. Hornung in his two volume work, the *Treasury of American Design,* which were both excerpted from the thousands of examples of American ingenuity contained in the whole index collection in the National Gallery in Washington, yielded but one nutcracker from the latter work. This piece, a cast iron dog, similar in appearance to the one pictured in Plate 1, was dated c. 1860–1880, and was inscribed with the words "Dog Tray Nutcracker" on its base.

This lack of written material about nutcrackers is very surprising considering that many thousands of individuals from all over the world have devoted a tremendous amount of their energy and skill over a period of several centuries to producing a vast array of fascinating and useful implements for the purpose of cracking nuts. Hopefully, this book will be a means of acknowledging in print the contribution they have made, many anonymously, to the history of domestic utensils.

Considering the difficulty in researching this subject, I believe I was successful in uncovering a good deal of information, and certainly know much more about nutcrackers than I did when I began my research. I still view this book, however, to be a work-in-progress. Having talked with and corresponded with numerous people in the course of this project, including museum curators, nutcracker collectors, antiques dealers, etc., unfortunately appears that those who were most anxious to be helpful were also frequently those who had the least amount of information to share. Conversely, those individuals who it seemed had fairly extensive knowledge on this subject were not inclined to part with such data. To those who were helpful, I am most grateful.

Accordingly, I have done my best with the information available, much of which was sketchy, some of which was out right contradictory, to arrive at the most accurate conclusions possible. You will note, however, that throughout the text I candidly admit to uncertainty over a few points and can only hope that the interest which this book might generate will lead to an exchange of ideas and information that will clarify and expand upon the research I have already done on this subject. I look forward to learning more as my research continues in the years ahead, as I am sure that collecting and studying nutcrackers will be a life-long pursuit. And, hopefully, as nutcrackers begin to receive additional attention, this will stimulate greater interest and more exploration into this fascinating field.

Before going any further, I should acknowledge the existence of hundreds, perhaps thousands, of nutcrackers which are non-figural (Plate 4). These too make for interesting collecting and are extremely diverse in design, including newer models powered by rubber bands and even by electricity. Some of these nutcrackers have special features which make them particularly effective at cracking certain varieties of nuts depending on the different sizes of the nuts and the relative hardness of their shells. I have chosen, however, to limit my collection and this book primarily to the figural and ornamental varieties, mentioning the others only occasionally in the following chapters. I will leave the writing of a book on non-figural nutcrackers to someone with expertise in this specialized area. I have also concentrated on "antique" nutcrackers, extending from the earliest times to the first few decades of the 20th century. Occasional mention is made of contemporary models to provide a more complete history of nutcracker development and to recognize the beauty and collectability of those pieces produced in recent years.

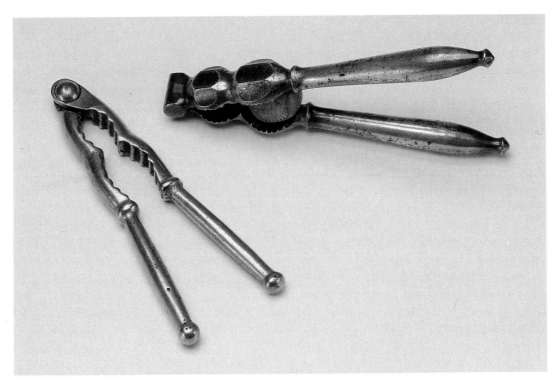

PLATE 4
Left: Small non-figural steel nutcracker – 5" long, 1" across, ⅜" deep. Mid-20th century.
Right: Large non-figural steel nutcracker – 5½" long, 1¼" deep, ¾" across. Silver-plated, badly worn. Early 20th century.

Chapter 1

HISTORICAL OVERVIEW

THE IMPORTANCE OF NUTS

The invention and development of nutcrackers is interesting and also quite logical considering the importance of nuts as a nutritional source. Over the centuries, nuts have been an important staple in the diets of many peoples around the world and have been used for several other purposes as well. That a variety of implements would be created by people in many different countries to crack open the shells of this important food, should not be surprising. However, as much as we enjoy eating nuts today, we take their existence and the existence of nutcrackers pretty much for granted. Therefore, some insight into the particularly high value placed on this food in years past is helpful in order to put the production and use of nutcrackers into historical perspective.

As we approach the 21st century, it is easy to forget how difficult housekeeping and homemaking were in the late 1800s and early 1900s before the advent of refrigeration. Early kitchens often lacked adequate storage and frequently had no provision for keeping foods fresh unless a cooler or an icebox was present. The icebox, of course, relied on ice as its name suggests for keeping food cold; the cooler, however, relied on air circulation. A cooler consisted of a passage in the wall of a dwelling fitted with strong wire shelves upon which food could be stored. During summer months, cool air carried from below ground up to the roof helped preserve the food. With food preservation and storage a serious problem during these early days, it is understandable that nuts became an important part of the diet because, when stored in a cool place, they could be kept up to two years without spoiling.

Further adding to the appeal of nuts is the fact that nut trees are hardy and prolific and nuts themselves are extremely rich in protein; so nutritious that they have been eaten in place of meat in some cultures. They have been made into a coffee substitute in others. Rich in nutrients as well, walnuts, for example, are high in Vitamin C and contain Vitamins A, B^1 and B^2, while almonds also contain Vitamins B^1 and A. Nuts are also very versatile in that they can be eaten plain or used as important ingredients in many dishes, including breads, cakes, pies, cookies, salads, candies, and soups.

Referred to by botanists as an indehiscent (not opening at maturity) fruit with a hardened endocarp, *nut* is actually a popular name for a type of seed or fruit with an edible and usually rather hard and oily kernel, which is grown in a shell of woody fiber. Technically speaking, the Brazil nut is not a nut, but a seed and a peanut is really a legume, and a variety of other foods we call nuts, are not nuts either. However, for the purposes of this discussion, all of these foods, commonly regarded as nuts, will be considered part of that group. Plate 5 shows the pods in which Brazil nuts are grown. The top portions of these pods have been carved away leaving openings through which the nuts can be seen. Ordinarily, the pods would themselves be cracked open to retrieve the individual nuts, a number of which are found in each pod. Not all nuts, of course, are grown several to a pod; some, like chestnuts, are grown within burrs which are covered with bristles on the outside. Still others must be harvested individually as in the case of almonds, each of which is grown as a single fruit, with a shuck which opens when ripe, allowing a pit or nut to fall out. Plate 6 depicts the humorous grouping of a "nut family" probably created in the last thirty years, representing examples of many of the more common varieties of nuts available today.

Nuts have been found in many Stone Age middens (refuse heaps) as far back as the Middle Paleolithic Age. They also were regarded as a delicacy in ancient times, served as a dessert. Affluent Romans, in fact, ate all kinds of nuts except the acorn, deemed acceptable only for the poor. For many years, nuts continued as part of the dessert course, hence the common saying "From soup to nuts."

Early Americans ate a variety of nuts, some native to America and others imported. Acorns, now considered poisonous and inedible were, in fact, consumed by both the Indians and the Colonists. North American Indians extracted a milky liquid from pecans and hickory nuts, while

PLATE 5
Brazil nut pods carved to expose nuts. 4" high, 4½" diameter. Late 20th century.

PLATE 6
Hand-crafted grouping of nuts, marked "The Nuts." (Left to right: pine nuts, chestnut, walnut, pecan, almond, hickory nut, Brazil nut, peanut, and pistachio nuts.) Base – 10½" long, 2¼" across, ¼" high. Mid-20th century.

in Europe walnuts and almonds were blanched, pulverized and soaked in water to produce a much-used milk consumed in many households until the end of the 18th century. Indicative of the extensive use made of nuts in earlier times is the following recipe for Walnut Ketchup, dated 1821.

WALNUT KETCHUP

Boil or simmer a gallon of expressed juice of walnuts when they are tender, and skim it well; add two pounds of anchovies, two pounds of shallots, one ounce of cloves, one ounce of mace, one ounce of pepper and one clove of garlic. Let all simmer until the shallots sink. Put the liquor in a pan until cold, bottle and divide the spices to each.

(Recipe excerpted from Linda Campbell Franklin's 1974 book *America in the Kitchen – From Hearth To Cookstove*, published by House of Collectibles, Inc.)

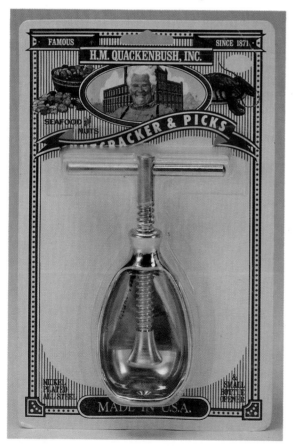

PLATE 7
Nickel-plated cast iron Quackenbush screw-type nutcracker. Reproduction of original design. Late 20th century (original dated 1871).

Another walnut recipe on the reverse side of the package which holds a modern reproduction of a famous Quackenbush nutcracker, originally dated 1871 (Plate 7), also highlights the frequent use of nuts in bygone years. This recipe would be especially appropriate during the holiday season.

SPICY SHERRIED WALNUTS

1½ cups packed brown sugar
2 tablespoons white corn syrup
¼ cup sherry
1 teaspoon pumpkin pie spice
¼ teaspoon salt
6 to 8 cups walnut halves
Granulated sugar

In saucepan, blend brown sugar, sherry, corn syrup, pumpkin pie spice and salt. Heat until sugar is dissolved. Stir in walnuts until well coated. Remove with slotted spoon and roll in granulated sugar. Spread on baking sheet to dry. Store in loosely covered container.

It should be noted that Henry Marcus Quackenbush from Herkimer, New York, designed a number of nutcrackers during his career. You may very well own a Quackenbush creation and not know it. Check for his initials HMQ. If you find them on a particular nutcracker, it's a Quackenbush!

In addition to the many uses of nuts as a food source, oil can be obtained from nuts and utilized for a variety of purposes. At one time, walnut oil was used extensively as a vegetable oil in France, although it is no longer used nearly as much. (The word *walnut* is thought to be a corruption of "Gall Nut," the name given to nuts which come from Gaul, as ancient France was called.) For centuries, walnut oil was also used for artists' colors, especially for mixing whites and delicate shades.

Another nut oil used in Europe in past years was beechnut oil, used both in cooking and as lamp oil. In West Africa, the shea and butter nuts yielded a fatty oil used locally for soap making.

The tagua nut, grown on palm trees in northwestern South America, primarily Panama, Ecuador and Colombia, has been imported during this century in large quantities. Once in the United States, these nuts have been made into buttons and other small articles. In making buttons, the nuts are sawed into slices, soaked in water to soften, stamped into desired designs and shapes, sometimes dyed assorted colors and then polished to be made ready for market. In 1991, the importance of the tagua nut took on greater proportions. A recent agreement between United States clothing manufacturers and a Washington-based international environmental group was entered into which involves the purchase of five million buttons made from the tagua nut. These buttons so closely resemble ivory that they are considered a natural substitute for it, and are being promoted in an effort to stop the slaughter of elephants and to give Ecuadorans an incentive to conserve the rain forests where the tagua trees grow.

Because of the many types of nuts which seem to flourish in one form or another in most parts of the world, and because of the numerous uses of nuts, both as a food source and in other capacities, it is not at all unexpected that nutcrackers became important implements in many regions. It should be understood, however, that the nutcrackers featured in this book were not manufactured to crack nuts in large quantities for commercial use, but instead were made mostly for use in private homes to crack nuts primarily for food consumption.

THE ORIGIN OF NUTCRACKERS

Nutcrackers are produced in the context of changing social, economic, political, artistic, moral and religious trends and conditions. As such, they reflect the history of the periods in which they were created. Studying the development of nutcrackers throughout the years will,

therefore, uncover a whole array of information about the people who lived during these times.

The date of the first nutcracker or nut crack, as they are sometimes called, is, of course, unknown. Early men and women undoubtedly tried using their teeth and their fingers first. Failing to crack some of the harder nut shells by these means, they must have resorted to two stones, and eventually tried a primitive hammer or mallet to crack open the shells. Plate 8 shows two relatively contemporary and decorative versions of hammers made specifically to crack open nuts.

It follows then that early nutcrackers were made to crack the smaller and harder varieties of nuts which would not succumb to pressure by the teeth or fingers. The very earliest reference to the existence of a nutcracker that I have seen is to Aristotle, the famous Greek philosopher and scientist, who reportedly owned a lever-type nutcracker around 330 B.C. The earliest written documentation regarding nutcrackers can be found in the writings of Jeanne d'Evreux who referred in 1372 to a device made of silver for "breaking nuts." The more widespread existence of these devices, designed and crafted expressly to crack

PLATE 8
Foreground: Nickel-plated cast iron squirrel nut hammer with nickel silver handle. 7¾"
long, 1¾" high. Early 20th century.
Background: Brass hammer with silver-plating and walnut-shaped base. Hammer – 2¾"
high, 6½" long. Base – 2¾" high, 3" wide. c. 1920s.

nutshells, can be traced in Europe to as early as the 1400s. The Louvre in Paris lists a gilded silver nutcracker in an inventory dated 1410. There are also references in the literature of the 1500s to "nutcrackers". The English poet, Geoffrey Chaucer (1343?–1400), mentioned a nutcracker in the *Canterbury Tales,* a collection of stories told by a group of pilgrims traveling from London to the shrine of St. Thomas à Becket at Canterbury. English author Sir Thomas Elyot referred to a nutcracker (Nucifrangibulum) in his writings in 1548, and in 1650, a notation in "Discolliminium" read "He was fain to make a nutcracker of it." (Reference in the Oxford English Dictionary to B. Discolliminium or a Most Obedient Reply to a Late Book Called *Bounds and Bonds*.) It is known as well that King Henry the VIII of England (1491–1547) presented an ornately carved nutcracker as a birthday gift to one of his wives, Anne Boleyn.

The subject of "nut-cracking" was even addressed by Leonardo da Vinci (1452–1519) who illustrated a variety of nut-cracking techniques and then proceeded to draw a nutcracking machine of his own design in the form of a press driven by horses.

The fact that nut eating and nutcracking were common occurrences in the days of Shakespeare was recently confirmed when excavations at the Rose Theatre unearthed numerous filbert shells. It can be assumed that the small hand-held pocket-sized nutcrackers often accompanied people to the theatre where nuts were consumed much as candy and popcorn are today.

Highly decorative wooden lever-operated nutcrackers have been produced in the French and Swiss Alps and the Austrian Tyrol for many years, very abundantly during the 19th century. They also were produced in the Black Forest region of Germany. In fact, Germany, for many

ILLUSTRATION 1

years has been a very prolific producer of nutcrackers or "Nußknackers" as they are called in that language. (The "ß" is pronounced as "s" and is sometimes spelled as "Nussknacker." This "ß" is a German character representing "ss"). Many of these nutcrackers were free-standing soldier-type figures made in the Erzgebirge region (see Illustration 1, map of Germany). Also known as the Ore Mountains, the Erzgebirge is a mountain range extending about 90 miles forming the border between Saxony and Czechoslovakia. This mountain range rises up from the Elbe River to a highest point of 4,000 feet. Although no one is certain when the first nutcracker was made in this region, records suggest that figurines equipped with a lever device could be found in German homes as early as 1725.

One geographer, K. A. Engelhard, reported in 1804 that from 1750 on, two or three hundred people had been making a living in the Seiffen, Heidelberg, Niederseifenbach, Einsiedel and Deutschneudorf regions of Germany by producing a line of toys which included nutcrackers. Engelhard also wrote, however, that even before 1750, some nutcracking models were produced in the Rhön Mountains of Thuringia. In the area of Seiffen, mention has been made of one family involved in wood-working as early as 1644. It also has been said that by 1700, there were 100 wood-turners in this village and that "vainly painted dolls, children's games and other carved pieces," possibly nutcrackers, from Seiffen appeared at the Christmas market in Dresden around the same time. Furthermore, the Steinbach family, a leading manufacturer of nutcrackers today, claims that the existence of "Nutbiters" was recorded three hundred years ago in the late 1600s in the Berchtesgaden area. Because of the importance of Germany as a producer of nutcrackers, Chapter 5 will provide more detailed information on the history of their production in that country.

Although it is clearly recognized that the "percussion" type of nutcracker, such as a stone or mallet used to crack nuts, pre-dates all others, these early implements were not designed for the sole purpose of cracking nuts. Instead, it is widely held that the earliest examples of utensils produced specifically to crack nuts were usually wooden, often the very strong boxwood which is excellent for fine carving. In fact in 1664, the English scholar and humanist John Evelyn noted the ideality of boxwood for nutcrackers in *Sylva*, a learned treatise on trees and forests. Many of these pieces, mostly lever operated, were ornately carved using techniques such as incising, chiseling and chip-carving. They were made in an enormous variety of shapes including human and animal forms. Nutcrackers were often beautiful examples of European folk or peasant art. Some were produced along with toys and other wooden objects by those engaged in the wood-working trade, while the amateur carver was responsible for creating a significant portion of these early specimens as well.

Finally, although nutcrackers produced from wood have been primarily mentioned, the availability of several other substances and manufacturing techniques has resulted in the creation of a broad assortment of implements made over the years.

In fact, extensive research performed in France on iron implements suggests that in addition to wood, wrought and chased iron lever-operated nutcrackers were being produced in Europe as early as the 15th and 16th centuries. The introduction of these iron nut-cracking utensils would have been simultaneous with, or possibly just a little later than, the advent of the very early wooden nutcrackers.

Nutcracking was also taking place outside of Europe. In particular, one East Indian language contained the word *pophalphodna*, a term widely used for *nutcracker* in part of India as early as the 13th century. In this culture, brass was a favorite medium for nutcracker production, dating back several hundreds of years. The topic of what compositions were used in the making of nutcracking utensils will be explored more fully in the next chapter.

Chapter 2

NUTCRACKER COMPOSITION

Throughout history most nutcrackers have been made from wood, brass, steel, and cast iron, but other mediums also have been used, including wrought iron, silver, pewter, aluminum, bronze, and amazingly, porcelain. One world famous nutcracker collection, owned by the late Hal Davis of California, contained a beautiful and very rare example made of Meissen porcelain. This eight-inch high nutcracker took the form of a letter press. Decorated with hand-painted pink roses, it utilized a screw activated by a handle with a porcelain knob at each end (Illustration 2).

(Mr. Davis' spectacular collection, inherited by his daughter, Claudia Davis from Hayden Lake, will be given more attention in Chapter 8.)

In so far as nutcracker construction is concerned, plating has been commonly used, especially for cast iron pieces. Plating mediums have included chromium, nickel, copper, brass, rhodium, and porcelain enamel. Silver-plated nutcrackers are quite prevalent too. The various substances used in the production of nutcracking implements are discussed in detail below.

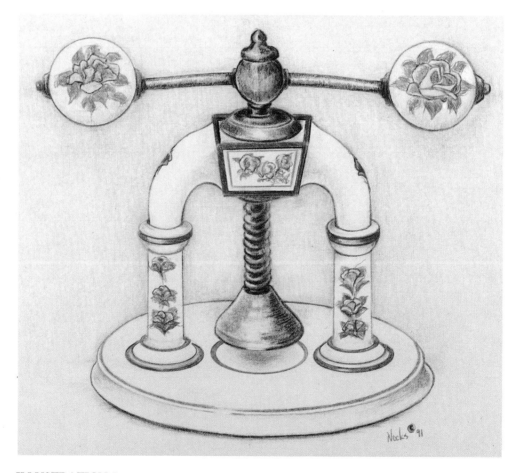

ILLUSTRATION 2
8" high nutcracker made of Meissen porcelain. From the collection of the late Hal Davis.

EARLY WOODENWARE OR TREEN

As previously stated, wood has been a very popular medium over the years for nutcracker construction and no discussion of the wooden variety would be complete without mention of the subject of treen. The word *treen* or *treene* is an old English word for trees and has been part of the English language since the 13th century. During this early time, the letter "n" was sometimes used rather than "s" to form the plural of a singular noun. For example, the plural of shoe was shoon and the plural of tree was treen.

Generally speaking, treen refers to the day-to-day wooden pieces used for eating, storage and preparation of foods. Definitions have been expanded to include a variety of household items including mousetraps, snuff boxes, stools, and even spinning wheels. Jane Toller in her 1975 book, *Turned Woodware For Collectors, Treen and Other Objects*, described treen as a "turned or carved object in wood, that has not involved the use of glue, or much fine and complex inlay work," further delineating that it is "nothing that could be termed a piece of furniture," and was preferably handmade prior to 1830.

Inventories and wills from the 16th and 17th centuries used the word *treen* to describe platters, bowls, and drinking vessels made of wood. Considering that many of these articles were made from parts of trees, it is not surprising that *treen* came to be used as the collective noun for all such woodenware.

It is widely acknowledged that one characteristic of treen is that most of these articles have been replaced over time by similar ones made of different materials such as plastic, metal or pottery. They are considered bygones – no longer useful because of changes in lifestyle. One bygone example is a wooden bed wrench once needed to pull taut the ropes supporting straw ticks and feather mattresses on bed frames. These objects became obsolete once metal bolts replaced the need for roping beds. Nutcrackers have been classified as bygones by some, but this is not actually correct. Rather, nutcrackers are unique examples of treen because they are still made and used today. Although wood is not the only medium used at present for nutcracker construction, wooden ones are still currently being produced.

Another way of classifying treen is to separate it into three categories – objects made on a lathe, objects made professionally with tools such as saws and gouges, and objects made by amateurs. The overwhelming majority of wooden specimens falls into the first group, having been produced with the aid of a lathe, but nutcrackers can and do fall into not one, but all three of these categories.

European Treen

Before the days of easy transportation, people who lived in rural areas of Europe were relatively isolated and were obligated to construct items for everyday use from available materials. Consequently, during early times, and, in particular, in the 1600s and 1700s, wood was used extensively in these country villages in the production of domestic utensils. Wood was so popular partly because it was so plentiful, but also because the cost of producing household articles from either glass or earthenware was prohibitive.

The pole and bow lathe was used increasingly in Europe from the 15th century on to make a variety of wooden objects necessary to the average home. The basic purpose of the lathe was to produce a circular movement so that an object fixed on the machine could be cut with chisel-like tools pressed against it. The tools used by the turner who operated the lathe were simple ones he made himself. The cutting ends of the tools were curved in a semi-circle with one tool used to shape the article and the other to hollow it. Unseasoned wood was taken directly from the tree and worked by a turner. The invention of the pole lathe was extremely significant. With earlier lathe models, the tools used became clogged with accumulated wood shavings during the turning process, rendering them unusable. The intermittent motion of the pole lathe, allowed for the tools to cut on a down stroke only, while the up stroke, which was against the tool, helped to clear away the shavings and prevent clogging. Also, the adjustability of the pole lathe rest permitted the tools to be worked at an angle with the grain of the wood and prevented scraping the surface of the turned article. The advantages in using the pole lathe encouraged the production of most treen by the means of turning.

Wood-turning craftsmen were known as coopers. Several classes of coopers existed with a group called the white coopers or dish turners who were responsible for household treen. With a shortage of ordinary table treen and a demand for its production, however, every cooper and many non-coopers made all varieties of woodenware without regard to specialization. The craft flourished well into the 19th century, producing many fine examples. Professionally carved treen fashioned from solid chunks of wood were made for the poor villager with the more ornate and finely carved pieces produced for the wealthy. European treen was often elaborately decorated and pieces were even occasionally mounted in metal.

Objects such as nutcrackers which have been turned on a lathe and then carved were usually the work of two individual craftsman (Plate 9). The turner would make only the basic shapes or rough forms, called *Docken* in German, which were then handed over to professional or casual carvers for completion. The handle of the 17th century nutcracker in this photograph was obviously worked on a lathe while the figural head was handsomely hand carved.

To identify a nutcracker which has been worked on a lathe, look closely at the handle. Almost all hand-held, wooden ones have been made in this way. The handles will exemplify a uniformity and regularity of form which would be very difficult to duplicate with a whittling knife. Many of the earlier specimens will have parallel bands encircling the handles, and the handles themselves will narrow or slightly taper at various points (Plate 10).

American Treen

Finding examples of American-made wooden nutcrackers is extremely difficult for a variety of reasons. Considering the scarcity of such nutcrackers in contrast to the abundance of Euporean-made wooden nutcrackers, it may seem odd that so much attention will be devoted to

PLATE 9
Wooden double-figure carved and turned on a lathe. Face on one side and seated figure on other side. Made probably of English walnut. 7¾" high, 2⅞" deep, 1⅜" across. 17th century.

this subject. I am convinced, however, that wooden nutcrackers produced on this side of the Atlantic do exist. It is only through understanding American treen, the circumstances of its production, and its characteristics that we can hope to explain the dearth of American-produced wooden nutcrackers and to attempt to correctly identify those nutcrackers carved by our ancestors.

Specifically, four groups of early Americans, apart from the Native American Indians, were responsible for producing wooden articles in this country. The first was composed of early settlers and farmers who made household items for their own use and that of their families. The second group was the coopers, who were engaged in making turned woodenware for sale to others. The third group was made up of hobbyists who whittled primarily for pleasure. They produced figural works of folk art along with more common domestic articles. This group included many individuals who carved as a leisure-time activity. Sailors, lumberjacks and miners, whose work was punctuated by intervals of inactivity, developed hobbies such as whittling. A fourth group, which also produced wooden folk art, was the professional carvers who made a variety of wooden articles such as weathervanes, toys and signs for sale to others. This group was made up of itinerant carvers, peddlers, local cabinet makers and carpenters who whittled as an adjunct to their primary trade.

EARLY WOODWORKERS

American colonists from the 17th century onward made a variety of wooden utensils for the household, in particular for kitchen and dining use. Items which were carved often were found among the domestic effects of the German, Dutch and Swiss colonists who brought a strong wood-carving heritage with them from their homelands.

Wooden nutcrackers were among the pieces of wooden tableware made in America, especially in the 1600s and early 1700s. Due to severe space limitations aboard early ships, few pieces of pewter, ceramic, glass, and silver tableware were brought to the New World. These materials were in short supply in frontier areas. Very plentiful, however, was wood. The vast number of trees encountered by the colonists were often considered a hindrance to a settlement. Cutting down trees to clear the land for housing and farming was a major preoccupation of these early settlers. The settlers, especially those from rural areas of Europe, were already familiar with producing wooden objects for home use. Finding the Indians using wooden utensils, they rapidly adopted the use of wooden-ware for themselves.

Every locality and each family made its own utensils from the wood at hand. Wealthy families eventually purchased china and pewter, relegating the treenware to use in the kitchen and in the servants' quarters. Less well-to-do people, especially those in rural areas, however, continued to use woodenware throughout the 1700s. According to Edith Miniter in her article, "When treen ware was 'The Ware'," in a 1930 issue of the magazine *Antiques*, whittling was an extremely common, almost all-consuming pastime for many early Americans – New Englanders, in particular. When worn out, the pieces were discarded and used for kindling. New ones were made in their place. This is one reason why examples of early American woodenware are in relatively short supply. Another reason is that wood deteriorates with frequent usage and exposure to the elements. Unfortunately, few American woodenware pieces survived from before 1700 and their precise dating has remained extremely difficult and sometimes impossible.

With the demand for woodenware so great during these early years, and wood as a raw material in such abundance, coopers who came to America from Europe also set about making all varieties of woodenware, continuing to make them for many years in the more isolated areas.

At first, this woodenware was produced completely by hand using knives, axes and the cooper's adze, a curved iron blade with a short wooden handle, while crude lathes were soon set up and used thereafter for making treen. One type of lathe, invented by Thomas Blanchard in 1820, was the gunstock lathe. It was used to turn irregular shapes and forms and to make woodenware in a variety of designs. In America, the cooper's craft eventually developed into an organized trade with a charter and a guild. Some of these coopers, especially in the more outlying areas, after completing the production of a variety of items, took to the roads to peddle them.

This commercial production of wooden articles by coopers actually began early in the 18th century. An advertisement in the *Pennsylvania Gazette*, dated 1732, attests to this act. It promoted a "Wood Turner from London" who made "all sorts of turnings in Hard Wood - Coffee Mills, Pepper boxes, Punch bowls, mortars, sugar boxes." Over the next hundred years, the ranks of the woodenware makers increased significantly, and by the early 1800s, many could be found in America.

Even after the introduction of machine-made goods, wood carving continued to flourish as a craft and as a folk art. Folk art has been defined as the work of self-taught artists producing goods for their peers (and themselves) in rural areas and small towns. Their work, to my mind, exceeded the rudimentary, and was invested with a creative, imaginative and often whimsical spirit.

PLATE 10
Three English screw-type nutcrackers, view of handles and apertures. Late 18th century to late 19th century.

Folk art sculptures, including wooden pieces, were most prevalent in the Northeast in areas where the middle class dominated, but also appeared, somewhat later in other regions. The popularity of wood, in the face of the increasing use and availability of other mediums such as iron, pewter and brass, is evident in the fact that the use of wood in the United States and Canada reached a peak in the 1800s.

EUROPEAN VS. AMERICAN TREEN

Strangely, almost no mention is made of wooden nutcrackers by authorities like Mary Earle Gould, who for many years collected, studied and wrote extensively about the subject of American treen nor by Erwin O. Christensen in his 1952 book, *Early American Wood Carving*, in which he discussed several categories of carving including a section on household articles, but devoted no attention to the subject of American-made wooden nutcrackers. The only reference to nutcrackers in Mr. Christensen's book was in a listing of Art Museums and Historical Societies which contained examples of American wood carving.

The Sturbridge Museum in Sturbridge, Massachusetts was credited by Mr. Christensen with having fifteen nutcrackers in its collection. According to Frank G. White, the current Assistant Director of the Curatorial Department at Old Sturbridge Village, only a very few nutcrackers are presently contained in this collection. Over the years, a number of nutcrackers at Sturbridge which were of English or European origin not of the usual type exported for use in the United States or of American origin but mid 19th century or later were removed as they did not meet the updated collecting criteria at the Museum which includes only objects made or used in New England prior to 1840.

More recent writers such as Robert Bishop, whose beautiful book, *American Folk Sculptures*, published in 1974, also omitted any mention of nutcrackers in his extensive coverage of the subject of American wood carving. This is typical of the lack of attention given to nutcrackers by American authorities on domestically-produced treen and folk art, while other kitchen and dining-related wooden objects such as pie crimpers and butter molds have received wide attention. This is in sharp contrast to English authors and authorities on woodenware like Evan Owen-Thomas, Edward and Eva Pinto, and Jane Toller who have made a point of including nutcrackers in their writings on European treen.

The rather consistent omission of nutcrackers by American writers is surprising. Nut-cracking utensils must occasionally have been among the wooden articles made by early settlers along with the trenchers (plates), mortars and pestles, boxes, and noggins (pitchers), which are frequently discussed. This lack of attention may stem from the fact that wood carving in this country is not representative of any one single style, and therefore, is not easily recognized. Early Americans were too diverse a people to be melded into one common style within a two or three hundred year time period. It may be that some wooden nutcrackers made in America by immigrants closely resembled nutcrackers made in Europe and frequently were thought to be of European origin. It is likely that these instances of erroneous European attribution have contributed to the omission of nutcrackers from discussions of American treen. Also, it may be that nutcrackers, much more so than other forms of tableware, were brought along to America with the early immigrants. Often given as gifts, nutcrackers probably possessed sentimental value. Their relatively small size and often decorative appearance made them more likely to be transported on the voyage across the Atlantic than other forms of treen, brass or iron. Assuming that numerous nutcrackers were brought here by early settlers, while other nutcrackers were imported for sale in America, these facts would have greatly reduced the need to domestically produce these utensils.

However, with the firm conviction that at least some nutcrackers must have been made in America, focusing on the characteristics of American wood-carving which can be identified is necessary. Therefore, despite the overall lack of uniformity in the "look" of American-made woodenware, studying a number of wooden articles deemed worthy of ornamentation, such as molds and wall boxes, provides some clues to American design. In general, American treen, especially tableware, is more elementary in form and execution than similar European examples. For the most part, Early American wood carving was utilitarian because the more elaborate ornamentation found on similar European pieces was too time-consuming to be executed by settlers of the New World facing a difficult, often harsh existence. Most of their energies were spent in activities relating to survival. Of course, once farmlands were settled, towns established, and the rigors of daily existence eased, slightly more attention could be paid to decorative wood carving.

Some wooden nutcrackers undoubtedly exist which can be documented through their long-term possession by a particular family or institution as being American-made, while others may be signed, dated or marked in some way which suggests an American origin. Others may embody traditionally American designs such as the American flag or an American political or historical figure which would help to verify that they were most likely produced in this country.

The tulip, acorn and eagle were popular motifs with Pennsylvania carvers and, therefore, may be incorporated in nutcracker designs produced in that region. As with many decorations used by the Pennsylvania Dutch, they were not strictly American in origin. The American immigrants, instead, copied what was familiar from their homelands, adding personal touches here and there. The tulip, for instance, had been brought to Europe from Asia Minor in the mid 1500s and became popular in Germany, England and the Low Countries (Belgium, the Netherlands and Luxembourg). The tulip was also widely grown in Pennsylvania and is thought to have a religious significance, representing the Trinity in the three petal design. As such, it is not surprising that the Pennsylvania Dutch colonists used this motif extensively in their decorative art because it was a fond reminder of their homeland and was religiously significant as well.

For instance, the eagle nutcracker in Plate 11 utilizes a typical American motif, but it was probably not produced in this country. It could be the product of an American immigrant carver but is more likely of Swiss, Tyrolean, or Scandinavian origin, possibly German, for the simple reason that it so closely resembles the other handle-held animal and human-shaped nutcrackers made in these countries in the late 1800s to early 1900s (Plates 12 and 13). (The Tyrol is an alpine region in Western Austria and Northern Italy.) Although the eagle has special significance to Americans, it is by no means an exclusively American design. Foreign nutcracker manufacturers have for some time included subjects of particular interest to people in the United States in their product lines. Figures like eagles, cowboys, and Uncle Sam are made by companies in foreign lands to appeal to American collectors who are enthusiastic purchasers of their merchandise. It bears repeating that an American subject may indicate, but does not guarantee, an American origin.

According to Erwin O. Christensen, American wood carving closely followed European traditions when performed by professionals responsible for ornamenting fine furniture and architecture. On the other hand, where wood carving served the needs of the home or was per-

PLATE 11
Wooden eagle nutcracker with glass eyes. Similar hand-held animal and human-head models are Swiss, Tyrolean, or Scandinavian in origin, but a small percentage may be German. 7½" high, 3½" deep, 1½" across. Late 19th or early 20th century.

PLATE 12
Left: Wooden nutcracker of bearded man with hat, lacquered. 8¾" high, 3⅛" deep, 2½" across. Swiss or Tyrolean, late 19th to early 20th century.
Right: Wooden nutcracker of man with stocking cap. 8" high, 3" deep, 2¼" across. Swiss or Tyrolean, late 19th to early 20th century.

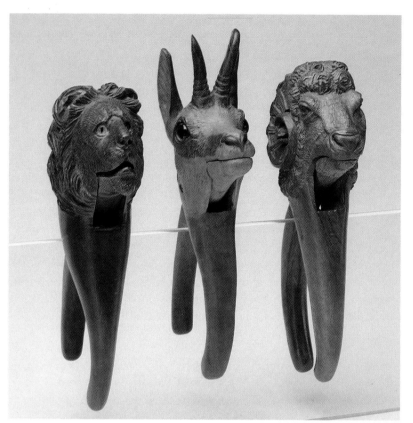

PLATE 13
Left: Wooden lion nutcracker with glass eyes. 9"
high, 4½" deep, 2¼" across. Swiss or Tyrolean,
late 19th to early 20th century.
Center: Wooden antelope-type nutcracker with
glass eyes and stained markings. 8½" high, 3½"
deep, 2" across. Swiss or Tyrolean, late 19th to
early 20th century.
Right: Intricately carved wooden ram nutcracker.
8¼" high, 3½" deep, 2½" across. Swiss or Tyrolean,
late 19th to early 20th century.

PLATE 14
Wooden folk art head. Old red paint in mouth. Lacquered,
probably at later date. 11" high, 7" across, 8½" deep (including
handle). American, early to mid-19th century.

formed for enjoyment and relaxation, a category into which most wooden nutcracker construction would presumably fall, it was closer to a native American expression and as such would be considered folk art.

Some nutcrackers may so obviously exemplify American folk art, in a naive or primitive style, that they are readily identifiable as the work of rural American carvers. One such example is the large head of a man carved to leave the tree branch clearly recognizable as part of the base (Plate 14). Note how crudely, yet powerfully, this piece was constructed. The tendency to minimize anatomical structure, such as in this example, is the mark of the American folk artist. The old cracks in this wooden bust-style nutcracker indicate that it is probably quite old, c. 1825–1850, with traces of original paint in the eye and mouth area. The surface was apparently lacquered at some later date. It is truly a remarkable piece for many reasons including its highly unusual form and its likely American origin. Especially fascinating is the use of a nail, hammered into the roof of the mouth. The nail head protrudes just enough to facilitate the nut-cracking process, a very clever and unexpected design technique. The raw strength which it exudes gives it a sculptural presence quite separate from its function as a nutcracker. This piece shows none of the refinement that typified the majority of European-produced wooden nutcrackers from the same period. It is also very different in size (11" high by 6½" wide) and overall design than the wooden hand-held models made in Europe during the 1800s which are usually 8" to 9" long and 3" to 4" wide. It is this lack of detail and ornamentation so common in European carving that is one of the best clues to distinguishing American from European produced woodenware.

In some instances, the general appearance of a piece is European, but an American origin is suspected. One of the only ways to distinguish it as European or American is to identify the type of wood used in the carving. If the wood was indigenous to America and not found in countries abroad, an American or North American origin would be fairly certain. European woods were eventually imported to America, but the likelihood of an exotic foreign wood reaching the rural areas and early settlements in this country, and being used in a nutcracker, seems quite remote.

A variety of woods, both soft and hard, were used by American carvers, including hickory, beech, cherry, oak, birch and chestnut. Maple, ash, walnut and fruitwood, considered hard and solid lumbers, were the best suited for nutcracker construction. Slightly softer woods, such as basswood, poplar and pine were usually used for chip carving, a one-handed technique done without the aid of a mallet.

An interesting nutcracker with possible American origin is the wooden dog pictured in Plate 20. Made around 1900, it is carved out of knotty pine and has a head and chest design which is not typical of most European-made treen animals. Knotty pine is not the usual material choice for hand-held European wooden nutcrackers of this vintage. Most were made of walnut or fruitwood. Again, the origin of the piece is uncertain and whether or not this nutcracker is American should not override and overshadow the general appeal of this lovable canine.

Identifying wood may be "easier said than done." It is not always practical, and can be extremely difficult, for the average collector to conclusively identify a particular wood in an item as small as most nutcrackers. Microscopic examinations are used by museums when a definitive wood-type analysis is needed. Such examinations require a carefully prepared section of the wood's end-grain to be cut off, and the risk of damaging the piece is significant. Instead of such complicated procedures, a few tips on distinguishing some of the more common woods used in nutcracker construction are provided in Chapter 7. It must be remembered, however, that many wooden nutcrackers (including their handles) have been stained and/or painted, which means that the actual wood is not visible except sometimes on interior sections or areas where the stain has been worn away with use.

CONTEMPORARY AMERICAN-MADE WOODEN NUTCRACKERS

Although this book is devoted primarily to the discussion of "antique" figural and ornamental nutcrackers, it should be acknowledged that a number of nutcrackers of high quality have been produced in recent years. This is especially important in the case of those wooden pieces which are American-made, because as previously discussed, the existence of many examples of antique wooden nutcrackers from the United States has been difficult to establish.

A handful of American companies over the last 15 years has attempted to penetrate the nutcracker market. Most have found it difficult or even impossible to develop a sufficient market to continue in business. One such company, Intermountain, based in Utah, sold a general line of nutcrackers as well as producing a five-foot solid wood piece. Another company, Christmas Village from Jonesboro, Arkansas, produced four models in the 1980s which were approximately 14" high. They were discontinued because they were considered too costly at the time.

The Milford, Ltd. in Raymore, Missouri is one American company which is currently producing very fine quality nutcrackers. Milford's line offers sixteen different designs – Benjamin Franklin, the Marquis de Lafayette, Uncle Sam, Captain Hook, Cicero, Sebastian, Davy

Crockett, George Washington, Ivan the Terrible, Keystone Bobby, Lamplighter, Molly, Palace Guard, a Beefeater, The Little General, and Saint Nicholas, shown in Plate 15. Each model has a limited edition of 5,000 pieces which are individually signed and dated.

This company is most certainly a family business. Walter Milford makes the body parts on a lathe; his wife, Susan hand paints them. Inspiration to make nutcrackers came from Susan Milford's childhood fascination with them. An old nutcracker brought out and used by her family on important occasions first intrigued Susan. After a special viewing of *The Nutcracker Suite*, her interest peaked further. She has become a highly proficient painter in the European tradition during her marriage to Walt Milford, an expert tool and die maker. The combination of their skills plus Susan's continued nutcracker fascination resulted in the formation of Milford, Ltd. and their first series, "The Cavalier Collection." Each figure in this collection is 12" to 15" in height. The detailed workman-

PLATE 15
Brightly painted wooden Milford Saint Nicholas nutcracker. 15¾" high (including base), 5¾" across, 4" deep at base. American, c. 1990.

ship is quite exceptional and many of the faces have benign expressions, rather than the fierce ones which often characterize German examples.

Another husband and wife team of nutcracker makers is Lee and Lois Anske of Sykesville, Maryland. Lee Anske learned his wood-carving trade while living in Germany in the early 1970s and has produced wooden folk art under the professional name "Yankee Chipper." He and his wife participated in the Smithsonian Institution's Holiday Celebration in the late 1970s, demonstrating nutcracker production for thousands of onlookers. Lee carved while Lois painted. While Lee was forced to take a few years off due to a carving accident, the couple devoted their time to other professional interests and grandchildren. Now, the Anskes are once again producing colorful free-standing nutcrackers in the forms of soldiers, chimney sweeps, elves, and kings. Made of sturdy basswood (linden), the Anskes models are not only decorative, but functional, capable of cracking any nut.

During this century, a number of American-made wooden nutcrackers must have been produced by amateur wood workers and carvers. Several references appear in the *Index to Handicrafts* which lists magazines that published articles on how to construct nutcrackers as a hobby or leisure activity. Articles such as these must have inspired many hobbyists to try their hands at nutcracker making. For example, the December 1930 issue of *Popular Mechanics* included an article by Kenneth Keith entitled "Grotesque Figures Crack Nuts." Six different nutcracker designs were shown – a peasant man and woman with hands in their pockets, an elephant, two charming clown-type figures (one with a long nose, possibly meant to be Pinocchio), and a pelican. The standing peasant nutcracker in Plate 16 very closely resembles the one pictured in *Popular Mechanics* apart from the addition of the attached wooden tray. It appears to date from the 1930s. Its creation may have been inspired by this or a similar article on "do-it-yourself" nutcracker making. In any case, it is not marked in anyway to identify its origin. It could be American or European since it represents a typical older style German peasant figure.

The cover of the November–December 1971 issue of *Chip Chats* magazine is reproduced in Plate 17. *Chip Chats* is the publication of the National Wood Carvers Association which is dedicated to the interests of amateur and professional carvers and whittlers. Its editor, Edward F. Gallenstein, was generous enough to search back issues of his publication to uncover the one instance which featured a nutcracker. This particular piece was carved around 1940 by Ed Lamping of Cincinnati, Ohio. Made from oak, it remains in the Lamping family and is used by Mr. Lamping's grandchildren. It was carved from 2½" thick wood with a 2" stock for the lever and a brass pin at the

PLATE 16
Painted wooden standing peasant nutcracker with attached tray.
Nutcracker – 10½" high, 5" deep including lever, 2" across.
Tray – 1½" high, 12½" deep, 6¼" across. Possibly American,
c. 1930s–1940s.

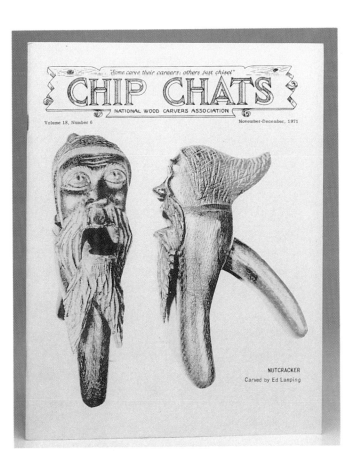

PLATE 17
Wooden nutcracker pictured on cover of *Chip Chats* magazine.
Nutcracker carved c. 1940.

fulcrum point. It was recommended in *Chip Chats* that a pattern could be made from the photographs and readers were encouraged to try their hand at making a similar piece in the tradition of the "typical Black Forest type nutcracker." Lamping's nutcracker is decidedly German in appearance as he was a native of Vechta/Oldenburg, Germany.

Gallenstein suggests that American-made wooden nutcrackers were probably produced of ash, oak or walnut. According to his vast knowledge of American woodcarvings, nutcrackers were not a popular item for carving in America. (To join the National Woodcarvers Association and obtain information on subscribing to *Chip Chats* magazine, write to the National Woodcarvers Association, 7424 Miami Avenue, Cincinnati, Ohio, 45243.)

Jim Hart of Basking Ridge, New Jersey, who whittles and carves as a hobby, produced the wonderful, humorous figure in Plate 18. His creation is not a nutcracker, but a clever carving of a squirrel attempting to crack a nut with a nutcracker. It is testimony to the creative spirit found in present-day American carvers and the continuing interest in nut-cracking as a carving theme. Contemporary German companies which manufacture nutcrackers will be discussed in Chapter 5. Several companies are currently in existence, producing models highly sought after by American collectors.

NON-WOODEN NUTCRACKERS

Cast Iron

Cast iron was used extensively for nutcracker construction in the 19th and early 20th centuries continuing to the present day. European countries produced many of this kind, although it was the United States which manufactured them in great profusion.

A large number of cast-iron table model nutcrackers of American origin were made originally in the 1800s and early 1900s. In fact, the United States has a long history of iron-making, beginning with the first successful iron works in Saugus, Massachusetts which dates back to 1643. Another iron works, the Bristol Furnace, located on the Rappahannock River about forty miles below Fredericksburg, Virginia, was established in 1722 with the help of George Washington's father, an ironmaster by trade. (The art of iron founding can be traced back to as early as the 15th century in Europe.) Several iron works could also be found in the 1800s, built in western Kentucky and Tennessee between and along the Cumberland and Tennessee Rivers so that riverboats and ferries were readily available. This area was a natural choice for the establishment of iron foundries as it was rich in iron ore, limestone for flux and wood for operational charcoal needed in the cold blast method of making "pigs" – a crude casting of metal. Pig iron was then melted into molds to form kettles, pots and other household necessities, such as nutcrackers.

PLATE 18
Painted wood carving of squirrel cracking nut with help of nutcracker. Carved by Jim Hart of Basking Ridge, New Jersey. 5½" long, 2¾" high, ¾" deep. American, c. 1988.

American-made cast iron nutcrackers come in many shapes with dogs, squirrels, and birds being among the most common. These nutcrackers are operated by pressing a lever, frequently the animal's tail. The tail is raised, the nut inserted in the animal's mouth, and the tail lowered, causing the lower jaw to crack the shell against the upper jaw. Some cast iron pieces are brightly painted in a manner similar to doorstops and children's banks, while many others are solid black in color.

Many cast iron nutcrackers were sold through mail order catalogues. Mail order first became popular in the late 1800s and early 1900s when general stores issued catalogues offering food, clothing, various housewares and hardware. The first Sears catalogue for the A.C. Roebuck Company was distributed in 1891. It consisted of 32 pages of watches and an 8-page insert devoted to jewelry and sewing machines. The response was apparently excellent because the following year's edition was increased to over 100 pages. Bearing the new name of *Sears, Roebuck and Company* for the first time in 1893, the catalogue reached almost 200 pages in length, covering a very broad line of merchandise.

Also popular was Montgomery Ward and Company which issued an early catalogue picturing a dog nutcracker, describing it as follows:

> H9054 Old Dog Tray, a large toy dog and nut cracker. Bright red base, black body, colored eyes, cannot be broken; a child of six can crack the hardest nuts, meats come out whole, enjoyed by young and old. Size, 13 in. long, 7 in. high, can be used to stand on floor to hold a door when not wanted as a toy or nut cracker; weight, 5¾ lbs.
>   Each .... 40¢

Compare the following description of a reproduction dog nutcracker, as pictured in a contemporary catalogue. This new nutcracker is considerably more expensive than the older model's original price. Authentic antique dog nutcrackers, however, often cost between $75.00 and $250.00, which is quite a bit more than new reproductions like the one described below.

> Labrador Nutcracker: This black lab is standing at attention just waiting to crack nuts for you. By lifting his tail, his mouth opens wide …well, you get the idea. Made of heavy cast iron, he measures 4½" high and 10" long (including tail) and is mounted on a sturdy iron base. Great for the pecans and hickory nuts you'll pick up this fall.
>   26517 Lab Nutcracker ....$18.50 delivered.

Apparent from the early Montgomery Ward advertisement, sturdy cast iron figural nutcrackers were used for more than one purpose. Beside cracking nuts, they served as toys for children, and doorstops.

Cast iron nutcrackers come in a large array of shapes, designs and subjects, but among the most interesting is the one in the shape of a little man with his hands in his pockets. Such a figure was patented in the United States on November 22, 1870 by Paul Ceredo of Dusseldorf, Prussia (Patent No. 109,495) and was called "The Automatic Nut-Cracker." Mr. Ceredo designed it according to the specifications represented in the drawing which accompanied his patent application. In this drawing, the figure appears to stand within an "A-frame" house or building of wood, with a receptacle or basket secured to the rear of the stand for holding nut shells. It was Mr. Ceredo's expressed intention "to render the apparatus ornate to such an extent as may fit it to be placed upon dining room tables." Surely, he succeeded in his creation of this delightful little fellow.

Three variations of this basic design are pictured in Plate 19, including a man in a red coat, a black man dressed in black and an elf or Santa Claus-like figure with a green hat. Each was supported by a thick wooden block attachment in the back of the figure and cracked nuts via their levered jaws. The elf is missing this base and none of the three have an accompanying house or rear receptacle. It is not certain whether any of them were originally made with the type of house or basket attachment pictured in Mr. Ceredo's patent specifications. I have been told that a Chinese man similar to the three figures in Plate 19 also exists, but have not been able to verify this report.

These same figural men (the hatless variety) were produced in brass, as well as cast iron. Such a nutcracker is pictured in Peter, Nancy and Herbert Schiffer's book, *The Brass Book*, published in 1978. According to the Schiffers, it is brass and iron and is English, mid-19th century. Unlike the cast iron examples in Plate 19, the brass man nutcracker has a second lever protruding from the lower third of his back upon which the upper lever rests when not in use. This second lever may add balance and stability to the piece.

Since Mr. Ceredo patented his little man called "The Automatic Nutcracker" in 1870 and the Schiffers date the brass man as mid 1800s which could, presumably include the 1870s, Mr. Ceredo's nutcracker figure may well have been the inspiration for the English brass version, or perhaps the reverse is true.

As mentioned earlier, the dog is an ever popular subject for makers of nutcrackers. A variety of dog nutcrackers are pictured in Plate 20. Many dog nutcrackers represent Labradors and St. Bernards, but other breeds can also be found including beagles, collies, boxers and span-

PLATE 19

Left: Painted cast iron nutcracker of standing man in red coat on wooden base. 9¾" high, 6½" long including base, 4⅛" across. American, patented 1870.

Center: Painted cast iron nutcracker of standing elf with beard. Probably attached to wooden base originally. 10" high, 5¼" wide, 8" deep including lever. Possibly American, late 1800s.

Right: Painted cast iron nutcracker of standing black man. Wooden support bolted to back of figure. 9" high, 5½" across, 5⅛" deep. Possibly American, late 1800s.

PLATE 20

Left: Wooden dog made of knotty pine with traces of paint. 7¾" high, 3¼" deep, 2¼" across. Possibly American, c. 1900.

Center: Cast iron green-painted dog, 4¼" high, 11" long, 2" across. Late 19th to early 20th century.

Right: Copper-plated cast iron dog. Illegible patent number on tail. 5" high, 11¾" long, 2" across. Possibly American, late 19th to early 20th century.

Foreground: Brass dog face nutcracker. 5½" long, 1½" across, 1½" deep. English, late 1800s.

iels. One dog-shaped cast iron nutcracker, resembling the dog in Plate 1, was patented in the United States on October 16, 1900, by Earl P. Sedgwick of Chicago, Illinois. Mr. Sedgwick's device, Patent No. 660,033, was intended to take the form of an "animal or other figure," but was represented as a dog in the original patent application.

On June 25, 1912, an inventor from St. Paul, Minnesota, Andrew M. Carlsen, patented a similar nutcracker with the intention that it represent a dog or a lion and unlike Mr. Sedgwick's earlier example, this would have an additional feature. This nutcracker (Patent No. 1,030,805) was constructed with an operating mechanism which permitted the cracking force and the stroke of the operating lever to be easily changed before and during operation for different kinds of nuts. Another Carlsen's design was an animal-shaped nutcracker whose tail would swing at the "natural point where a tail usually swings and to use said tail as the operating lever of the cracker."

Confirming the continuing popularity of dog nutcracker designs is a model created by Anna T. Marcinek and Helen M. Marcinek of Chicago, Illinois. A patent was granted to them (Patent No. 3,491,814) on January 27, 1970. Similar in outward appearance to the Carlsen and Sedgwick dogs, the greatest variation in the Marcinek invention appears to have been that the body of the dog contained a pick which extended from the top of the head through the interior of the body at an angle. The pick could be removed for use and then replaced within the body of the dog for storage.

Cast-iron nutcrackers, it has been said, were sometimes distributed in the first half of this century as an advertising device. Stove manufacturers and salesmen apparently gave cast-iron nutcrackers with porcelain enameled surfaces to clients as promotional devices. See the black and white spotted porcelain encased cast-iron dog in Plate 21. Possibly meant to represent a dalmatian, this nutcracker may be such an advertising piece, although no manufacturer's name is present.

Strangely, crocodiles and alligators were also frequent subjects for nutcracker construction (Plate 22). Distinguishing one from the other is no easy task. Crocodiles are amphibious reptiles found in the waters of all warm regions of the world and are the largest living reptiles, growing up to 30 feet. Alligators are reptiles of the crocodile family, found mostly in the rivers of tropical America and along the lower Yangtze River Valley in China. In appearance, the differences lie in the snout and teeth. The alligator has a broad snout and its upper teeth overlap the teeth of the lower jaw. The snout of the crocodile is sharply tapered and the teeth are more in line. On nutcrackers, it is impossible to use the "teeth overlapping" test to distinguish alligators from crocodiles, and the only criterion is

PLATE 21
Black and white porcelain enamel-plated cast iron dog. 5¾" high, 11" long including tail, 3⅝" across. Probably American, early 20th century.

the tapering snout. The large copper-plated brass figure and the black-painted aluminum piece would appear to fall into the crocodile category, while the other models do not seem to taper as much.

Of the nutcrackers appearing in Plate 22, two are cast iron. With realistic details, including pointed teeth and scales, many of the cast iron specimens were made in the late 1800s to early 1900s. Among them is a large painted green alligator of fairly recent vintage. This model and the small nickel-plated example are noteworthy for their design. Neither have any pins holding their two composite and separable parts together. The nickel-plated nutcracker is disassembled in the picture. To put it back together, the lower jaw piece and the scaled back is slipped over the head of the figure. This nutcracker and the large painted cast iron model contrast the other models as their two parts are permanently pinned together.

I have seen a smaller version of this green cast iron alligator, dated 1875–1900, attributed to manufacture in the Northeastern or Midwestern United States. Apparently this design originated quite early. United States

patent records reveal that design patents have been granted for alligator/crocodile nutcrackers going back to March 15, 1864 when Eli W. Blake of New Haven, Connecticut, administrator of the estate of inventor Edward F. Blake, received a patent (Des. No. 1920) for an alligator nutcracker whose "head turned sideways at right angles or nearly so to the body" and whose tail was looped for ease of transport. This looped tail was also a feature of a nutcracker patented on February 19, 1929 by Lampert Bemelmans of Miami, Florida. Mr. Bemelmans secured a design patent (Des No. 77,734) for an alligator whose tail, although forming the top lever, was curved up over the back of the figure rather than laying flat. It was also distinctive for having large screws serve as the eyes and a decidedly geometric look. Another alligator patent was obtained on October 23, 1934 for a model very similar in appearance to the small brass alligator in Photo 22. This patent was granted to Abraham Rothenberg and Philip Mann of Los Angeles, California (Des. No. 93,675).

Also in this picture is an interesting black painted aluminum nutcracker which cracks nuts under its tail

PLATE 22
Background: Aluminum crocodile highlighted with black paint and marked "EMIG 1462" on underside of base. 2½" high, 8½" long, 3¼" across. Late 20th century. Large copper-plated brass crocodile. 12⅛" long, 1½" high, 3" across. Early 20th century. Large cast iron alligator predominantly painted green. 2½" high, 14" long, 3¾" across. Probably American, mid-20th century.
Foreground: Small painted cast iron alligator marked with "T" on roof of mouth. Painted with black and flesh-toned paint. ⅞" high, 6¼" long, 1¾" across. Probably American, c. 1920s–1930s. Small nickel plated alligator with indecipherable patent numbers on underside of lower jaw. 8½" long, 1¾" high, 2" across. Plated with white brass or patkong. Mid-20th century. Small brass alligator that was produced and reproduced in great quantities. 7¾" long, 1¾" high, 1¾" across. Often made in China, mid to late 20th century.

rather than in its mouth. The feet of the base are made in the shape of four walnuts. Returning to the subject of cast iron, note the smallest of the crocodiles which is painted cast iron. Only 6¼" long and ⅞" high, it is surprisingly powerful for its size, cracking open small varieties of nuts very effectively.

Certain figures are repeated often in cast iron nutcracker designs, but this medium was used to produce some very unusual shapes as well. The fish and dragon in Plate 23 are especially appealing and interesting examples of this variety. Note the brightly colored green glass eyes on this shark-like fish and the intimidating teeth. Nuts are quite efficiently cracked in the shark's ominous looking jaws. It is marked with what appears to be the word "Nestor," "R^{D}751619" and "Made in (Name of Country)." Although the country's name is not clear, the registration number indicates that it was made in England around 1930. (The letter combination "R^D" refers to a numbering system used in England to denote a "registered design." See the section "Patent Dating" in Chapter 7 for more information about the British patent system.) A noteworthy feature of this fish is the use of glass eyes in a cast iron model. Glass eyes are used fairly often in wooden figural nutcrackers, but only occasionally in cast-iron pieces. (Plate 2, page 7 includes a cast iron squirrel with glass eyes.)

The gold-painted dragon is also a wonderful cast iron piece made around 1900–1910. Fairly large for a figural

PLATE 23
Cast iron dragon with old gold paint. 5½" high, 14" long, 3⅛" across. English, c. 1900–1910.
Nickel-plated cast iron fish with green glass eyes. Marked "R^{D}751619, Nestor" 2½" high, 8½" long, 2¼" across. Made in England, c. 1930.

PLATE 24
Cast iron horse nutcracker with traces of copper plating. Letter "A" forms horse's muzzle and two "L's" form eyes. 4¼" high, 7¼" long, 1" across. English, c. 1930.

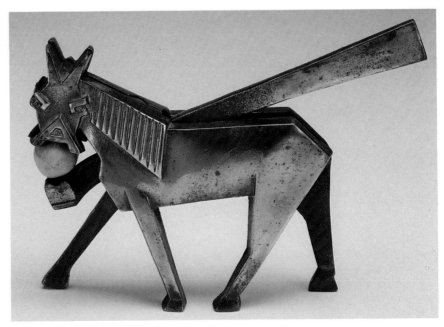

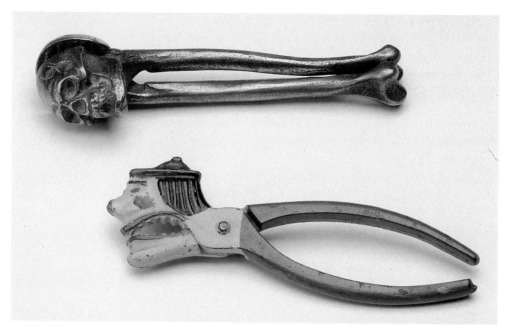

PLATE 25
Nickel-plated cast iron skull and cross bones nutcracker marked "BANKS.WAY HB, R^D740410." 6"
long, 2" deep, 1¼" across. Made in England, c. 1928.
Cast iron painted clown nutcracker. 5¾" long, 1¾" high, ¼" across. c. 1920.

PLATE 26
Wrought iron frog nutcracker with glass eyes. Marked "Germany" on underside of base. 6¼" high, 8¾" deep including base, 6¾" across. Early 1900s.

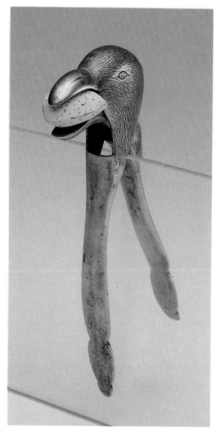

PLATE 27
Hand-finished cast steel bird with etched feathers. Marked with small "x" on lever. 6" long, 2½" deep, ¾" across. Late 19th or early 20th century.

nutcracker, it measures 14¼" in length and 5½" in height and was made in England. It is marked with a barely discernible English trademark on its handle which reads "Rᴰ" followed by a series of indecipherable numbers.

Another unique free-standing example is the horse in Plate 24. It is incised with the Patent No. 273,480. This number does not correspond to either a United States utility or design patent for the invention of any nutcracker. (It may refer to a Canadian or Australian patent, but is more likely a British patent, referring to the same patent number under which the brass and cast iron dogs in Plate 34 were made.) Nonetheless, it is a striking piece which still bears traces of a copper finish. The large letter "A", which forms the horse's muzzle is unusual and probably representative of a name. The eyes suggest two letter "L's" which are also distinctive. This nutcracker operates by the levered tail that cracks nuts in the horse's mouth.

Although the vast majority of figural cast-iron nutcrackers are free-standing, hand-held implements were also made of cast iron, but were much less common than the free-standing variety. The skull and cross bones in Plate 25 is a particularly interesting and macabre example of this type. Also in this photo is a rather unusual brightly painted hand-held cast-iron clown nutcracker. Made possibly in the 1920s, it retains most of its original paint, but contains no other markings.

Wrought Iron

In addition to the mass produced nutcrackers, such as the cast iron variety sold in stores and through mail order catalogues, many items were made by local craftsmen. In fact, the majority of early kitchen utensils were made from iron by American blacksmiths who created numerous objects such as cooking forks, pot hooks, trivets and an occasional nutcracker from wrought iron. Hand-wrought iron and steel figural nutcrackers are certainly less common than those made from molded cast iron. According to one French theory, the concept for the lever-type nutcracker was derived from the pincers used by blacksmiths.

Similar to the simple look of most colonial-made woodenware, the Old World decorative elements and designs were also missing from Early American wrought ironwork. Even the Pennsylvania German smiths, who produced decorative items, stressed utility rather than ornamentation in their work. Iron articles produced for the wealthy generally lacked decoration as well.

Cast iron, because of the process by which it is made, is inflexible and brittle, and it breaks rather than bends. Broken pieces will expose an inside which is gray and coarse in texture. Wrought iron, however, is pliable and bends easily because it retains much of the carbon removed from cast iron during manufacture. Also, unlike cast iron, wrought iron is apt to have slight irregularities on its surface caused by hammer marks.

An unusual wrought iron frog nutcracker with large orange and black glass eyes, seated on a lily pad, is shown in Plate 26. Notice the thinness and curve of the hand-hammered legs and the hammer marks on the surface of the frog. This frog is marked "Germany" and was probably produced between 1900 and 1910. Not only interesting as a wrought iron example, it is extremely unique because, although cracking nuts in its jaws, it contains no levered handles. Instead, pressure is exerted on nuts inserted in its mouth by pushing down directly upon the frog's nose with a spring-type mechanism hidden within the body. The nose snaps back into place. (The screw-type nutcracker section in Chapter 4 contains information on hand-wrought iron nutcrackers.)

Steel

Steel refers to any of the numerous alloys of iron and 0.1% to 1.5% carbon in the form of iron carbide. Often it is used in combination with other metals such as chromium, nickel, or manganese alloyed to impart special physical properties. Steel nutcrackers will not be discussed at length as they were, for the most part, non-figural. Furthermore, steel nutcrackers are discussed elsewhere within the text, under other headings such as steel plated with silver and screw-type models made of cut-out and chased iron and steel. However, worthy of mention are the wrought steel nutcrackers from 18th century Europe. Although not figural, they were certainly highly decorative. These included delicately modeled ones, some with handles finishing in acorn-shaped knobs, or those also made to be used as tobacco stoppers. Tobacco stoppers were used from around 1700 onward to press down the half-smoked dottle which caked in the bowls of clay pipes. Other mid-18th century steel nutcrackers have aesthetic appeal. Their simple designs often included curvaceous handles and decorative markings on their outer handles.

Occasionally, a figural steel nutcracker is found. The workmanship on those with a good deal of hand finishing can be quite exceptional. An example of a beautifully cast and hand-finished steel nutcracker is shown in Plate 27. A significant amount of work was done after the piece was cast to strike a pattern simulating feathers onto the bird's head. The incised eyes and some decorative details on the interior of the lower beak were also added. Only marked with a small "x", it is unfortunate that no other identifying marks are present. The simplicity of the overall design would suggest that it was made in America, probably during the late 1800s or early 1900s. (See two other figural steel nutcrackers in Plate 73, pg. 70. Also pictured are a variety of bird nutcrackers including a nicely cast nickel-plated parrot's head and a steel bird-shaped model with hand-finished cast handles with decorative eagles.)

Brass

Throughout history, braziers, the craftsmen who worked in brass, fashioned many items from this alloy of copper and zinc. However, brass had only rare appeal to the aristocratic tastes and was primarily enjoyed by the middle and lower classes.

In the 14th century, Austria, France, Germany and the Low Countries had thriving brass industries, but it was not until the late 1500s that England began producing brass. Before Europeans knew how to distill zinc in the 18th century, their brass was made from the crushed metallic zinc ore, lapis calaminaris. After perfecting the distilling process by the end of the 18th century, England became the world's foremost brass manufacturer. However, in less than a century, brass fell into low repute due to its mass production. Many fine examples made during this peak production period were discarded as scrap.

PLATE 28
Left: Brass Shakespeare nutcracker. One side is a figure of Shakespeare on a balcony with the dates 1564–1616. The other side has a portrait bust of Shakespeare with his name and some indecipherable writing. "No. 554" appears on the interior of one lever. 5" long, ¾" across, 1" deep. English, c. 1884.
Right: Brass Fagin and Bill Sikes nutcracker. Fagin is on one side; Bill Sikes on reverse side. 4¾" long, 1" across, 1½" deep. English, late 1800s to early 1900s.

Brass resists corrosion and is stronger and harder than the metals from which it is made. Brass had many uses in colonial America, but little of it was alloyed here because the raw materials were too scarce. Therefore, most brass came to the colonies from England as ingot sheets which were then hand hammered into various objects.

The American merchant fleet needed mathematical instruments such as quadrants, compasses, and sextants. Consequently, instrument makers thrived in seaport towns. Their products required brass as did clock parts and a whole category of articles termed "furniture" which included pins, buttons, buckles, upholsterer's nails, thimbles, cork screws, candlesticks, and nutcrackers.

In 1780, James Emerson was successful in fusing zinc and copper in the ratio of one-to-two to produce a high quality of brass. Ten years later, the Waterbury Brass Works opened in Connecticut and the existence by the late 1700s of several brass foundries in America allowed brass to be cast as well as hand hammered. The founders cast most brass articles rough, in sand or iron molds, and finished them by hand. By the beginning of the 19th century, several makers of brass existed in United States. Some signed their work with impressed marks.

The Victorian era, 1837 to 1901, witnessed the widespread use of cast iron, but brass was also popular for fashioning nutcrackers. During this era, brass nutcrackers were generally larger and more elaborate than those produced in earlier periods. English brass is ordinarily simple in design and seldom follows the elaborate shapes and patterns of silver. This held true for decorative but nonfigural brass nutcrackers. Many of the hand-held type, ornamented with a variety of figures, were made in Great Britain during the reign of Queen Victoria. Some of them utilized British themes in their designs, as shown in Plate 28. Shown are two Charles Dickens characters, Fagin and Bill Sikes from *Oliver Twist*, and William Shakespeare. Other examples of brass nutcrackers are pictured in Plates 29 and 30.

The brass clown face on the left in Plate 30 is marked "England" on the interior of the handle. The "Made in (Name of country)" designation identifies a piece as having been produced c. 1910 or later. From 1891 to 1910, a variety of wares, including nutcrackers, stated only the name of the country of origin (i.e., "England", "Germany", etc.) in order to comply with the McKinley Tariff Act of America. Consequently, nutcrackers made before 1891 will ordinarily bear no reference to national origin. These designations of national origin were applied to items imported into the United States only. Nutcrackers or other merchandise brought to America by immigrants from their homeland would not be marked since they were not specifically made for export.

PLATE 29
Brass full-length cat nutcracker. 5" long, ¾" across, 1¼" deep. English, late 19th to early 20th century. Brass grandfather's clock nutcracker marked on interior of handle with illegible letter, possibly company's name, and "Made in England." 5½" long, 1¼" across, ¾" deep. c. 1925. Brass cat with large bow nutcracker. 5½" long, 1½" across, 1¼" deep. English, late 19th to early 20th century.

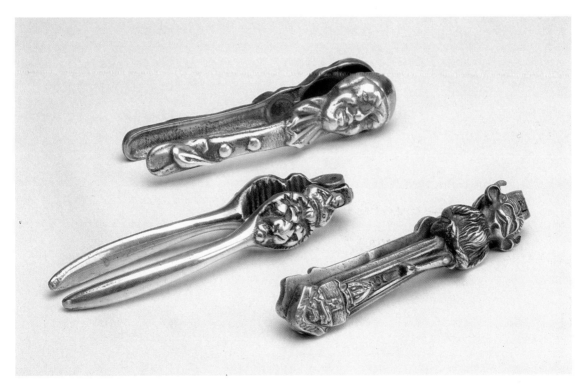

PLATE 30
Brass double-faced clown (Pierrot) nutcracker marked "England." 5¼" long, 1½" deep, 1" across. Late 19th to early 20th century. Brass lion with crown nutcracker. 5⅝" long, 1⅞" across, 1" across. English, late 1800s to early 1900s. Brass devil or horned monkey nutcracker marked "R^D596549." 5½" long, 1" across, 1¼" deep. English, c. 1912.

Also, impressing the country of origin on nutcrackers applied only to those made from brass, cast iron or some other metal. Wooden nutcrackers made from 1891 on rarely have the country of origin carved into their surfaces. A paper label was probably used, and most have long since been removed or fallen off. Deliberate removal of such paper labels is now legally prohibited.

Returning to Plate 30, the horned monkey or devil-like figure on the bottom right was also produced as a doorknocker. (Similarities between nutcrackers and doorknockers are discussed more fully in Chapter 7.) According to T. Q. Franks in her article written in 1911 for *Country Life in America* entitled "The Quest of the Knocker," this grotesque design represents a gargoyle from an English cathedral.

Most iron and brass nutcrackers are cast rather than hand-wrought. Some very interesting hand-wrought brass examples do exist. The whale in Plate 31 is especially well done with sleek lines and nice details. The pins which hold the levered jaws together serve also as the whale's eyes. Marked on the interior of one handle with letters which appear to read "HA PIND," it was obviously the work of a proud craftsman. Unfortunately , the origin is unknown. According to the wear and the design style, this piece was probably made around 1900–1910 when the Arts and Crafts influence produced hand-wrought items with simple geometric lines, but it is difficult to be certain.

Hand-fashioned steel and brass utensils, such as the whale, lack the seams made from the molds in which cast iron and cast brass pieces are formed. On many molded pieces, seams are sanded down so that they are not readily apparent. See Plate 32 for a seam which is visible on the interior handle and head of the brass eagle nutcracker on the far left in this photograph. Next to it is an almost identical nutcracker in which the seams were sanded

down. This particular design is an extremely popular one, made almost certainly in England around 1890–1910. Although produced rather prolifically, slight variations do exist, such as the splayed handles on some and the straight handles on others. I have seen this piece described as a multi-use opener. In addition to cracking nuts, the various recesses could be used for other purposes, such as cracking lobster claws.

On the right side of Plate 32 are two brass rooster or cockerel nutcrackers which are very similar in their handle design to the eagle nutcracker. These may have had multiple uses, too. Being so similar in form and appearance, it would seem logical that they were made around the same time, probably the late 1800s or early 1900s. I have seen, however, the cockerel dated as early as 1800 by at least one authority. This could mean one of three things. First, the dating of this piece around 1800 could be incorrect. Secondly, the cockerel and possibly the eagle might actually have been produced in the early 1800s rather than 90 to 100 years later. Lastly, these nutcrackers may represent designs which were first made around 1800 and were reproduced over the subsequent hundred year period. I would tend to think that due to the fact that these specimens are quite common and were produced in great quantity, the vast majority were probably made over a period of 25 to 30 years between the late 1800s and early 1900s, even though the design may have originated at an earlier time. Also, those exhibiting poorer workmanship were probably made later. I have recently seen the cockerel design reproduced and being sold at decorator shops. These recent reproductions, although made of brass, are lighter in weight and lack the detail of the older ones.

In Plate 33, a brass hand-held elf or gnome nutcracker is pictured along with a slightly larger copper-plated cast iron nutcracker and a wooden example of similar design.

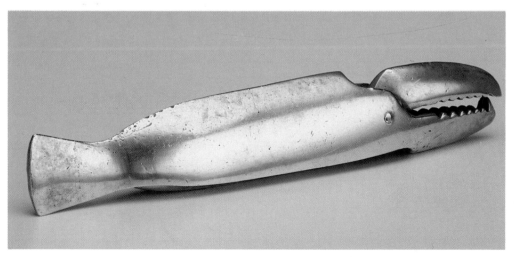

PLATE 31
Hand-wrought brass whale nutcracker marked "HA PIND." 6¼" long, 1" high, ½" across. Early 1900s.

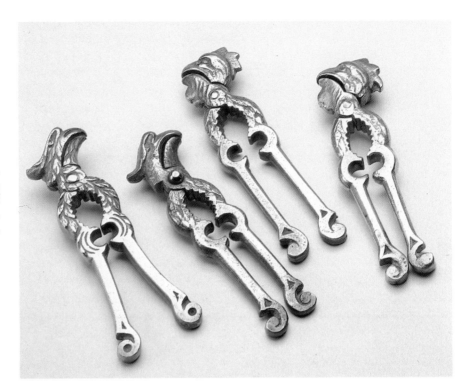

PLATE 32
Pair of brass eagle nutcrackers. 5¾" long, ¼" across, 1¼" deep. Probably English, late 19th to early 20th century. Pair of brass rooster nutcrackers. 5⅞" long, 1¼" deep, 1" across. Probably English, late 19th to early 20th century.

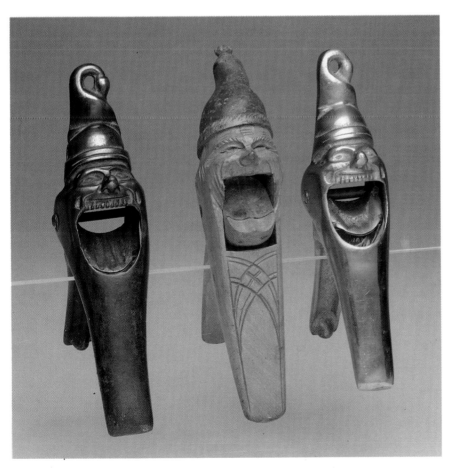

PLATE 33
Left to right: Copper-plated cast iron elf nutcracker marked "RD No. 776837" on interior of handle. 7⅜" long, 1⅞" across, 2" deep. English, c. 1932. Painted wooden elf with red stocking cap nutcracker. 7½" long, 1⅝" across, 2" deep. German or Swiss, early 20th century. Brass elf with stocking cap nutcracker. 7" long, 1⅝" across, 1¾" deep. Probably English, early to mid-20th century.

Some nutcrackers, like these, can be found in a variety of mediums, including brass. American inventor Anders L. Mordt from Guymon, Oklahoma, patented two hand-held nutcrackers with human head designs on February 6, 1912 (Patent Design Nos. 42,143 and 42,144). He did not state in his specifications from what substance the figures were to be made. One figure wore a beret-like cap, while the other had short wavy hair. Presumably, they could have been made out of brass, cast iron and/or wood.

Likewise, two inventors from Minnesota patented a hand-held German military-type nutcracker wearing a helmet with a visor (Des. No. 83,881). John T. Skogman of Minneapolis and Clifford L. Hansen of St. Louis Park patented their design on April 7, 1931. It was designed as a nutcracker or "analogous article" and incorporated a "Λ" in the bottom of the front handle which could serve as a stand for display. In addition, an elf or peasant-like nutcracker, donning a ski cap, was patented on August 1, 1933 by Christian Swensen of Duluth, Minnesota (Des. No. 90,428). In keeping with the brevity of most design patent descriptions, neither of these hand-held designs specified the intended composition.

The common standing dog nutcracker comes in more than one composition – brass, cast iron, and rhodium-plated cast iron. All were made in England in the same identical size and design from the 1920s–1940s (Plate 34).

The two cast iron dogs are marked with an English patent number (273,480) which reveals that their design was patented in 1927 by three English inventors, George Day, Fred Alexander Rimington, and Frederick Taylor.

Interestingly enough, nutcrackers were also produced with the same design, but in different sizes. In this case, the jesters in Plate 35 were made of brass, probably in England, in the early 1900s, although no identifying marks are present on either piece.

Worthy of special mention is the rather strange looking brass nutcracker in Plate 36 which comes in its own decoratively tooled leather pouch. This figure, possibly a lion, represents an animal in a caricature style with elongated legs which form the handles of the nutcracker. The saying on the pouch reads "Use my jaws for Nuts & Claws." This English nutcracker is apparently recommended for a dual purpose – to crack both nuts and lobster claws. A registration number appears along the bottom half of one of the legs, just above the foot. Worn away to some extent, the letters appear to read "R^D 6924-4" or "5924-4" which would suggest that it was registered in either 1911 or 1922 and produced around that time. The back of the leather pouch is marked with a small gold leaf within which is the name, Arden Forest. The letter/number combination "C66" appears directly below the leaf, but once again, what it means is not clear.

PLATE 34
Small rhodium-plated cast iron dog nutcracker. Marked "Made in England" and "Patent No. 273,480." 3¾" high, 9" long including tail, 1½" across. Patented in 1927.
Small cast iron dog nutcracker with traces of red polychrome paint. Marked "Made in England" and "Patent No. 273,480." 3¾" high, 9" long including tail, 1½" across. Patented in 1927.
Small brass dog nutcracker. 3¾" high, 9" long including tail, 1½" across. Probably English, c. 1930.

PLATE 35
Left: Large double-faced brass jester
nutcracker. 7¼" long, 2" deep, 1¼" across.
Probably English, early 1900s.
Right: Smaller similar model.

PLATE 36
Brass figural nutcracker in leather case. Back of case is marked "Arden Forest" with a gold leaf and
"066." 4¾" long, 1⅜" across, ⅝" deep. English, c. 1911–1922.

Confirming the use of nutcrackers as souvenir items are the brass examples in Plate 37. These horses are obviously nutcrackers, as the corners of the base on each piece are in the form of a different variety of nut (peanut, walnut, almond and Brazil nut). They have an unusual cracking surface which resembles a press with ridges top and bottom. Apparently souvenirs from the mid 1900s, one is marked "Miami Beach, Florida" in a small circle in the middle of the base near the horse's hooves and the other has a similar circle marked with just "Florida" in the center. The existence of the famous Hialeah race track in Florida no doubt inspired the production and sale of these horse-related nutcrackers. American-made, these brass pieces are marked "Pat. PEND." on the Brazil nuts on their bases.

Another brass nutcracker (Plate 38) depicts a rather elongated monkey whose tail forms the lever which operates the jaw. This figure is marked with the letters "R^D" followed by "706124." The numbers on this piece identify it as having been registered for production in 1924. (Appendix I contains a list provided by the British Patent Office which gives R^D numbers and the corresponding years of manufacture from 1839 to 1989. This list can help to date English-made brass and cast iron nutcrackers during this period. Mention should be made that the R^D marking should not be confused with an R^E designation which represents "Reissue Design" in the American patent system, according to the United States Patent Office.)

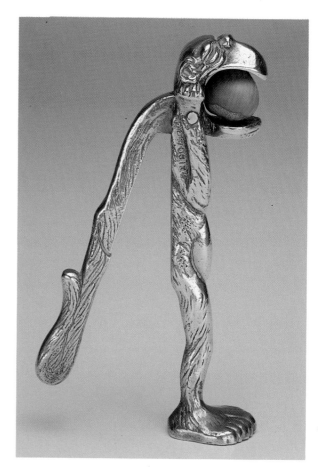

PLATE 38
Brass monkey caricature nutcracker marked "R^{D}706124." 5⅝" high, ⅞" across, 1⅛" deep. English, c. 1924.

PLATE 37
Brass standing horse nutcracker marked "Miami Beach, FLA." and "PAT. PEND." 4¾" high, 8" across including lever, 3" deep. Mid-20th century.
Brass running horse and jockey nutcracker marked "Florida" and "PAT. PEND." 4⅜" high, 8" across including lever, 3" deep. Mid-20th century.

Silver Plate

Silver alone is basically too soft a metal for overall nutcracker construction and of the few that were made, most were produced around 1800. I have heard, however, of one fascinating sterling piece in the shape of a crocodile. The mouth moved from side to side rather than up and down to crack open nuts. Some early nutcrackers, like the one listed in the 1410 inventory in the Lourve, were made of silver, in that case gilded silver. The vast majority of so-called "silver" nutcrackers were not made of silver but were actually silverplated brass or steel.

The process of plating base metals with a silver veneer has been practiced for hundreds of years. Roman coins were silvered as early as 304 A.D. Until the 1700s, silverplating was accomplished through chemical amalgamation. In the early 1700s, a method of attaching leaves of pure silver to brass and copper evolved in France.

The technique referred to as "Sheffield plating" was discovered quite by accident in 1743 in Sheffield, England. A cutter, repairing the handle of a knife, touched some copper with heated silver and the two metals fused together. They could be hammered or rolled as one entity. Thomas Boulsover is credited with this discovery.

The English process of close-plating, a less costly method of plating than French plating on brass and copper, involved applying silver leaf over base metals such as iron and steel. Close-plating was not used extensively in Sheffield and Birmingham, England until around 1800. In 1809, Edward Thomason of Birmingham developed an improved method of close-plating utilizing rolled silver foil rather than silver leaf which was quite costly and, therefore, not widely used. Employing this process opened up a huge new market where articles formerly made of expensive silver could now be produced more cheaply.

Identifying and dating decorative silver-plated nutcrackers is made somewhat easier by the frequent existence of identification marks representing the various manufacturers. The practice of marking silverplated items dates back in England to 1784 when it was made legal to make a strike identification mark upon plated ware, a practice extended by the Sheffield Assay office to close-plated steel in 1806. It is possible by tracing registration marks for an individual firm to attribute periods of manufacture and to date particular articles like nutcrackers which were produced by these companies.

One such manufacturer of silver plate on steel was the William Hutton Company of Birmingham which first registered a mark with the Assay Office on November 19, 1807. The mark consisted of "Hutton" in script to the left of an open-topped triangle with a pair of ears. This mark is often found on a variety of flatware, skewers, snuffers and nutcrackers. Over the years, the Hutton Company registered many variations of this original mark through the time when its goods became electroplated. A variety of books is available which list the marks of silverplate manufacturers and the dates which correspond to such marks to aid in the identification process.

In 1841, Elkingtons of Birmingham, England developed a technique for laying a coating of silver on a base metal using an electric current. This process soon replaced the English method of making Sheffield plate. (Originally the word "plate" was derived from the Spanish word "plata" which means silver.) Unlike Sheffield plating which was done on copper, electroplating was usually done on nickel silver. (Also called "German Silver." It refers to an alloy of copper, zinc, and nickel with the highest content being nickel to give it a silvery-white color. It has no actual silver content.) Such pieces ordinarily bear the letters EPNS or EPWM which stand for "Electroplated Nickel Silver" or "Electroplated White Metal." These metals were similar in color to the silver plating and could also be easily replated. By 1845, electroplating was being used in the United States where this new method was readily adopted. Unlike England, there was no Sheffield plating business to convert. Silverplaters in the United States started from scratch and, within a decade, were manufacturing electroplated silver in huge quantities. This Elkingtons method produced silverplate economically because it did not require the expensive dies needed for the old Sheffield plating process and handwork was kept to a minimum. Therefore, silver plate could be sold at prices affordable to almost everyone.

In distinguishing Sheffield plate from electroplated reproductions, look for traces of wear which are usually more abundant on the true Sheffield. Also, the silver used in Sheffield has a bluish-grey tone, whereas a more silvery look is achieved through electroplating. Old examples of Sheffield plate, dating from the 1700s and plated on copper, will show signs of wear, particularly at edges and corners where the silver has been worn away and the copper has "bled" through.

Numerous companies, from the prestigious Gorham firm on down, made and sold silverplate. The deposit of silver on the base metal was so standardized throughout the silver-plating industry that the same quality was made by almost all the companies. Therefore, pieces of silverplate, including ornately decorated nutcrackers, can be evaluated primarily, or in many instances entirely, upon their aesthetic appeal and uniqueness of design.

As early as the 1890s, the Gorham Company in the United States made a variety of collectible silverplated tableware, including toothpick holders, napkin rings and nutcrackers. Early in the 20th century, many decorative nutcrackers sold in America for between $1.00 and $1.50

each – much less than what these treasures are worth today. Two silver-plated nutcrackers are shown in Plate 39. One has decorative engraved handles and is marked "Wallace Bros." The other, a plain silverplated steel nutcracker, has impressed marks on the interior of one handle which read "(T) (P) & (S)" and stand for the English company which manufactured it. This piece, although not ornate, is interesting because it is convertible. The handles can be flipped back and forth to accommodate smaller nuts on one side and larger nuts on the other. Tiny pointed triangular prongs create a rough surface on both sides of the cracker to help hold nuts in place.

Some manufacturers did produce sterling rather than, or as well as, silverplated models. A case in point is the Reed and Barton company, based in the United States, which produced sterling nutcrackers. Specifically, they manufactured sterling nutcrackers in 1905 with matching nut picks in the "Intaglio" pattern. The handles of this nutcracker were sterling, but the parts of the implement used for cracking were made of a stronger metal.

Older electroplated silver can be replated without fear of obliterating either decorations or identification marks, but replating the old Sheffield silver will destroy the patina and charm of these beautiful pieces.

Pewter

Aluminum nutcrackers are not terribly common, sterling silver specimens are even harder to find and porcelain nutcrackers are extremely rare. Pewter is also very unusual. Therefore, the subject of pewter will be addressed only as an example of a medium with some potential for nutcracker construction, but apparently very little actual use. *Pewter* is a term used loosely to encompass Britannia metal and all such alloys regardless of tin content. In ancient times, however, *fine pewter* was an alloy of specific proportions of tin and antimony and was used extensively for various tableware including dishes, saucers and plates. An organization for regulating the pewter craft in England dates back to the year 1348 and many pewter articles were made as early as the 1300s.

For many centuries, pewter was the poor man's silver, used extensively for household utensils. Numerous objects were produced from pewter molds from the beginning of the 18th century. The pewter articles produced in Europe included tobacco stoppers, snuff boxes, candle snuffers and children's toys. The scarcity of examples of early pewter is attributed to the strict regulations of the Trade Union in England called the Pewters' Company. Its members were not permitted to mend broken pieces of pewter

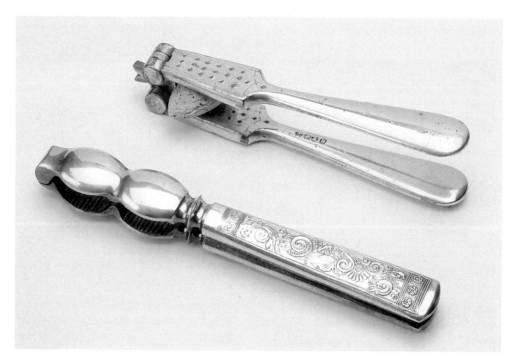

PLATE 39
Silverplated non-figural nutcracker marked "(T) (P) &(S)." 5" long, ⅞" deep, ⅝" across. English, late 19th century.
Silverplated non-figural nutcracker with decorative handles. Marked "Wallace Bros." 5¼" long, ¾" across, ¾" deep. Late 19th to early 20th century.

which were brought to them. Instead, they were obliged to put the damaged pieces in the melting pot and re-cast the pieces from current molds.

Very few pieces of pewter were produced in the 1700s in America due to the fact that tin, which is the primary constituent of pewter, was scarce in the colonies. The English guilds confined the export of pewter to the finished items manufactured in England. American craftsmen were limited to the recasting of old pieces that had originally been produced abroad and through long, hard usage were no longer functional.

I have yet to find any nutcrackers in pewter, but I have read of one screw-type nutcracker depicting Christopher Columbus. It is 7" in height with a circular bottom through which the screw descends from a beautiful pewter bust of Columbus. Not having seen this nutcracker firsthand, the bust is most likely pewter, but the nutcracking ring is made of stronger metal. This nutcracker was a souvenir of the World's Columbian Exposition held in Chicago in 1893 (Illustration 3). It was probably intended to be more decorative than functional.

Christopher Columbus is once again the subject of nutcracker construction. In 1992, the prestigious Steinbach Company of Germany produced a wooden nutcracker depicting Columbus with his left hand resting atop a globe. The globe is standing atop a plaque commemorating the 500-year anniversary of Columbus' 1492 voyage to America. (Plate 86, page 85).

I would be surprised if a few other pewter nutcrackers do not exist, although pewter is generally too soft a medium to produce such sturdy objects intended for heavy use. Lead was added to a lesser alloy known as "lay" (or ley) and that metal was used for hollow and shaped objects which would be expected to receive rough long-term use. It would seem likely that nutcrackers might have been fashioned from this more durable form of pewter.

ILLUSTRATION 3
Christopher Columbus screw-type pewter nutcracker was a souvenir of the World's Columbian Exposition held in Chicago in 1893.

Meat skewers with ornamental heads were also produced in pewter. The prongs of these meat skewers were often reinforced with an iron core. This technique of strengthening a piece of pewter with an iron center might also have been applied to nutcracker production.

Maker's marks on pewter, called "touches," aid in identifying the origin and age of the nutcracker. Generally, the smaller the mark the earlier the piece of pewter. A small circle with beads or dots around it is representative of 16th or 17th century pewter. Four small shield-shaped punches containing silversmith marks, such as "Lion Passant" or initials, are usually found on 17th or early 18th century specimens.

Bronze

Bronze is an alloy of copper and tin and sometimes other elements such as zinc, lead or nickel. The proportion is usually ninety parts copper to ten parts tin. It is quite heavy and is often reddish rather than yellow in color. Aging sometimes causes a deep brown patina, but sometimes no darkening occurs. Bronze is an excellent casting metal and is frequently found in figural forms. In fact, it must be cast and cannot be worked in sheets. There are two casting methods: cire perdue and sand casting. Cire perdue (the lost wax method) is superior to sand casting. This process requires a clay model to be made for each bronze to be cast. Reproductions are often made of spelter or zinc, which is a lighter and poorer quality base metal.

Beautiful bronze nutcrackers were not created in the same profusion as wooden, brass and cast iron examples. An especially striking copper-plated bronze dog is pictured on the right in Plate 40. Notice the rich patina of the bronze where the copper has worn away. This patina enhances the appeal of this charming retriever. Unlike the majority of standing dog nutcrackers, this one is shown in a striding position.

The squirrel holding a nut is also bronze (Plate 40). The smooth surface and very angular style of this piece sets it apart from other squirrel nutcrackers I have seen. It was mass-produced, as I have seen more than one piece like this one, and it seems to reflect an Art Deco style.

More expensive to produce than either brass or cast iron, it is not surprising that bronze nutcrackers are fairly rare in comparison to these other mediums. To distinguish bronze from iron, a magnet can be used. The magnet will adhere to iron but not to bronze, chromium, aluminum, lead, copper, or brass. Although cast iron pieces can be quite heavy, bronze is heavier yet.

PLATE 40
Copper-plated bronze striding dog nutcracker. 11¼" long including tail, 5¾" high, 3⅝" across including base. Late 19th to early 20th century.
Bronze squirrel nutcracker. 5¾" high, 9⅜" long, 2½" across. 1920s–1930s.

Chapter 3

THE SIGNIFICANCE OF NUTCRACKERS

NUTTING PARTIES

In America, during the late 1800s and early 1900s, nutting parties were popular outings held in the autumn. Because many kinds of nuts grew in abundance in various parts of the country, farmers often permitted people to hold nutting parties on their land to gather them for free. Boys and girls would go in groups into the woods and fields to gather these fruits. Ordinarily, the boys climbed the trees and beat them to bring down the nuts while the girls together with the boys competed in gathering a supply of the fallen nuts.

Following the nut gathering, the groups often went to one of the farm houses for an evening of dancing and simple games such as a candy-pull. No doubt, nutcrackers were put to good use at these parties where the guests anxiously tasted a sampling of the day's gatherings.

Through these nutting parties, many families secured an ample supply of chestnuts, beechnuts, hickory nuts, black walnuts and butternuts for the winter evenings ahead. The clearing of the woodland, the loss of many chestnut trees to disease and the move of many people to cities signaled the decline of this once popular festivity. The commercial growing of nuts in America, primarily pecans, hazel nuts and walnuts, began around 1900 and also negated the need for people to gather their own nuts each year.

LITERARY REFERENCES AND ARTISTIC RENDERINGS

As noted earlier, both Chaucer and Elyot made mentioned of nutcrackers in their writings. The writings of Benjamin Franklin also included a reference to nutcrackers. In correspondence to his wife in Philadelphia, dated February 2, 1773, Mr. Franklin wrote from London: "*When seeing me one day crack one of the Philada. Bisquits into my Tea with the Nutcrackers, (the child) took another and try'd to do the same with the Tea-Tongs.*" Writings of Benjamin Franklin, ed., A. H. Smyth (New York, 1907). (Tea-tongs are small silver or silver-plated tongs used to lift tea from the caddy to the pot. They are similar to tongs used in the 20th century to transport sugar cubes.)

In the mid-1800s, British author Edward Lear wrote a charming children's story called *The Nutcrackers and The Sugar-Tongs*. In this delightful tale, the nutcrackers and the sugar-tongs decide to abandon their places at the table and go off on horses, leaving the Victorian household behind in chaos and confusion.

In 1851, the German writer Heinrich Hoffman wrote a poem about the nutcracker which includes these words:

The King, mighty,
handsome and tall
with scepter, crown and red
britches
A proud lord, full of majesty
By jove, what a rarity!

In the same poem, the nutcracker says to himself:

King Nutcracker,
that's my name
I crack hard nuts
and eat the sweet
insides.
But the shells, ugh –
I throw to others,
Because I am the King!

Even Russian literature is not without reference to nutcracking. In Alexander Pushkin's 1905 work *The Tale of Tsar Saltan*, a recurring passage refers not to a nutcracking implement but to a nut-cracking squirrel:

On an island, far away …
Dwells a squirrel strange and rare,
Full of frolic, all day long,
Cracking nuts, it sings a song.
Nuts, most wondrous to behold -
Shells of purest yellow gold,
All the Kernels - emeralds bright.
Sentries guard it day and night.

In addition to the illustrations made to accompany stories and poetry involving nutcrackers, at least one painting is noted as having a nutcracker depicted along with the human subjects of the piece. It was painted by Burne-Jones (Sir Edward Coley) who was an English painter and designer (1833–1898), a follower of the Pre-Raphaelite brotherhood and a major figure in the Arts and Crafts movement. The picture, entitled *Lorenzo and Isabella* included a wooden nutcracker in the form of a man with a ruff and a beaver hat. (A ruff is a broad starched collar of fluted linen or muslin worn by both men and women, especially in the 16th century.)

English authority Edward Pinto possessed an identical wooden nutcracker in his collection of treen. After seeing the painting and comparing it to his nutcracker, Mr. Pinto theorized that despite its early appearance, which initially suggested it had been made around 1620, it did not actually show significant signs of age. Most likely it was made more than two hundred years later. Furthermore, in addition to the nutcracker in Mr. Pinto's collection, he had seen two other similar pieces and believed that this nutcracker was designed by Burne-Jones specifically for the painting, which has been on display at the Tate Gallery in London.

HOLIDAY FESTIVITIES

Nuts and nutcrackers have played a prominent role in a variety of holiday celebrations. For instance, in northern England, Halloween is known as "Nutcrack Night." Traditional customs of this holiday include games in which both nuts and apples are used extensively.

For many centuries, the cracking and eating of nuts around an open fire has been a traditional part of the Christmas festivities. Wherever the custom of hanging up Christmas stockings has been practiced, nuts also have been a standard stocking filler, although more often in bygone years than at the present. Nutmeats have been for centuries an important ingredient of Yule plum puddings, cookies, candies and fruit cakes. It seems natural then that in years past, especially in Europe, nutcrackers served as special Christmas gifts for children and grown-ups alike. They continue to be popular today, having found particular appeal in the United States.

THE NUTCRACKER SUITE

The Nutcracker and the Mouse King was written by the writer, composer and painter, Ernst Theodor Amadeus (E.T.A.) Hoffman (1776–1822) and remains to this day one of the most popular tales associated with Christmas. Considered a long short story, it was first published in 1816 in a children's collection, *Kindermärchen,* along with other stories by C. W. Contessa and Friedrich Baron de la Motte

Fouqué. Sometimes confusing is the fact that some years later another nutcracker-related story was written by an author with the same surname of Hoffman. This physician and poet was Dr. Heinrich Hoffman (1809–1894), a neurologist in the Bavarian city of Nuremberg, who was inspired in 1851 to write the now classic story of a nutcracker and a child after visiting one of his young patients. The name of the child in this tale is Reinhold and the story is translated from German as *King Nutcracker and the Poor Reinhold.* It tells of a child who is restored to good health with the help of a nutcracker.

Alexandre Dumas Pére (1802–1870), a dramatist and novelist, adapted E.T.A. Hoffman's story, *Nutcracker of Nuremberg,* into *Casse Noisette.* (*Noisette* is French for nut.) This French version inspired composer and conductor Peter Ilyitch Tschaikovsky (1840–1893) to compose his much acclaimed *Nutcracker Suite.* The music was first performed in St. Petersburg, Russia, in 1892 as the feature of a Christmas festival.

The original E.T.A. Hoffman story had not been meant as a fairy tale for children, being considered by the author himself as much too frightening for the young. It was the story of a little girl named Marie Stahlbaum, daughter of a doctor who was a member of the town council. Marie, whose family appeared devoid of love, had an unusual affection for her nutcracker doll. The nutcracker was in the form of a Prussian soldier or Hussar from the Napoleonic Wars. (Soldier nutcrackers like the one on the cover of this book and the two in Plate 41 continue to be popular today.) Hoffman's story is really a story within a story, filled with dark undertones and cynicism about human beings and family relationships.

In direct contrast to this moody and somewhat sinister piece is Tchaikovsky's ballet which was indeed meant for children as well as adults. This story centers around a little girl named Clara. Her favorite Christmas present, a nutcracker, is given to her by her elderly and eccentric godfather, Drosselmeyer. In some accounts, the nutcracker is a soldier with large jaws, while others describe it as little man with a long nose (Plate 42). The little girl's nutcracker is accidentally broken by her brother, and after an evening party, she remains to say good-night to her injured toy. One version of the story has the parlor invaded by mice during the time Clara is visiting her nutcracker. Another interpretation has Clara dreaming later that night that her gifts have come to life and that they are being attacked by an army of mice. Both versions agree, however, that when the Nutcracker soldier appears to be losing a duel with the Mouse King, Clara intercedes by throwing her slipper at the mouse, causing the army of mice to retreat. Suddenly, the Nutcracker is transformed into a handsome prince resembling Drosselmeyer's nephew who had accompanied his uncle that evening to Clara's

PLATE 42

PLATE 41

Pictured are two inexpensive, but colorful contemporary soldier-type nutcrackers. These German soldier nutcrackers have been popular for many years and are widely sold in department stores each year during the Christmas season. The crowned figure could actually represent royalty. The smaller nutcracker measures 10½" high, 3½" across, 2½" deep including base and the larger measures 15½" high, 5¼" across, and 4¼" deep. Stickers on the bottoms of the bases read "Made in China."

PLATE 42

Silhouette of young girl and nutcracker doll, artist unknown. Early 20th century.

PLATE 43

Toy soldier ornaments marked "(c) KSA" on bottom of base. 4¾" high, 1¾" across, 1¾" deep. Late 20th century.
Football player ornament marked "Roman" and "Made in Taiwan" by sticker on bottom of base. 4½" high, 2½" across, 1½" deep. Late 20th century.

PLATE 43

home. Clara is persuaded by the prince to accompany him to a wonderful Fairy Kingdom where they are entertained by sugar plum fairies and other fanciful creatures.

This is the story dramatized in the Nutcracker ballet. The literary version, however, contains another tale told to the little girl on the following day by her godfather, Drosselmeyer. This story goes:

There once was a princess named Pirlipat. Because her parents had quarrelled with mice, the mice swore revenge upon her. Therefore Pirlipat's bed was watched every night by guardians...except that each of these guardians held a big, purring cat. Alas, one night all the cats and all the guardians fell asleep at the same time, and the Mouse Queen turned the princess into a dwarf. A wise clockmaker (named, by a strange coincidence, Drosselmeyer) discovered that Pirlipat would be restored to her natural beauty if a young man cracked the Krakatuk nut. This was easier said than done, for not even a cannon could penetrate its hard thick shell. Nonetheless Drosselmeyer found a young man who could do it. By another strange coincidence, it was his own nephew.

(Here, says Dumas, is the origin of the old saying, "That's a hard nut to crack.")

Just as everybody was planning to live happily ever after, nephew Drosselmeyer accidentally stepped on the Mouse Queen's tail and was himself transformed into a dwarf. This spell could be broken only if he slew the Mouse Queen's son and heir, the seven-headed Mouse King.

When the little girl heard this, she was convinced that her nutcracker was really the bewitched nephew, Drosselmeyer. She supplied him with a sword borrowed from a tin soldier, the Mouse King was slain, and she and nephew Drosselmeyer sailed off to Confectionery Castle in a seashell drawn by dolphins. Then she woke and found herself at home in bed.

Time passed. Several Christmases later, Drosselmeyer introduced her to his real nephew, a handsome fellow who was able to perform the curious parlor trick of cracking nuts with his front teeth. The girl was sure this was her childhood Nutcracker Prince. They were married, and again went off to a candy kingdom. There they are still living today.

(Excerpted from Jack Anderson's book, *The Nutcracker Ballet* published by Mayflower Books in 1979.)

With approximately 130 ballet companies across the United States performing the *Nutcracker Suite* annually, and an estimated two million Americans attending a performance of this classic ballet each year, it is little wonder that nutcracker collecting is more popular than ever in this country. Many homes at Christmastime prominently display nutcracker soldiers. Recently, German nutcracker manufacturers have included characters from the ballet, such as the Nutcracker Prince, the Mouse King, Herr Drosselmeyer, and the Toy Soldier, in their collections. Meanwhile, the Horchow Company of Dallas, Texas, featured a 59" hand-carved, hand-painted toy soldier style nutcracker in its November–December 1991 catalogue.

Miniature nutcrackers in a wide assortment of forms, including toy soldiers and football players, also have been made as tree ornaments (Plate 43). The tiny football player was made in Taiwan by a company named Roman and stands next to the box in which it was purchased. This example provides a good opportunity to mention the packaging of contemporary nutcrackers. Retaining the boxes in which new nutcrackers are packaged is always recommended if they contain some wording identifying the manufacturer or the nutcracker type or model. As with most collectibles, having the original packaging enhances the future value. All tags, booklets and other descriptive materials which accompany a nutcracker also should be saved.

Returning to Plate 43, the toy soldiers in this picture are unmarked except for a stamp on the bottom of one which reads "(c) KSA." Although cute, they are not noteworthy apart from the fact that their levers move in such a way as to crack nuts in the stomach cavity rather than in the mouth. The bottom of the stomach is grooved to hold a nut secure – a rather interesting detail on pieces which were obviously inexpensively mass-produced.

There can be no question that the *Nutcracker Suite* together with annual Christmas celebrations have done much to popularize nutcrackers. Contemporary examples, advertised as Christmas gifts, come in a wide assortment of designs which are expanded each year. Recently, the ever-popular Mickey Mouse has taken the form of a nutcracker. Figures are also taking the form of different professionals and hobbyists such as doctors, tennis players and golfers. These items are so collectible that they are no longer considered merely Christmas decorations, but are enjoyed year-round in numerous homes.

Chapter 4

CONSTRUCTION AND DEVELOPMENT OF NUTCRACKERS

TYPES OF NUTCRACKERS

Four basic mechanical principles are employed in the design and function of nutcrackers with some interesting variations. These four basic varieties are the percussion, direct pressure, indirect pressure and screw-type nutcracker. The direct and indirect pressure nutcrackers are sometimes referred to as direct and indirect "action" and both ordinarily involve the use of one or two levers.

Among non-figural nutcrackers, credit must be given to a Texas pecan grower and nutcracker collector, Hayward Rigano, who manufacturers a nutcracker specifically for the cracking of pecans. This piece, called the "Miller Cracker," is marked with its name on both the top and bottom and with "Fort Worth, TX, 76119" and the patent No. 3965810 (Plate 44). It was patented by Jess Miller of Fort Worth, Texas on June 29, 1976 and utilizes a "twisting" motion which is similar to the screw type. It is different enough to be considered distinct from the other four categories of nutcrackers but rare enough not to establish a fifth classification.

Although there are only four fundamental nutcracker design principles, there has been a remarkable array of style variations. Nutcrackers that exemplify these design types and demonstrate their original approaches are described next.

Percussion

The "percussion" or "strike" type of nutcracker is an extension of the caveman's practice of cracking a nutshell by banging at it with a rock. The type of nutcracker which utilizes this principle is the nut hammer. Nut hammers, as opposed to hammers and mallets in general, were made specifically to crack nuts and appear to be a 19th and 20th century innovation, although earlier ones may exist.

Nut hammers can be found in sets which combine a hammer and a separate base upon which the nut is put for cracking. A particularly fine example is pictured in Plate 8, which includes a small, rather common-looking, hammer and a base in the form of a nut. Common, that is, except for the fact that these pieces were made with a thick silver plate, probably during the 1920s as the style reflects a Deco influence. A real nut can be balanced or carefully held upon this base while the small mallet is used to crack open the shell.

Other nut hammers are individual instruments with no matching base. A squirrel figural hammer is shown in

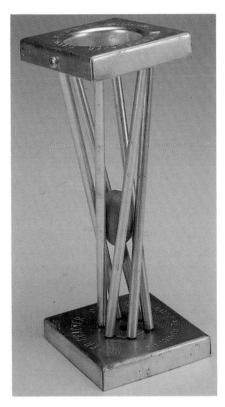

PLATE 44
Aluminum Miller Cracker for pecans. Marked "Miller Cracker, Fort Worth, TX 76119 – Pat. 3965810." 7¼" high, 3" wide, 3" across. Patented in 1976.

Plate 8. The nut is merely set on a hard flat surface, such as a table or cutting board, and hit with the hammer to crack open the shell. Of course, the possibility exists that this nickel-plated squirrel-shaped mallet originally had a matching base which was lost over the years.

Another variation of the nut hammer is the "knee warmer" which is an interesting example of a non-figural, percussion type. The "knee warmer" nutcracker derives its name from the fact that it combines a hammer and a curved metal base which is intended to fit just above the bent knee of the person doing the cracking. The nut is cracked on a protruding curved metal center similar to the pedestal found in some nut bowls. These cast iron "knee warmers" were probably American and made mostly in the early 19th century. They are usually 3½" to 6" long.

The most common form of nut hammer, widely produced in the 1900s, is the wooden or metal nut hammer with matching wooden bowl. The center of the bowl is in the shape of a pedestal. The nut is placed upon the pedestal or anvil. The nut meats and/or shells can be retained in the circular "doughnut" of the bowl.

A patent was granted in the United States for this type of bowl design on June 16, 1914 to the inventor Ralph A. Parsons of Denver, Colorado (Patent No. 1,099,996). Mr. Parsons' bowl was designed to have the anvil of "denser material than the bowl and the bowl though of lighter material (probably wood), ... adapted to sustain blows communicated through the anvil." The anvil was unique in "having a hammer surface broad at one end and tapering to a narrow end to accommodate nuts of different sizes…" The bowl was to be constructed to permit stacking of one bowl within another for storage purposes, the bottom of each bowl having "an opening so that the anvil portion of one may fit within the bottom of the one next above it in the stack." Several bowls, possibly in sets, would be available so that each guest could have a separate bowl.

Many variations to this general design can be found, some very plain, others more decorative, including the one on the left in Plate 45, marked "Nippon" on the bottom, which was made in Japan around 1920. The nut bowl on the right, rather than utilizing a nut hammer, employs a metal press type cracker which is permanently affixed to the center of the bowl. It is not technically a percussion cracker, but a direct pressure design, included here to contrast percussion and direct pressure nut bowl and cracker combinations. The handle on this piece is moved back and forth to create pressure on a nut placed within the grips of the central press. The black lacquered bowl is decorated with an Oriental design in gold and silver relief. United States design patents were granted on August 19, 1919 to Jesse S. Kepler of Dayton, Ohio, and Milton O. Kepler of New York, New York, for both the ornamental design of the nutcracker and the design for the

PLATE 45
Wooden nut bowl and mallet marked "Nippon" on bottom of base. 7" across, 2½" high including removable pedestal. Japanese, c. 1920. Wooden lacquered nut bowl with metal cracker. 10½" diameter, 5¼" high. American, patented in 1919.

shape of this particular bowl (Des. Nos. 53,713 and 53,712, respectively). A third design patent was also granted to these two inventors on the same date (Des. No. 53,711) for a slightly different bowl design which utilized the same nutcracking device in the center. (Nut bowls are discussed in "Other Nut-Related Utensils" at the end of this chapter.)

Direct Pressure

Another variety of nutcracker operates by "direct" pressure applied in front of the fulcrum. Many early examples of this type exert direct crushing force by two levers pivoted at one end like a hinge.

The mermaid in Plate 46 is an especially appealing example of the direct action principle. Her body, propped on one elbow as she reclines on her side, forms the top lever of this nutcracker, probably made about sixty years ago. The mermaid/merman theme apparently dates back to the 1600s. A rather unique and comparatively small wooden merman was included in the writings of Edward Pinto. (Comparatively small as opposed to other wooden figural nutcrackers from that time period.) It is from the 17th century and is English or Continental in origin. This merman, however, operated by indirect action, a form of nutcracker construction which will be described later.

Metal nutcrackers employing this direct pressure principle have been common over the years. Although there are wooden nutcrackers that used such a pivot, they were not very popular because they were usually not strong enough to withstand the exertion pressure. Of those wooden direct pressure nutcrackers, some interesting varieties, however, do exist. One unusual type was constructed from a single piece of hardwood, selected for its springiness. The handles were fashioned from a piece of wood which was connected across the top by a relatively thin strip of common wood. One such example even had teeth carved into the cracking apparatus. Although extremely clever in design, they are nonetheless not very strong nor very practical, and few of them, made mostly in the 1600s, 1700s and early 1800s, have survived to the present day. This variety of nutcracker is primarily simple in design and not heavily ornamented.

Perhaps even more rare is the type of nutcracker made from three pieces of wood. Produced in the 18th and 19th centuries, the two handles or arms of this variety were tenoned and loosely pegged with the third piece or strap mortised through. Incised decoration was sometimes found, particularly on the strap component.

A truly wonderful and very unusual example of a wooden direct action nutcracker is pictured in Plate 47. Found in England, it was probably made in the early 1900s. The bird's long orange beak serves as the handles and the nuts are cracked in its mouth. With glass eyes, a black head, and an overall sleek and simple line, it is a very striking piece.

Although the double-lever variety of nutcracker is ordinarily the type associated with "direct action," another wonderful example of direct action is pictured in Plate 48. This model, made of brass-plated cast iron, cracks nuts in its stomach rather than its mouth and is in the shape of a kangaroo with a rather pleasant face. It operates by tilting back the top half of the figure which is hinged at the back to the lower torso. Nuts are placed in the "pouch" and using the upper torso as a kind of lever, the nuts are compressed between the top and bottom sections of the figure. Like the shark nutcracker (Plate 23 on page 31), this cast iron kangaroo is marked "Nestor," probably representing the name of the English manufacturer. This name appears on the underside of the tail, and a series of indecipherable numbers are present on the bottom of the kangaroo's right foot.

PLATE 46
Brass mermaid nutcracker marked "Made in England." 5" long, 2⅛" high, 1" wide. c. 1930.

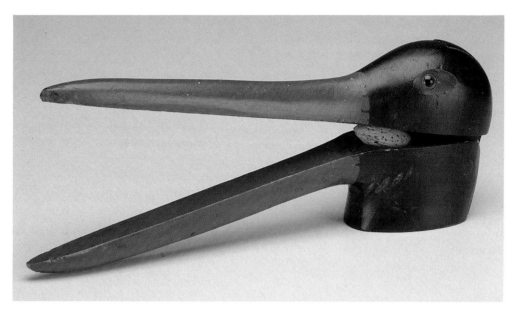

PLATE 47
Wooden orange-beaked bird with glass eyes and original paint. Found in England. 8½" long, 1½" across, 3" high. Early 20th century.

PLATE 48
Brass-plated cast iron kangaroo nutcracker marked "Nestor" on underside of tail and indecipherable registration number on foot. 5½" high, 6½" deep, 4½" across. English, c. 1930.

The predominantly orange and black elephant-shaped nutcracker (Plate 49) is another excellent example of the direct action type. The trunk of the elephant is used to exert pressure directly as it is first raised and then lowered to crack the nut placed in its mouth. Almost certainly American-made, this brightly painted pachyderm was manufactured in the 1920s or 1930s and is very Art Deco in appearance. Although widely produced in the bright orange color, the elephant is reported to have been made in blue as well. This cast iron piece closely resembles the wooden elephant, mentioned earlier, that appeared in a 1930 *Popular Mechanics* magazine article on nutcrackers. Creatures like this elephant typically crush the nutshells in their mouths, but I have seen at least one example of a direct action model, also represented in this magazine article, in the form of a clown which was pivoted at his feet and cracked nuts by "sitting" on them (Illustration 4).

Another humorous and very clever aluminum nutcracker pictured in Plate 50 is in the shape of a nut. This piece operates by lifting the top half from its hinged side and then cracking a real nut which is placed on a small stand with teeth in the interior of the aluminum nutshell. Although this piece was made in Taiwan, probably in the last ten years or so, this same basic design was utilized by an inventor almost one hundred years ago. Corties Collins of Dallas, Texas patented a design on May 25, 1897 (Des. No. 27,093) for a nutcracker which looked much like a powder compact. With two curved halves, it was held together by a common hinge, much like the aluminum nut. As a Texas inventor, Mr. Collins, adorned the nutcracker with the star of Texas. (Coincidentally, a signifi-

ILLUSTRATION 4
Sitting clown nutcracker pivots at his feet and cracks nuts by "sitting" on them. Seen in a 1930 issue of *Popular Mechanics* magazine.

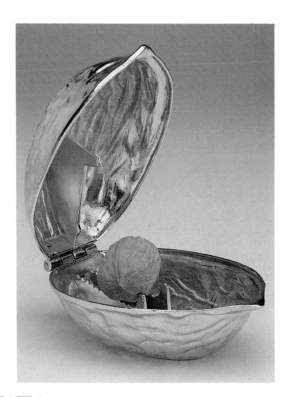

PLATE 49
Painted cast iron elephant nutcracker. 4¾" high, 9¾" long, 1¼" across. Probably American, ca. 1920s–1930s.

PLATE 50
Aluminum nutcracker in shape of a nut. Sticker on bottom marked "Made in Taiwan." 2¾" high, 5" long, 3⅜" across. Late 20th century.

cant percentage of nutcracker inventors and manufacturers seem to have come from the state of Texas.)

One very rare nutcracker which is not easily classified, but which does utilize a form of the direct pressure principle is pictured in Plate 51. This cast iron "Tough Nut" sailor nutcracker of English origin (c. 1897) applies pressure directly to a nutshell, but utilizes no lever per se. Instead, the nut is placed in the hollow belly of the sailor and the sailor's head is then pressed down to forcefully drive his long neck into his stomach to crush the shell. This nutcracker, although direct action, combines a nutcracking technique which is a somewhat similar principle to that found in the screw type. The application of direct pressure pushes the neck downward in a single thrusting motion rather than a turning action. Without a lever or fulcrum, an argument supposedly could be made that this type also resembles a percussion instrument as nuts are smashed in the sailor's belly with a force similar to the strike of a mallet. To my mind, however, it is most like the direct action type. An extremely interesting model, this "tough nut" sailor was also produced in brass.

A non-figural example of this "plunger" type cracker was patented in the United States on April 11, 1922 by Homer W. McClung of Barryton, Michigan (Patent No. 1,412,249). Mr. McClung's device was composed of a hollow dome with a long cylindrical neck. The dome was fitted with an opening for inserting a nut, a plunger for cracking and an anvil upon which nuts could be placed to be cracked. At least one nutcracker I have seen employs both a lever and a plunger. This model is described in Chapter 7 under the "Patent Dating" section.

Indirect Pressure

The "indirect" variety of nutcracker, by contrast, applies pressure behind the fulcrum. Nutcrackers with this indirect pincer action usually employ two levers which are pivoted off-center. This type of nutcracker often takes the shape of an animal or human head, sometimes with glass eyes. The lower jaw of the head is attached to the shorter of the two levers. Once a nut has been placed in the jaws of the nutcracker, pressure is applied by pressing down on the lever attached to the lower jaws. Simultaneously, the

PLATE 51
"Tough Nut" Sailor marked "Tough Nut" on cap and "PATENT 29795?" on back of nutcracker base. 7¾" high, 4¾" across, 3⅛" deep. English, c. 1897.

other stationary lever attached to the crown of the head is held firmly to create resistance to the downward thrust of the lower lever, causing the nutshell to crack.

The lower jaws of lever-operated nutcrackers are pivoted together by boxwood or iron pins and are activated by manipulating the top lever. Frequently, pins are visible at either side of a nutcracker's head, but many have been made in which the pins are concealed from exterior view. From those that I have seen, the earlier pieces (pre-1850) have pins showing more often, while most examples made during the Victorian Era and beyond have the pins concealed from view. This is by no means an absolute and many exceptions to this generalization do exist. An example of this is shown in Plate 52. The wooden cat nutcracker shows concealed pin construction while the rabbit nutcracker has a visible wooden pin. Both were probably made within thirty years of each other in the late 1800s or early 1900s.

Of the many charming and amusing nutcrackers which operate by indirect action, most of these are of the double-handled variety where the levers also serve as the handles. Some are clearly representational, depicting humans and animals with exacting and realistic detail, while others are strictly caricatures such as the strange-looking boxwood man with a bowler hat (Plate 53). So unusual is this piece, that it seems quite possible that it was modeled after a particular person or literary character, who with his mouth open, appears to be either laughing uproariously or crying out in pain. This boxwood man is but one example of the humorous and sometimes grotesque quality of many of these devices. Another, less ambiguous and more common example is a large boxwood dwarf or elf-like figure who is riding the handles of his nutcracker (Plate 54). He, without doubt, is depicted in a high-spirited mood complete with a glint in his eye.

In addition to human and animal heads, seen in Plates 12 and 13 on page 21–22, ogres were also popular subjects for early levered nutcrackers. In fact, one of the earliest known boxwood pieces which survived was made in the shape of an ogre. It was made around 1500 and is probably

PLATE 52
Small wooden rabbit head nutcracker with glass eyes. 8⅛" high, 2½" deep, 1¾" across. Swiss or Tyrolean, late 19th to early 20th century.
Small wooden cat head nutcracker with glass eyes. 6½" high, 2¼" across, 3" wide. Swiss or Tyrolean, late 19th to early 20th century.

PLATES 53, 54
Left: Wooden man with bowler hat nutcracker. Made of boxwood. 8½" high, 2½" deep, 2" across. Probably English, mid to late 19th century.
Right: Wooden laughing elf nutcracker. 11" high, 3⅞" deep, 2¼" across. German, Swiss or Tyrolean, late 19th to early 20th century.

French in origin. One of the most curious lever-action nutcrackers I have seen is carved with a jester and other grotesque figures. Highly decorated, this example also was inscribed with all the letters of the alphabet. It is believed to be 18th century Dutch.

Another fascinating and unique indirect pressure nutcracker was made in 1892 by T. J. Hitchcock of Oswego, New York. A surgeon by profession, Dr. Hitchcock created this brass piece in the form of Admiral Dewey complete with mustache and goatee. (Illustration 5). The handles are shaped like a traveling scalpel, an especially clever and appropriate choice for a physician.

In addition to double lever indirect pressure nutcrackers, others employing the same principle exist which utilize only a single lever. In these models, the head is part of the base and the lever cracks the nuts in the jaws of the figure. A cast iron example on the left in Plate 55 is in the shape of an eagle's head. It was patented on May 15, 1860 by Samuel J. Smith of New York, New York (U.S. Patent No. 28,311). This nutcracker operates with a "cam lever that is acted upon by a coiled spring arranged in such a relation to a curved fixed jaw, and operated by a lever having an eccentric motion, that two jaws will be obtained for cracking nuts." The Smith bird exhibits a lever in the shape of a feather and its base is meant to be secured to a wooden stand, bench or table. It was also meant, according to Mr. Smith "to be painted to suit the fancy … and when finished will present a very neat and elegant appearance and serve as a convenient nut cracker." (Excerpted from

Mr. Smith's patent application, the Letters Patent No. 1249, dated June 12, 1860.) The fact that my bird nutcracker (Plate 55) has neither the feather handle nor any signs of having been affixed at one time to a stand, indicates that it is a later copy of Mr. Smith's original invention. The eagle is unmarked in terms of a maker, but I have seen this model signed "Lehigh Foundries, Easton, PA." Apparently this nutcracker was produced by that company at one time.

Another nutcracker, very much like the Smith eagle, but with a shorter beak and heavier neck is shown on the right in Plate 55. This piece was painted and is believed to be a more recent 20th century variation of the original Smith design.

Similar to the cast iron eagles is a nickel-plated dog or wolf head nutcracker. It is marked with the words "PAT'D June 1920" but shows no patent number (Plate 56). It was patented by Anthony W. Geigand and Joseph J. Geigand of Buffalo, New York (Des. No. 55,460) on June 15, 1920. This model also possesses one lever and the animal's neck is attached to a wooden base (unlike the two eagles).

Some cast iron single-lever nutcrackers operate by a coiled spring in the interior of the piece. This spring creates tension when the tail is depressed and then allows the tail to snap back into place after a nut has been crushed. See Plate 57 for an interior view of a cast iron squirrel.

In contrast to the many "head-shaped" nutcrackers, some human form examples exist. They are full-bodied

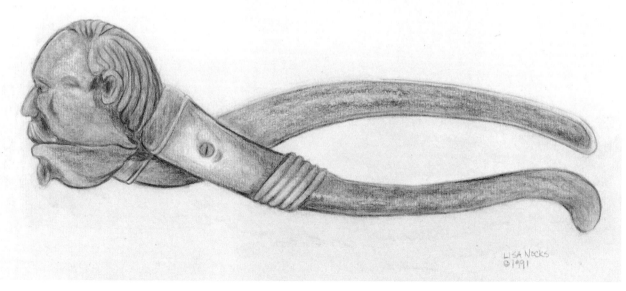

ILLUSTRATION 5
Nutcracker of Admiral Dewey made in 1892 by Dr. T.J. Hitchcock of Oswego, New York. Face is complete with mustache and goatee.

PLATE 55
Left: Cast iron eagle head nutcracker. 10¾" long including lever, 4⅛" high, 3" across. American, patented 1860.
Right: Painted cast iron eagle nutcracker. 10" long including lever, 5⅛" wide, 4¾" high. Probably American, early 20th century.

PLATE 56
Nickel-plated cast iron wolf or dog head nutcracker. 10" long including lever, 3⅞" across, 4⅞" high. American (patented 1920), c. 1920s–1930s.

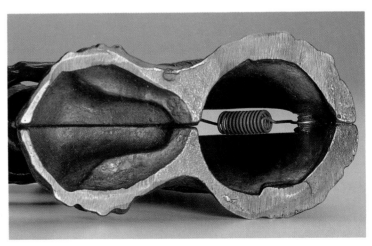

PLATE 57
Interior view of brass-plated cast iron squirrel nutcracker. See description under Plate 2 for nutcracker details.

and most are free-standing (Plate 58). This amusing peasant man, with his arms crossed and a smiling face, balances well on his feet but can utilize the lever for added stability. Full-bodied animal forms also exist. I have seen a wooden bear nutcracker, which is a wonderful example of this type. Standing upright on his hind legs and arms crossed against his chest, this bear is truly a special piece.

Animal-shaped nutcrackers whose levers are part of the figure itself, usually the tail, are common among cast iron and brass dog, squirrel and alligator models, but less typical of other animal forms. The full-bodied seated brass cat in Plate 58 is a delightful exception, utilizing its tail as the lever. The bird in Plate 59 is yet another example of a free-standing nutcracker whose lever is part of the overall design, in this case the bird's tail. Representing a jackdaw, a black and gray bird found in Europe and Asia which can be tamed and taught to talk, this nutcracker is an extraor-

dinary example of carving. The interior of the mouth has been stained a reddish brown color to add to its sense of realism.

Certain standing examples have levers which, when not in use, become flush with the figure, helping form the base upon which they stand erect. The figures in Plate 60, the rather stern-looking peasant woman with Dutch shoes and similar peasant man, both were made around 1920–1930. Their levers are concealed as part of the figure when not engaged in nut-cracking (Plate 61) and are pulled outward when in use. The peasant or Breton man was found in Brittany, a former duchy and province of the Armorican peninsula in northwest France. The peasant woman, being so alike in appearance, may also come from that region. The man is unusual because he has a hole in his mouth that goes all the way through to the back of his head.

PLATE 58
Left: Wooden full-bodied peasant man nutcracker. 6½" high, 3½" deep, 2" across. German, Swiss, or Tyrolean, early to mid-20th century.
Right: Seated brass cat nutcracker marked with indecipherable registration number. 5¼" high, 1½" across, 3⅝" deep. English, c. 1930s.

PLATE 59
Wooden jackdaw nutcracker with glass eyes. Stained and painted wood. 8⅝" high, 2⅛" across, 4½" deep including tail. English, c. 1860.

PLATE 60, 61
Left: Wooden standing peasant woman and man nutcrackers. Man - 7¼" high, 2⅜" across, 1⅛" deep. Woman - 8½" high, 1¾" across, 1¾" deep. Both are probably Breton, c. 1920s–1930s. Right: Rear view of peasant figures.

Cross-Over Lever Type Variation

Another nutcracker which should be mentioned is really a variation of the lever-type indirect action nutcracker. This unusual form of construction, called the cross-over lever type, dates back primarily to the 1600s. Made from carefully chosen pieces of hardwood, they have a crooked branching grain at the head end. This crooked piece of wood is used for the cross-over mortised arm. Into this piece, the straight arm is loosely tenoned and levers against a hardwood peg in the tenon (Illustration 6). Many of these nutcrackers are rather plain in appearance, but some are decorated with incised designs. I have never seen a figural nutcracker of this kind. They are, however, interesting and beautiful because of their unique construction.

One known chip carved cross-over specimen which is dated May 1677, is inscribed with the initials "A" and "K", the names Ambros and King and the words, "If All Bee Trew As Weemen Say Ye Night Is Sweeter Then The Day." Made of boxwood, this nutcracker is believed to commemorate a marriage between two individuals with the names of "Ambros" and "King."

Screw Type

Another type of nutcracker is the "screw type." Many wooden examples were initially made in the late 1600s. This variety operates by the tightening of a screw which is usually in the center of the nutcracker. By applying increased pressure against the shell of the nut, it finally cracks. The interior of the nutcracker is hollow and the hold is threaded to receive a wooden screw which is activated by turning the single handle of the nutcracker. The screw head is flattened to create a smooth surface upon which the nutshell is crushed when pressed against the opposite side of the hollowed area.

Many nutcrackers manufactured in England are of the screw variety. Carvers from Switzerland, Austria, Germany and France also produced beautiful examples of this type. A large number of these nutcrackers, made in the 1800s, are either figural or are adorned with designs taken from nature such as variously shaped leaves and flowers. Plate 62 depicts three examples of wooden screw type nutcrackers – a delicate hand carved in such a way as to grip something oval in its palm (possibly meant to depict a nut), a squirrel holding a nut between its paws, and a

ILLUSTRATION 6
Cross-over lever nutcracker dating back to the 1600s. The bent piece of wood is used for the cross-over mortised arm. The straight arm is loosely tenoned and levers against a hardwood peg in the tenon.

PLATE 62
Left: Wooden bird screw-type nutcracker. 6⅝" long, 2" across, 1½" deep. Probably English, mid to late 19th century.
Center: Wooden screw-type nutcracker in the shape of a hand. Possibly made from fruitwood. 7" long, 1¾" across, 1¾" deep. Probably English, mid to late 19th century.
Right: Wooden squirrel screw-type nutcracker. 7" long, 1⅝" across, 2¼" deep. Probably English, mid to late 19th century.

lovely bird which utilizes its tail as its handle. I have seen all three of these designs repeated on several occasions which suggests that they were popular subjects widely produced during the mid to late 19th century. A wooden screw-type crocodile of similar construction was also prevalent during this same era. (Plate 10 on page 19 shows the interior cavities of three screw-type implements.)

Three views of a fascinating fruitwood screw-type example can be seen in Plates 63, 64 and 65. The nutcracker has a laughing face on one side. An identical face with its mouth opened to accept nuts is shown on the other with an interesting profile from the side view. It is possibly Punch from the story of "Punch and Judy" and probably English-made, c. 1820. This extremely clever design was also made to stand without assistance – a rare feature for wooden screw-type pieces.

Another exceptionally beautiful and unusual screw-type English nutcracker is shown in Illustration 7. This nutcracker is in the form of a wonderful bird perched on a cage. The bird serves as the finial on top of the screw component. This piece is probably from the 1700s rather than the 1800s even though it was in the 19th century that most of the more elaborate screw-type designs appeared. Very decorative cut-out and chased iron and steel screw-activated nutcrackers were produced in the 1700s according to Henry René d'Allemagne (1863–1950), who spent most of his life studying and collecting ironwork. They were made with an openwork case and a screw-type vise at the center in the form of a press. These pieces, probably made in Europe, had finial-like tops, some of which were quite ornate. (Illustration 8).

It was Monsieur d'Allemagne who wrote a catalogue in 1924 of the ironwork collection in Le Secq des Tournelles Museum in Rouen, France. This collection, which included nutcrackers, was established by his friend, Henri Le Secq des Tournelles, who donated his entire ironwork

PLATES 63, 64, 65
Left: Front view of wooden double-headed nutcracker depicting "Punch" from the story of "Punch and Judy." Made of fruitwood. 6½" long, 2¼" across, 2" deep. English, c. 1820. Center: Rear view shows open mouth as nutcracking area. Right: Side view shows interesting profile of nutcracker.

collection as a gift to the city in 1917. Monsieur d'Allemagne contributed many pieces from his own collection to the museum as well.

We are certainly indebted to Monsieur d'Allemagne as it is through him that we have become aware of the fascinating and beautiful iron and steel nutcrackers from this period. Unfortunately, his intention to include an extensive text of material along with his catalogue was never realized and some details, such as specific origins and dimensions of individual pieces and other related information, are not available.

More contemporary screw-type nutcrackers also have been made of iron. These cast iron pieces are ordinarily non-figural like the nickel-plated one in Plate 66 which is a very popular design. This style of nutcracker called the Ideal Nut Cracker was patented on August 6, 1918 (Patent No. 1,274,856) by Frank B. Cook of Chicago, Illinois. (It closely resembles the Quackenbush nutcracker in Plate 7 on page 12.) In Mr. Cook's patent specifications, his nutcracker had ball-like ends on the handle and what appears to be a somewhat wider cracking receptacle; the overall design, however, is exactly the same as the one pictured.

ILLUSTRATION 7
Bird on cage screw-type nutcracker. Bird serves as the finial on the screw component. Probably from the 1700s.

PLATE 66
Nickel-plated cast iron non-figural screw-type nutcracker. 4½" long, 2¼" across, 1" deep. American, patented 1918.

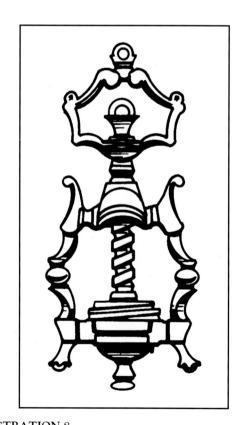

ILLUSTRATION 8
Screw-type nutcracker made of openwork iron case with vise in the center to form press.

The same form of nutcracker was featured in an advertisement in the January, 1921 issue of *Good Housekeeping* magazine. It read:

Gets the Kernel Out Whole!
Cracks any Pecan, Walnut, Brazil Nut, Filbert, etc. - **without crushing kernel!** No scattered, flying shells, pinched fingers or lost tempers.

IDEAL NUT CRACKER
Just a quick easy turn of the handle brings the kernel out whole. So simple a child can do it. No levers, springs or clamps. Lasts forever. Thousands in use. Money back if not pleased. Order early for Xmas.
Style 2. Plain nickel plated 60¢
Style 4. Highly polish'd 85¢
Postage paid anywhere in U.S.
COOK ELECTRIC CO.
906 W. Van Buren, Chicago, Ill.

Screw-type nutcrackers, similar in appearance to the chased iron and steel shown in Illus. 8, were also made of brass while more contemporary screw-type models have been made from brass as well. One such piece, utilizing an unusual and exceptionally charming design is pictured in Plates 67 and 68. It was produced in England and registered in 1956 (Reg. No. 881165). The figure is made of brass and is approximately 4" tall and 3¾" wide at the base. The screw mechanism, hidden behind the little girl's skirt, is activated by twisting her torso around.

Another very unusual and beautifully designed screw-type nutcracker is in the shape of a cat (Plate 69). It was made in Austria (c. 1910) by Wiener Werkstatte, an organization of craft workers which existed in Vienna from 1903 to 1932. The organization was formed to promote and distribute high quality designs in the Secession style. Secessionist design rejected the conservative standards of the Vienna Academy. It was connected to Art Nouveau in its use of nature-related and curving lines, but the style was often more restrained and geometric. It is sometimes described as "rectilinear Art Nouveau." The jewelry, metal work, furniture and leather goods produced were from designs by Josef Hoffman, Koloman Moser and other noted designers of the time. The cat is a very geometric form that uses its tail as the screw component. The screw is placed at an interesting angle rather than perpendicular to the base. Made of a combination of brass and nickel-plated brass, it is not only unique, but humorous as well.

PLATE 67

PLATE 68

PLATES 67, 68
Top: Front view of brass nutcracker resembling girl with hoop skirt. Marked "Made in England" and "Pat. App'd for Regd DE 3 881165." c. 1956. 3¾" high, 2¾" across, 1¼" deep.
Bottom: Rear view shows nutcracking mechanism.

Like some lever-operated nutcrackers, a number of screw-type models have a humorous touch. In fact, one of the funniest nutcrackers I have seen is that of an irate wooden monkey with paws covering his ears to deaden the sound of the nuts as they are being cracked. This screw-type nutcracker, probably of Swiss or Austrian origin, is a tribute to the imagination and sense of humor of its carver. Another truly ingenious wooden screw-type example is in the shape of a fish. Made so that a nut can be inserted in the fish's mouth, the nut shell is then broken by pressure from a screw that forms a kind of fin atop its head. This piece is beautifully carved to show the eyes and the many scales and markings on the fish's body. In addition to the detailed carving, the whole design is quite wonderful utilizing the fish's tail as the handle.

Scrimshaw

When most of us think of scrimshaw, the decorations on whales' bones and teeth, and the articles made from them, come to mind. Frequently, these designs involve a nautical theme. Scrimshaw, however, is a technique which also has been applied to wood as a form of ornamentation. English examples of scrimshaw, in particular, include nutcrackers.

The art of scrimshaw involves engraving a design with a sharp knife, and then filling the lines in with a pigment or ink. Much antique scrimshaw found today is from the 1800s, but the particular type of scrimshaw decoration found on early nutcrackers was done primarily one hundred or more years before in Scotland and England. This would suggest that scrimshaw is an old practice, which began with the use of wood, dating back to a time before whaling even had begun.

Be aware that on old scrimshaw, the color of the pigment or ink used should now be faded. Contemporary makers of scrimshaw, attempting to duplicate an older look, often use a lighter-brown pigment which is a uniform color all over, showing no signs of normal wear.

The nutcrackers decorated with scrimshaw also are occasionally dappled with spots of dark stain to simulate tortoise shell. The tortoise shell effect is sometimes found on other treen from the 1600s which is thought to be the work of sailors from various countries.

A tradition of spending leisure hours carving developed early among sailors on the whaling vessels of many countries. When the whaling industry was at its peak, the ships were frequently at sea for several years at a time, affording the sailors many long hours between catches and ports, to spend in carving. Knives were the sailor's most precious possession. They worked with scraps of wood left

PLATE 69
Brass cat nutcracker marked "Austria" on bottom and attributed to Wiener Werkstatte. 4¾" long, 3¼" high, 1⁵⁄₁₆" across. c. 1910.

over from the wood brought aboard for use in repairs and in coopers' shops where casks to hold whale oil were made during the voyage. These scraps of wood were the only carving material on hand until the whales were caught and their teeth and bones became available.

Despite the availability of bones and teeth, some sailors preferred carving wood. These sailors would use their share of the precious whale bones to trade for choice pieces of mahogany and other exotic woods in the South Sea Island ports. Since wood was in short supply, only small objects could be made for loved ones waiting at home port, like boxes, rolling pins, cane heads and nutcrackers. Some items were carved of wood and had whale bone for decoration, using nautical or patriotic themes in the ornamentation. Ships, anchors, dolphins, and rope designs were popular motifs as were folk art symbols such as hearts, birds, stars, and stylized flowers and foliage patterns.

ILLUSTRATION 9
One of the earliest dated nutcrackers is from the 16th century and depicts Hercules astride the Nemean Lion. It is an example of indirect lever action.

Cross-over type nutcrackers frequently made of yew wood and incised with scrimshaw-type decoration were made during the 1600s through the 1800s. Sometimes the decoration took the form of fish, animals, English flowers or tropical palms. The 17th century examples are typically 4½" to 6½" in length and considerably smaller than the larger and coarser examples from the 19th century which are similarly decorated and usually made of yew wood.

CHRONOLOGY OF NUTCRACKER DEVELOPMENT

Much information which would undoubtedly shed more light on the development of nutcrackers unfortunately has been lost over the years. Certain trends in production can be identified which help to chronicle their history.

The very first nutcrackers were purely utilitarian in design and purpose. As soon as the functional features of these implements were perfected, beginning as early as the 1400s, they began to take on a more ornamental form. So ornate and rich in detail were many of the nutcrackers produced over the next 500 years that they developed into an art form. The many beautiful and diverse examples created from the 15th through the 20th centuries attest to this fact.

It is no surprise that the earliest nutcrackers were of the percussion variety, such as a rock or mallet. As stated earlier, these "implements" were not created expressly for nutcracking. Common sense would seem to dictate that people would try to crack open nuts with the simplest tools first before moving on to more creative ways of accomplishing this task. Actual "nut hammers" were a later invention. Less certain is which variety of nutcracker came next after the percussion.

Authorities are divided on which is the earlier invention – the screw-type nutcracker or the indirect action lever-operated nutcracker. There are early examples of both, but the majority seem to agree that the lever-type nutcracker is the older form. Many of the earliest dated nutcrackers are of the indirect action lever variety, which seems to add weight to the theory that this form preceded the screw-type. A fine example is Hercules astride the Nemean Lion (dated 1570) in Illustration 9. This truly extraordinary nutcracker, however, is not typical of 16th century workmanship, which usually took the form of draped human figures with the jaws hinged to the back handle.

Some controversy also exists as to whether the screw-type nutcracker preceded or postdated the advent of the direct action lever-operated nutcracker. Generally, the belief is that the direct action type was the earlier form with the screw-type appearing in the mid 17th century.

Actually, of the two forms of lever-operated nutcracking designs, the direct action is usually thought to have existed before the indirect pressure type was invented. This, however, is somewhat speculative. They both first appeared around the same time. Nonetheless, it is quite certain that both kinds of lever-activated nutcrackers (indirect and direct action) were made before the introduction of the screw-type model.

It should be noted that because screw-type nutcrackers were less likely to be dated than lever-activated types, it is more difficult to conclusively determine when the screw variety was first introduced. The surface area upon which to sign or date a piece generally is more limited on screw-type nutcrackers than on the lever-operated type. First, there are two handles which offer space upon which to carve a date on a wooden lever-activated nutcracker rather than the single handle of the screw variety. Secondly, the screw handle is curved all the way around and frequently is incised with bands or gouges to form design patterns, reducing the space for making identifying marks such as initials and dates.

ILLUSTRATION 10
Ornately carved French "King" nutcracker from the 15th or 16th century. Nutcrackers from this era were frequently made from boxwood.

In any case, it is known that beginning in medieval times, lever action nutcrackers were made frequently from the very strong and tough boxwood. Some of these early medieval specimens, from the 15th and 16th centuries, depicted French kings and other royalty holding shields often embellished with the fleur-de-lis (Illustration 10) and incorporating another common symbol, the lion. The finest of these lever-type nutcrackers were made primarily in France, Italy, and the Low Countries, and from there were transported to other countries, including England, where they were prized very highly. This is not to say that other countries, such as England, did not produce nutcrackers of their own during this same time period.

As mentioned earlier, a number of wrought and chased iron nutcrackers that operate by either direct lever action or indirect action have been attributed by French ironwork authority Henry René d'Allemagne to the work of 15th and 16th century craftsmen. Many of these are ornamental, like the one which incorporates the head of a man with a wonderful French stocking-like cap (Illustration 11). It would, therefore, seem clear that wooden and iron lever-operated nutcrackers were both produced as early as the 1400s, but apparently the wooden varieties were produced in greater quantity.

The earliest wooden specimens from the 1500s have jaws only large enough to accommodate the filberts and cobs which were the popular dessert nuts for many centuries. Because walnuts were soft-shelled and, therefore, more easily cracked with the fingers than other varieties, there was no immediate reason for the makers of early nutcrackers to create a cavity in the mouth large enough to hold this popular nut. Many early specimens, however, have a secondary hollow or oval recess in the back of both levers to accommodate a walnut for cracking. Beginning in the early 17th century, the existence of such a secondary recess became even more common. This secondary recess was not only larger to accommodate nuts such as walnuts, but also permitted stronger pressure than could be achieved by means of the jaw action. The nutcrackers in Plate 70, made in the late 1800s and early 1900s, possess this secondary recess as the inclusion of such a mechanism for cracking larger nuts has continued into this century long after the jaws on such nutcrackers were enlarged to crack open bigger nuts.

As for the early wooden screw-type nutcrackers, many seem to be ornamental rather than figural, but examples do exist which were made in the shape of a human head with the nuts cracked by screwing them against the mouth of the figure. These early screw-type nutcrackers are usually quite small, varying in size from 2½" to 4" in length. Some of the 18th century chased iron and steel screw-activated nutcrackers are quite similar in design to wooden ones made in the 17th and 18th centuries.

PLATE 70
Shown are the secondary recesses of a bear nutcracker, on the left, and a lion nutcracker, on the right. (Full descriptions of these items are captioned with Plate 12 and 99.)

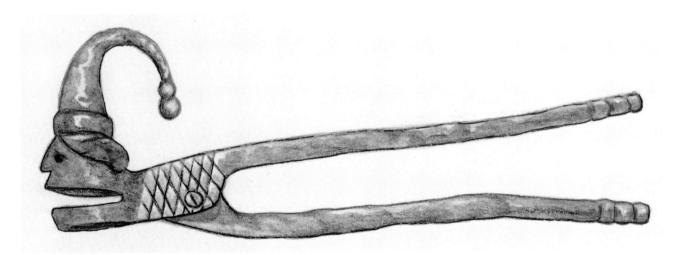

ILLUSTRATION 11
This iron nutcracker, a man in a French stocking cap, is the work of 15th or 16th century craftsmen.

With the screw-type nutcrackers so popular in the mid to late 17th century, it was the double-handled lever-operated variety of nutcracker which was revived and produced fairly extensively in the 18th century. The difference was that metal was used more often than wood during the 1700s. Wood had been very prevalent in early nutcracker construction, and wooden examples did continue to be made during the 18th century.

In fact, in the 1700s, wooden nutcrackers could be found with ivory teeth and utilizing various techniques to reinforce their strength with the use of metal. Jaws were sometimes lined with metal or brass to increase durability, a practice carried into the 1800s. The jaws of one English piece from the 1800s was studded with metal pins to aid in gripping a nut. The nutcracker in Plate 71 has copper-covered metal plates fitted to each side with several hand-wrought metal screws and pins holding the plates in place. Resembling a kind of armor, these plates strengthen the overall design of this piece and have probably contributed to its survival from the late 1600s or early 1700s to the present day.

Another way in which metal was combined with wood to add durability to a nutcracker involved the base of the piece. Bases of standing wooden nutcrackers were

PLATE 71
Wooden nutcracker of head and torso with copper-coated metal plates. It has glass eyes and is made of yew-wood. Marked with initials "TS." 8¼" long, 2" deep, 1¼" across. Probably French, late 17th century.

sometimes weighted with lead to add stability and prevent the figures from tipping over when cracking nuts with hard shells. Illustration 12 shows an unusual standing specimen with a rather somber expression. This nutcracker is an interesting design, combining a figural head with a long cylindrical neck which rounds off to a ball at the base. Probably 18th century English made, this piece has both brass-lined jaws and a lead-weighted base.

Charming examples of 18th century wooden nutcrackers include nut vendors, sometimes polychromed, carrying baskets or sacks of nuts. See Plate 72 for such an example, probably mid to late 19th century in origin. Such nutcrackers were often sold at fairs in many European countries, including Holland, Switzerland, and Germany. A notation in the diary of Sophie V. la Roche, made on September 4, 1786 while she was crossing the English Channel from Rotterdam to Harwich, refers to just such a fair or kermis. (A kermis or kermess is an outdoor festival of the Low Countries usually held for charitable purposes.)

ILLUSTRATION 12
18th century English nutcracker with lead weighted base and brass lined jaws.

"… The young Suffolk farmer (a fellow traveller) was indeed, one of the brightest, and amused himself with his nutcrackers, which were carved and painted like mannequins with large mouths and which he had bought for his children as portraits of young Dutchmen at Rotterdam kermis…"

One piece, made in the late 18th century, was a brightly painted gentlemen with blue coat, red breeches and white waistcoat and hose and was sold at such fairgrounds.

Curiously, some 18th century indirect action lever-operated nutcrackers, carved as full human figures, cracked nuts in a torso cavity rather than in their mouths. Nutcrackers which crack nuts in their mouths were also

PLATE 72
Wooden nut vendor nutcracker marked on handle "MÜRRE IV." 8⅛" high, 3¹/₁₆" across, 4" deep. Probably German, mid to late 19th century.

produced during the same time. I have not personally seen any indirect action human figure nutcrackers from the 19th and 20th centuries which crack nuts in the chest or abdominal cavities, like those from the 1700s. (One exception is the cast iron "Tough Nut" Sailor in Plate 51 on page 54. It was made during the late 1800s. This one does not operate by use of levers but by cracking nuts in its belly. Another exception can be found in the two soldier nutcracker Christmas tree ornaments in Plate 43 on page 47.) Rather, ones made during the 1800s and 1900s use their jaws for nutcracking or occasionally an opening in the neck on some contemporary German models.

While wooden and hand-wrought steel or iron nutcrackers have been continuously made since the 1400s (with some peaks and valleys in production), other mediums were also used in nutcracker construction. Silver, as previously noted, is too soft to be practical for nutcrackers construction, so only a few have been made throughout the years from this substance. Some nutcrackers were made with sterling handles with steel hinges and ends.

Silver-plated nutcrackers, including Sheffield plate, could be found among the wealthy for a number of years and were mass produced in the late 1800s and early 1900s with the introduction of electroplating. Brass, which had been used for many years to produce nutcrackers, became a favored metal for this purpose during the Victorian era. Cast iron nutcrackers were produced in great quantities, especially in America, but also abroad from the 1850s to the 1930s. Most figural nutcrackers produced from the 1940s to the present day are either wood or cast iron, with brass being used to some extent.

The advent of one type of nutcracker did not eliminate the production of the other forms. Lever-activated nutcrackers still continued to be made after the appearance of the screw-type. The percussion variety, although considered to be the earliest form, has continued to be produced into the 20th century. Nutcrackers have been made in a variety of mediums over the years, often overlapping production. During the Victorian era, the love for ornamentation and elaborate dining traditions lead to the heavy production of brass, cast iron, wood and silver-plated nutcrackers. Therefore, a combination of factors, along with the type and composition of a nutcracker, must be taken into account when determining its age.

DESIGNS AND MOTIFS

Nutcrackers have been made in what seems like an almost infinite variety of forms and patterns with some designs much more prevalent than others. Human forms have been used almost from the very beginning with animal shapes being common as well, especially in the 1800s and early 1900s.

Most ornamental nutcrackers are clearly representational, often depicting in great detail, an animal or human form. Others are more stylized, relying on line rather than detail to suggest a particular figure. The brass nutcracker on the bottom right in Plate 73 could not be mistaken for anything other than a bird, but is certainly less graphic than the other bird nutcrackers in this photo. In fact, the tiny circles or incised punch marks covering the whole length of this nutcracker are an added and rather interesting decoration, but do not necessarily relate to the bird motif. The hood adornment covering the head may correspond to the practice of covering the heads of falcons and hawks while in captivity. The other birds in this picture are easy to identify including the two parrots with rectangular bases which are virtually identical in form, but the cast iron piece is slightly larger in size and painted gold-brown. The green parrot is painted aluminum, not cast iron. Both are probably American. The other parrot in the photo is a hand-held nickel-plated cast steel example with clearly defined beak and feathers. The brass pelican is English, marked with an indecipherable British registration number. The nutcracker with the double eagle handles is noteworthy as an excellent example of a cast steel piece, made with exceptional detail and refinement. A product of the 1920s or 1930s, made by the Hoffritz Company, its handles are nickel-plated steel while the cracker part is chromium-plated steel with a gold wash. It is reversible and can be used for different-sized nuts depending upon which side of the fulcrum the handles are placed for cracking.

Many nutcrackers have been made which although not figural are very ornamental with a variety of designs

PLATE 73
Back row: Green and gold aluminum parrot nutcracker. 10" long including lever, 2" across, 5¼" high. Early to mid-20th century. Gold brown cast iron parrot nutcracker with traces of old paint. 10" long including lever, 2¼" across, 5½" high. Early to mid-20th century.
Front row: Brass pelican nutcracker marked with indecipherable registration number. 5½" long, ¾" across, 1⅝" high. English, late 19th to early 20th century. Nutcracker with chromium and nickel-plated double eagle handles in Deco style. Marked "Hoffritz NY" and "Germany." Gold wash on chromium-plated top portion with handles nickel-plated. c. 1920s–1930s. Brass hand-held hooded bird nutcracker. 6" long, 1⅝" high, ⅜" wide. Possibly English, late 19th to early 20th century. Nickel-plated hand-held cast steel parrot nutcracker. 7" long, 1½" high, ⅜" across. Late 19th to early 20th century.

including architectural forms. Other nutcrackers combine the figural and the ornamental (Illustration 13). One standing figure has a human head and torso combined with a bottom decorated in a guilloche-style pattern on all four sides. Guilloche is an architectural ornament formed of two or more interlocked bands with openings containing round devices. From the 1500s, this piece could be Flemish, French or Italian.

A fascinating nutcracker design was patented on January 2, 1934 by Arthur Meng of Cleveland, Ohio (Des. No. 91,277). Almost futuristic in appearance, it represented a robot-like figure (Illustration 14) with a female torso and graceful arms extended to either side of the body. Unfortunately, as is generally true of design patents, the description which accompanied the drawing did not elaborate on how this model was meant to operate nor from what substance it was to be made. I can only speculate that the arms were intended as the levers and the nuts were to be cracked in what appears to be a cavity in the center of the torso at the base. Whatever the planned mode of operation, it is exemplary of yet another extremely imaginative and diverse nutcracker design.

ILLUSTRATION 13
Nutcracker with human torso and guilloche-style base from the 1500s. This piece could be Flemish, French, or Italian made.

ILLUSTRATION 14
Robot-style nutcracker patented by Arthur Meng on January 2, 1934.

ILLUSTRATION 13

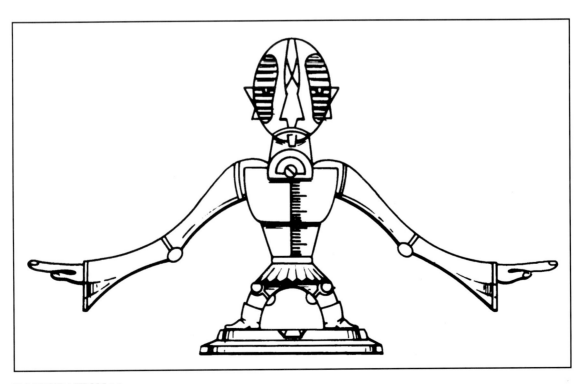

ILLUSTRATION 14

Figural nutcrackers can be found in the shape of anonymous and sometimes grotesque human beings, and sometimes in the form of gnomes and elf-like creatures. Nutcrackers also have been made to resemble famous persons including Bismarck, von Hindenburg, Rutherford B. Hayes, Napoleon, British Prime Minister Gladstone, Frederick the Great, Louis Philippe, and Woodrow Wilson. In fact, the making of nutcrackers in the form of a variety of famous individuals was a speciality of Swiss carvers in the 1800s.

OTHER NUT-RELATED UTENSILS

In addition to the great variety of nutcrackers, it should be noted that other "nut-related" utensils also have been popular. Every well-to-do Victorian home had a silver service complete with several types of spoons and numerous serving pieces, including specialized pieces such as pea servers, asparagus tongs, sardine shovels and cucumber servers. This was in addition to a selection of toothpick holders, card holders, mustard jars, syrup pitchers, knife rests, and covered butter dishes. Naturally, a variety of nut-related utensils were also necessary to the Victorian life-style.

These serving and accessory pieces were often highly specialized but many were offered in standard silver and silverplate production patterns. Included, in addition to nutcrackers, were nut picks, nut scoops or nut spoons, and nut dishes. Nut sets were also made with matching nut scoops, nut picks, nutcrackers, and occasionally nut dishes. The relative scarcity of these nut sets, compared with the overwhelming popularity of nuts during this period, indicates that the majority of people preferred to assemble their own nut sets rather than purchasing them off the counter. Some nut sets have become disassembled over the years, with individual parts going their separate ways.

Nut spoons, which were actually more like scoops, were used to transfer nuts from a storage container to a nut dish. They were not used for eating nuts and the term *spoon* can be misleading. Resembling a ladle, a nut spoon can be distinguished by its relatively short handle. The bowl of the spoon is usually wide, not too deep, with tall sides to prevent the nuts from spilling out of the spoon. Some of these spoon bowls were shell or heart-shaped, either solid or decorated with pierced-work ornament.

Many different kinds of nut picks can be found. Nut picks are small toothpick-like implements with sharply pointed tips used to spear nuts from the nut dish or to assist in the removal of meat from cracked nuts. Although produced in large quantities, they were not always effective at spearing the more solid kinds of nuts, like Brazil nuts. Over the years, nut picks were made in a variety of designs, ranging from very plain to quite ornate.

Wooden-handled nut picks date back to the 18th and early 19th centuries. Silver and silverplated nut picks became very popular during the reign of Queen Victoria. Many had decorative floral and leaf designs on their handles. A selection called "Assyrian" was made by Rogers and Brothers of Waterbury, Connecticut and featured the head of a lady at the top of the handle with a spiral shaft above the pick. Pearl-handled picks with silverplated mountings are very collectible, in contrast to the more common plain silverplated and nickelplated picks. Some nut picks came in sets with matching nutcrackers, all with decorative handles. A typical set included twelve nut picks and two nutcrackers. Other nut picks were sold as part of a fruit and nut set which included a knife, a nutcracker and a pick. Plate 74 shows a typical nutcracker and nut pick set. Some of the picks have slightly different designs on their handles which may indicate a marriage of pieces from different sets.

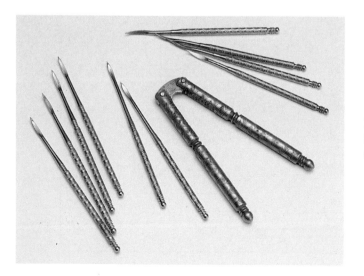

PLATE 74
Steel nutcracker and nut pick set. Nutcracker - 5" long, 1⅛" across, ¼" deep. Early 20th century.

Ornate nut dishes were also prevalent. The dishes were made with either flat bottoms or feet. Some were mounted on pedestal bases reflecting the Victorian enchantment with the Classical Revival style. These nut bowls were made of glass, pewter, silver, or more commonly, silverplate. Some nut dishes were produced in crystal glass imitating cut glass patterns. Large quantities of nut bowls, especially silver or electroplated examples, were made from 1850 to the early part of the 1900s, mainly in America, but also in Britain.

Silverplated nut bowls were sometimes silver-lined, while others were gold-lined. Ornately embossed decorations often depicted fruits, flowers, and birds. Many nut dishes were decorated with the image of a squirrel. Many times the squirrel would be eating a nut, while perched on the rim or at the handles of the bowl. Some of these bowls

were made in the shape of leaves. One very unique example was produced in 1893 by B. F. Norris, Alister and Company. The bowl was in the shape of half of a large nut shell. Its handle was in the form of a tree branch with a leaf and a curious metal squirrel atop the upper half of the shell. Plate 75 shows a beautiful silverplated Victorian nut bowl made with a squirrel standing where the handle is joined in the middle. This bowl was made around 1893 by the Woodman and Cook Company from Portland, Maine. It is triple-plated and bears traces of the gold lining which once adorned the piece.

Wooden nut bowls, some of which came from Germany, were often beautifully carved and made sometimes with more ornate features like silver feet and/or lids. One exceptional example I have seen had silver feet and finials in the form of nuts. Other wooden nut bowls were popular

PLATE 75
Silverplated nut bowl with traces of original gold wash. 7¼" high, 8" wide. American, c. 1893.

PLATE 76
Wooden nut bowl with attached cast iron squirrel nutcracker. Marked "Copy Right 1916" on underside of nutcracker. Has traces of original copper plating. Bowl - 8¼" diameter. Nutcracker - 9" long, 4¼" across, 2⅛" deep. c. 1916.

over the years, like the one in Plate 76 which has a nutcracker actually attached to the bowl. This attached copperplated cast iron lever-operated nutcracker is in the form of a squirrel on a branch, a common nutcracker design. A detached example of the same piece is also shown in this photograph. Made in the early 1900s, this piece is by no means a design unique to the 20th century. A similar example involves an alligator astride a bowl. This wooden specimen, probably Swiss or Austrian, was popular in the late 1700s and early 1800s. What is fascinating is that the alligator cracked nuts by means of a screw mechanism rather than a lever.

A variation of the squirrel and nut bowl design is a large black aluminum squirrel nutcracker sitting on an attached aluminum leaf (Plate 77). The leaf serves as the bowl for either serving the nuts or catching the shells. This piece, like many others, has been reproduced. An advertisement in the April 1985 issue of *House Beautiful* magazine showed a very similar nutcracker with the leaf facing in the opposite direction. It was available from the Moultrie Manufacturing Company in Moultrie, Georgia.

Over the years, an assortment of nut bowl designs have incorporated a squirrel nutcracker into the overall form. Two such models were patented in the United States in the early 1920s. A design patent was granted to Frederick C. Baker of Portland, Oregon, on February 14, 1922 (Des.

No. 60,394) which utilized a squirrel nutcracker on a pedestal in the center of a bowl. Julius L. Emery of Altoona, Pennsylvania, also received a design patent on January 16, 1923 for a squirrel nutcracker perched on the side of a bowl shaped like a tree stump (Des. No. 61,801). A very stylized squirrel seated on a rectangular base upon which an oval bowl is attached was designed by Arthur F. B. Starke of Shelby, Montana. Mr. Starke's design patent was granted on May 5, 1931 (Des. No. 84,117) and was sketched in a geometric and angular fashion to suggest a squirrel but omitted anatomical details of any kind.

Less ornate and generally newer examples of nutcrackers can be found which combine a type of metal nutcracker or pair of nutcrackers sold with a separate wooden bowl. Furthermore, as mentioned during the discussion of nut hammers earlier in this chapter, and pictured in Plate 45, another type of wooden bowl has a pedestal center upon which nuts can be cracked using a matching wooden mallet or a nutcracking device affixed to the center of the bowl.

Pottery nut bowls also exist; often hand-painted with nut and acorn leaf designs. Especially in Japanese pieces marked "Nippon" or "Noritake," the nuts are painted on the bowls in relief to simulate real nuts (Plate 78). (*Nippon* is the Japanese word for Japan. Pieces of porcelain marked "Nippon" were made between 1891 and 1921. A few

PLATE 77
Black painted aluminum squirrel on leaf. 11¾" long, 8" tall, 10" across. Mid-20th century.

PLATE 78
Noritake lustre nut bowl. 7⅛" across, 2¾" high including squirrel. Japanese, c. 1920s–1930s.
Noritake hand-painted peanut bowl. 7⅝" diameter, 2⅜" high. Japanese, c. 1920s–1930s.
Small individual hand-painted Nippon nut bowl. 3" diameter, 1½" high. Japanese, c. 1920.

PLATE 79
Nippon hand-painted squirrel nut bowl. 8¾" diameter, 3" high. Japanese, c. 1920.

PLATE 80
Limoges nut bowl marked "D & C" and "France" on the bottom. 8½" long, 6½" wide, 2⅞" high. c. 1890s. (From the collection of Nancy Marchuk.)

manufacturers continued to use "Nippon" on ceramics after 1921, usually as part of the company name.) They occasionally come as a set with six or eight smaller matching bowls. A small individual footed nut bowl also is pictured in Plate 78 along with a Noritake lustre bowl with a squirrel perched on the rim and acorns in relief in its interior. The Nippon bowl in Plate 79 is the ultimate "nut bowl" with a squirrel eating a nut beautifully painted in relief on its interior. Japanese nut bowls marked with the "M" mark circled by a wreath were most likely products of the Morimura Brothers, a distributing company in New York during the 1920s and 1930s. The company did not use this mark after 1941.

Although Japanese nut bowls are quite plentiful, European examples can also be found. The Limoges example in Plate 80 is especially attractive with its hand-painted leaf and nut pattern on the interior and exterior of the bowl, gold pedestal legs, and matching gold rim. Made during the 1890s in France by the Delinieres Company, it was produced for distribution by Endeman & Churchill of New York and exemplifies the beauty of European design.

A more recent example with peanuts used as three-dimensional decoration is shown in Plate 81. Produced in Portugal, this green-colored piece confirms the continuing interest in nut bowls throughout the world.

Pottery nut bowls even have been combined with figural cast iron nutcrackers, as in the case of the dog with the pottery dish (Plate 81). Made in England in the 1930s, this piece was constructed so that the nut meats and/or shells fall into the bowl after the dog has performed his nut-cracking job. Both the dog and the bowl are bolted to a wooden base.

The tin dish in Plate 81 is yet another example of a nut bowl, this one made by the Kelly Company of Cleveland, Ohio, to promote Mammoth salted nuts. This piece has value as an advertising collectible in addition to its appeal as a nut bowl.

Considering the large and interesting assortment of nut-related paraphernalia, it is tempting for nutcracker collectors to branch out and include a selection of these other pieces in their collections, a temptation to which I have already succumbed.

PLATE 81
Green peanut bowl. 6⅛" diameter, 2⅝" high. Portuguese, late 20th century.
Mammoth salted nut tin adverting bowl. 5⅝" diameter, 2¼" high. American, mid-20th century.
Cast iron dog on wooden base with pottery nut bowl. Marked on lever "Made in England" and "Patent No. 273,480." 11¼" long including tail and base, 4⅜" high, 2¾" across. c. 1930.

Chapter 5

GERMAN NUTCRACKERS

IMMIGRANTS TO AMERICA

A large variety of nutcrackers can be found in the United States. As previously stated, many of these are not of American origin. Some of these nutcrackers reached our shores as souvenirs and gifts purchased by Americans while on European trips. Others were imported for sale in this country. Still other nutcrackers were brought to America by immigrants who cherished these implements.

The October 1988 issue of *Victoria* magazine included an article entitled "Serving as an Art." This article told of the arrival from Russia of the parents of needle artist Debra Minsky Jackson. As immigrants to the United States, Ms. Minsky's parents arrived in America many years ago, carrying only four possessions with them – a pair of candlesticks, a cherished pocket watch, and an old English nutcracker.

Nutcrackers, such as the one brought to America by this Russian couple, have been passed down through families and in many instances are still in excellent condition. Often the more decorative examples were considered too fragile to be put to use, or used only on hazelnuts or soft-shelled pecans that are relatively easy to crack. The nutcrackers surviving in good condition to this day are those that have been cherished over the years for their aesthetic appeal and sentimental value.

Because of the widespread popularity of nuts, most countries have made nut-cracking utensils over the years. Some nations, however, have either devoted a great deal of time and attention to nutcracker production and/or have a distinctive nutcracker style. Most prominent among these international influences is Germany.

GERMAN LEGEND AND THE FIRST NUTCRACKER

According to German legend, to own one of the many wooden nutcrackers produced in that country would bring good fortune to its owner. Whether this legend is true or not, the desire to have a German nutcracker (or a whole collection of these figural masterpieces) has resulted in a long history of nutcracker production for this nation. Over the years, many German nutcrackers have found their way into other European homes and have been exported to America also.

The origin of the first German nutcracker is steeped in legend. One lovely story, according to Kenneth W. Althoff, author of *The Legend of the Nutcracker and Traditions of The Erzgebirge*, has no historical basis but remains popular to this day. (Mr. Althoff is the Chief Executive Officer of Midwest Importers of Cannon Falls, Inc. in Minnesota, a company which imports and distributes, among other items, nutcrackers.)

The legend tells of a farmer who lived long ago. He was an extremely wealthy man, but stingy and lonely. His heart was professed to be as hard as the walnut trees on his property. Busy as he was, the farmer had little time to spend cracking these nuts to reach the nut meats at the center. He offered a reward to anyone who could find an easy way to crack them. Many humorous and creative suggestions were made including that of an old soldier who proposed shooting the nuts to crack them open. Other ideas included a veterinarian's suggestion that if walnuts were put under a hen, they would hatch, while a carpenter was in favor of using a saw to open the nut shells. It was an old puppet carver from the village of Seiffen, which is located about 120 miles south of Berlin, who finally came up with an idea that pleased the farmer.

The puppet carver had a beautiful brightly painted puppet with a large mouth and sturdy jaws strong enough to crack open walnuts. The miserly farmer was so appreciative of this nut-cracking invention that he rewarded the entire village of Seiffen. The reward was that during the holidays he would give all its residents chocolate with nuts, German fruit cake, and even walnuts painted gold to be used as Christmas decorations for the trees. The farmer purportedly gave the wood carver his own workshop to make the most beautiful nutcrackers in the world. As the story goes, not only were the nuts cracked by the nutcrackers, but the farmer's heart was opened as well. Thus came the kindness and generosity he bestowed on the carver and the villagers. Perhaps this story did not happen exactly as it has been told, but I prefer to believe that there is a basis in fact for this charming legend.

NUTCRACKER-RELATED SAYINGS

Nutcrackers have been popular for so many years in Germany that in addition to inspiring a selection of stories and even an occasional poem, they also have spawned a number of well-known sayings. Among these sayings are "The harder the nut, the sweeter the kernel" and "Nuts are given to us by life, we have to open them ourselves."

To understand the significance of these sayings as they relate to the people of this country, and to the long and sometimes arduous development of the wood-working craft responsible for producing beautiful German nutcrackers, we must begin with events which took place as early as the 1400s and 1500s.

A HERITAGE OF WOOD CARVING

The Erzgebirge region, until recently part of East Germany, has for many years produced some of the most beautiful wooden items made anywhere in the world. The reasons for this are many including economic, geographic and historical influences stemming back, in part, to the mining industry in Germany.

A long heritage of hard work was founded in the mining of metal beginning in this area as early as the 1200s. In fact, the word *Erzgebirge* is a combination of the word *Erz* meaning ore and the word *Berg* meaning mountain. Mining naturally developed as a primary occupation for many of the people in the Erzgebirge, not only because of the rich deposits of silver, iron, tin and nickel, but because of the abundance of timber needed for supporting the ceilings of the mines. The mountain streams provided a resource for producing power required for pumps in the mines and for the mechanical equipment used to remove the ore. Over a period of many years, however, this once seemingly limitless supply of metal was depleted and families who for centuries relied upon mining to make a living were forced to turn to other professions, a primary one being wood-working.

Wood-working was a logical choice as many miners were gifted carvers as well. In fact, mine-workers often had spent hours away from the mines pursuing various wood-working projects. Carving items for practical use initially, they soon mastered the art of ornamental carving and the modeling of wooden figures. Over the years a cottage industry was established in which the wood was carved by the men and then painted by the women. Wood-working had been practiced as a craft in this region long before

many displaced miners turned to it as an occupation. It was in the 11th century that carving first began to spring to life in Northern Europe with Germany at the center of the carving activity. This was the result at first of generous church patronage and later was supported by wealthy merchants and private patrons who wanted their homes adorned with beautiful carvings.

The Oberammergau region of Germany, long associated with its re-enactments of the Passion Play (the Passion and Death of Christ) which was first performed in 1633, has for many years been the European center of classical carving. Thousands of carvers have been educated there since 1835 when more than 200 families in the region practiced this craft. As late as 1969, about 1,000 craftsmen were being trained in the art of carving in this area of Germany, where today nutcrackers, as well as other wooden items, are produced for sale throughout the world.

INFLUENCE OF THE LATHE ON NUTCRACKER CONSTRUCTION

Although the importance of the lathe was briefly mentioned earlier, the role it played in the development of the woodworking industry and in facilitating the production of nutcrackers cannot be overstated. In fact, the long history of nutcracker production in Germany did not really begin until the introduction of the lathe in the Erzgebirge region of Germany in the late 15th and early 16th centuries.

The Elector of Saxony and King of Poland, Augustus the Strong, popularized the techniques of wood turning and the lathe became widely accepted in the Black Forest areas which were rich in timber. Consequently, a new independent brand of the wood-working trade, that of the wood turner, quickly developed. So prosperous was the carving industry which arose in the Oberammergau region in Germany that the carvers asked the Abbot of Ettal in 1520 to publish a decree permitting wood-carving to be done only by native craftsmen and their legal children. Because of this decree, the same family names have been prominent throughout the ages as practitioners of this fine craft, but many beautifully carved pieces were anonymously produced by others.

The first lathes were not motorized, but instead were operated like old sewing machines driven by the tip of the feet. The earliest products were simple wooden articles such as wooden plates, staffs, spindles and household items made on the lathe or cut by the saw. In the 1600s, small toys began to be produced including jumping jacks. A variety of handmade pieces initially made by craftsmen in their homes were made later in factories. Then around 1750, the lathe began to be worked by the same hydraulic power employed in the mines for so many years. It was this water power which allowed five to fifteen lathes to be hooked together. About the same time, toys from the Erzgebirge were being sold at Christmas fairs in large cities throughout Germany.

Toward the end of the 18th century, changes took place for the wood carvers of the Oberammergau. These changes forced them to turn to different ways of marketing their wares.

First, hard times forced many of these carvers to take their goods abroad to sell. The Oberammergau is located on the old military road of the ancient Romans from Verona to Augsburg and many villagers set out with their "craxes" on their backs containing all the carved figures, crucifixes, toys, and nutcrackers that they could carry to houses of commerce in other countries. Some 18th century toy salesmen, unable to carry samples of all their available merchandise from village to village, instead took toy sample books or toy model books, similar to catalogs, along with them. Frequently, they would stay for a while in foreign lands like Russia, Poland, Hungary, Norway, Austria, Denmark and Prussia, often returning home as well-to-do people from the proceeds of their trade.

Secondly, the areas of Berchtesgaden, Thuringia and the South-Tirols also began producing wooden merchandise for the same markets with factories built for inexpensive production on a large scale. Consequently, many carvers of the Oberammergau began selling their goods at wholesale through a "Verleger" in their own villages who bought their merchandise, paying them in advance, and subsequently selling the products on the retail market.

In 1860, there was another new development as lathes were attached to large transmissions of steam engines. Because propulsion was provided by strings of hemp, rather than a wide leather belt, the lathes ran to the left (rather than to the right which is true today), which is an advantage in the production of the very small component parts found in many German nutcrackers. Around 1912, the villages of the Erzgebirge region were connected to the electrical net and lathes have been driven by electric motors to the present day.

The wood turner's role in the production of nutcrackers continues today. Due to the development and refinement of machinery, the turner now works not only by hand but with partly and fully automatic equipment, including computerized lathes. These lathes from Italy, currently being used by the Christian Ulbricht Company, can be programmed to produce specific body parts at high speeds. To make a fine quality nutcracker today, there exist as many as 130 separate procedures. First, the wood must be carefully selected – usually birch, beech, linden, maple or pine. Next, it is cured and dried for 3½ years and then machined on the lathe. Interestingly, part of the process involves the use of large eight-sided wooden rotating drums into which hundreds of unfinished limbs, heads, etc. are loaded. After 24 to 36 hours of constant rotating, the action of the pieces rubbing against each other has a smoothing effect which negates the need for sanding. Once smoothed, the parts are assembled and painted to produce a finished nutcracker. Some nutcrackers are still carved by hand, but the majority are produced entirely on the wood lathes as has been true for many years.

Again, because the manufacture of toys has remained basically a domestic craft, the names of certain manufacturers have become prominent. Among early toy makers, the name of Albrecht Fuchther was well known for various items, including nutcrackers. How exciting it would be to find a nutcracker with his name carved into it!

EXPORTATION OF WEST AND EAST GERMAN NUTCRACKERS

After World War II, the Communist takeover resulted in the nationalization of the entire East German economy. This affected the producers of nutcrackers as well as other forms of business.

A significant influx of German nutcrackers into the United States occurred during the post-war era of the late 1950s. Because of the strength of the dollar, these nutcrackers were relatively inexpensive. Seven models were produced under the Seiffener Volkskunst label. Limited numbers of nutcrackers were made by small companies and family units of East Germany because the demand was low. The typical German households owned one nutcracker and only occasionally bought others as Christmas gifts. The East German economy recovered slowly during the next few years without the benefit of the Marshall Plan as in West Germany. Desperately in need of funds in order to buy from the West, East Berlin began to export more products from the Erzgebirge region. Consequently, East German nutcrackers became more visible in West German retail stores and also began to be imported in greater variety by Americans.

Soldiers from America stationed in West Germany purchased many nutcrackers as souvenirs to send to family and friends back home. In the mid-1960s, several manufacturers from East Germany resettled in West Germany and resumed the production of nutcrackers. The competition between East and West became quite intense, made even more difficult by the East German government's subsidies to their industries.

One story of note describes the eventual success of Volkmar Matthes from the Spielwarendorf (Toy Village) Seiffen. His business, which was started in a spare room of his apartment, seemed doomed until an American customer suggested that he take his products to GI settlements. His products became an instant hit and he proceeded to produce 25 different models in regular and three-foot heights. Two trucks left his factory on a daily basis headed for GI bases. Made rather simply and inexpensively, Mr. Matthes' nutcrackers have not generally been considered very collectible nor have they been available for sale in the United States.

By the mid-1980s, the market for nutcrackers changed with many retailers looking for greater variety, good quality and reasonable prices. The market exploded as supply could not be kept up with the high demand. The bottom fell out, however, as the dollar began to decline late in 1985, and the price of most nutcrackers rose very rapidly due to the exchange rate. In response, the manufacturers lowered prices as much as possible, while importers and distributors cut their profit margins.

Various labor problems in Germany further complicated the situation. One casualty of these economic problems was the Otto Ulbricht Company, which closed its doors in November of 1985. Manufacturing a line limited to a very simple small piece and one large model which was available in different colors, this company chose to sell only domestically. In retrospect, some believe that restricting sales to the German market and not selling abroad, especially to the United States, contributed extensively to the company's bankruptcy.

Before the collapse of the Berlin Wall, nutcrackers made in East Germany were produced by government controlled companies which set both wages and prices. They were marketed by the Aussenhandel, a state-run cabinet with its seat in Berlin. These nutcrackers were produced almost entirely for export rather than as a domestic commodity. After the reunification of Germany, the government-run factories were placed in holding companies and marketed for sale. Formerly, the prices of East German nutcrackers were generally only half or less the cost of West German pieces of comparable size. However, the prices of items produced in former East German factories are now attaining free market value. The government subsidies are gone and prices are now reflecting the true cost of doing business. In fact, most local residents can no longer afford to buy their own merchandise, but increased tourism from more affluent Western Germans is helping to offset the lack of spending by local inhabitants.

Additional negative effects of the transition from Communist control include the closing of many small workshops in Eastern Germany that were over-staffed with socialist-style work forces. Others are floundering in their attempts to compete in a new business environment. Competition from businesses in Hong Kong and Taiwan who produce less expensive copies of German folk art has added yet another glitch.

The story of Matthias Schalling, a young German businessman, who recently reclaimed a small woodworking factory which his great-grandfather had started in 1904, highlights the plight of many Eastern Germans who are trying to compete in the post-unification business world. The equipment installed in Mr. Schalling's work shop during the Communist period were unwieldy Russian and Bulgarian models not appropriate for intricate wood working. These machines will have to be replaced because they are outdated and use excessive electricity. With funds so low, however, it will be difficult to make these renovations.

On the positive side of post-reunification business is that the wood-workers can now sell all of their merchandise as they see fit and designs no longer need government approval. Under Communist rule, 97% of their goods were sold for lower prices by the government to other countries with hard currencies like France, the United States and Great Britain. The remaining 3% were usually inferior products which could be sold in East Germany.

With this new found freedom to manage their own businesses, one thing seems certain to the Eastern Germans – exporting their goods is the key to survival, with export to the United States especially important. A real controversy erupted during the 1991 Christmas season when one eastern German company, Holz-und Drechslerwaren G.m.b.H. from the village of Rothenthal, produced an Operation Desert Storm nutcracker in recognition of the recent Mid-Eastern conflict. Outfitted in a helmet, dressed in camouflage and armed with a tiny rifle and boxes of imitation munitions, many traditional German nutcracker manufacturers were horrified, believing that this was a case of going too far to attract an American market. Available for Christmas, 1991 in shops catering to the United States military in Western Germany, plans were also underway to export these nutcrackers to the United States. Distributors seemed to give the nutcracker a lukewarm reception. It was released too late to be of much interest. The consensus appeared to be among many that although "soldiers" are a traditional nutcracker motif, the symbolism for the Desert Storm model was different. Traditional nutcrackers were intended to spoof authority figures, not to glorify military victory.

As seen from this situation, one of the challenges facing German manufacturers is retaining creative integrity while effectively competing in business. A delicate balance must be struck between making folk art and the necessity for mass production and intensive marketing.

According to Manfred Schubach, a former United States distributor of German-produced nutcrackers, only a few contemporary East German nutcrackers produced before the reunification were worth collecting. The range in quality of the East German model was from excellent to commonplace. They were ordinarily traditional in design, usually decorated with real rabbit fur for hair with glossily painted hands, faces, bases and levers. Most often made of linden wood, they carried few accessories and often had interchangeable body designs, arms, legs and hats with distinguishing touches in the different colored paint and trims. Most of these nutcrackers ranged in height from 8" to 16" although some were as tall as six feet. A few animal models were made such as mice and rabbits, but they are more difficult to find. The woodsman in Plate 82 was produced in East Germany by a craftsman who suspended production for a while during Communist rule, but has since resumed manufacturing. Nicely carved and with few accessories, this nutcracker is a good example of quality East German workmanship.

In recent years, nutcrackers produced in East Germany were usually mass produced and of poorer design than their West German counterparts. To assist in identification of East as opposed to West German nutcrackers, it should be noted that beginning in 1972, all East German export products, including nutcrackers, were labeled "Exports" and often had a paper label or an ink stamp which read "German Democratic Republic" or "Erzgebirge." These markings may make these nutcrackers highly prized in the future since the reunification of Germany has resulted in a new name, the Federal Republic of Germany.

Now that eastern German manufacturing is no longer government-controlled, foreign importers and distributors will have to deal with thirty-seven individual family-owned businesses which produce nutcrackers, rather than a single centralized government body. This will, no doubt, complicate the situation, until business relationships are firmly established with the separate companies.

According to recent estimates, there are still about 200 full-time and about 800 part-time wood-workers in the Erzebirge region.

COLLECTING CONTEMPORARY GERMAN NUTCRACKERS

Interestingly, many German nutcrackers have grim or even fierce faces, due in part to the horizontal position of their mouths, structured that way to accept nuts. Adding to this look is the fact that the teeth are often painted outside the jaw, especially on more contemporary examples. These ominous figures depict characters such as kings, policemen, foresters and military officers.

In Germany, there is a saying, "He has to crack a hard nut." This means a person is faced with a difficult problem or is in trouble of some kind. The miners and other residents of the Erzgebirge had many tough nuts to crack during their lives – difficult working conditions, meager compensation and the presence of authorities who often

made harsh demands. Therefore, some theorize the German people enjoyed representing the unpopular officials as mean-looking nutcrackers who would then be forced to do their bidding by cracking nuts. Christian Steinbach, current owner of the Steinbach Company in Germany, one of the foremost producers of nutcrackers for many years, has his own thoughts on this subject. In his recently published book, *Steinbach GMbH*, on the Steinbach company, he states that "... nutcrackers are symbolic figures. They will help you to crack the 'spice of life'. Strong, powerful, genuine and loyal like their forefathers over the centuries, they do their duty. Always ready to ward off evil from their owners. They are kind companions, venerable and respectable figures, *but never objects of ridicule*, as an Eastern ideology claimed for a time."

PLATE 82
Wooden carved woodsman nutcracker made in East Germany. Real fur hair. Base - 3¾" across, 3½" deep, ⅝" high. Nutcracker - 10½" high, 6" deep, 4¼" across. c. 1989.

In any case, as nutcrackers became popular throughout Europe and in other parts of the world, more varied figures were added including nightwatchmen, sellers of birds and cloth, bakers, and even mushroom pickers. Recent examples have included musical components, such as the "Chopin Musical Nutcracker" by the Steinbach Company which depicts Chopin seated at a keyboard playing *Tristese* revolving on his stool to take a bow. Another, also by Steinbach, is of a whimsical clockmaker. Among his tools and clocks is a hand-operated music works. In fact, musical or music box nutcrackers are a specialized area of collecting for some enthusiasts.

Another East German nutcracker produced in the late 1980s is a soldier on a rocking horse (Plate 83). Because of the close proximity of the nutcracker's mouth to the horse's neck, it would difficult to actually crack nuts in the soldier's jaws. It was obviously meant to be primarily an ornamental piece. Note the rabbit fur used around his cap. Reportedly, 1990 was the last year that the company, Erzgebirgische Volkskunst, produced this model using real fur to adorn its nutcrackers. A welcome change, I am sure, to all animal-lovers.

The other Erzgebirgische Volkskunst nutcracker in Plate 83 is a red-headed witch with green skin and a black and orange costume. A broom in one hand, a cat perched on her hat and a basket of apples in her other hand, this friendly-looking witch is all ready for Halloween. Her paper label on the bottom of the stand reads "Erzgebirgische Volkskunst" and "expertic," a term referring to the trademark association for arts and crafts in Olbernhau. Founded in 1968, it promoted the continuation and preservation of traditional crafts in the German Democratic Republic and protected trademark rights as well.

In addition to the time-honored nutcracker designs, including soldiers, guards, nightwatchmen, and kings, contemporary companies have also introduced nutcrackers representing more current figures like oil sheiks, literary characters including Sherlock Holmes and Dr. Watson, and American historical or political personages like Uncle Sam and the cowboy.

Those who specialize in collecting German nutcrackers and who take a traditional approach often suggest that when beginning a collection, a King should be purchased first and displayed where he can watch over his subjects.

PLATE 83
Left: Handpainted wooden witch nutcracker made in East Germany. Paper sticker on bottom reads "Erzgebirgische Volkskunst" and "Made in German Democratic Republic (expertic)." 12" high, 3¾" across, 3⅜" deep. c. 1989.
Right: Wooden soldier on rocking horse nutcracker made in East Germany by Erzgebirgische Volkskunst. 6½" long, 7¾" high, 2" across. c. 1989.

The second piece should be a soldier or the like who is outfitted with a weapon to protect the King. The third nutcracker is the good luck piece, often a chimney sweep, thought to bring good luck in European countries. A drummer should be added next to drum out the good news that tells everyone about the collection. More nutcrackers with weapons should then be added to protect the King, followed by a butcher and baker to provide food for his majesty. A nutcracker with a musical instrument to entertain the King is also recommended, after which the collector must rely upon his own imagination in acquiring additional pieces. Christian Steinbach's book, referred to earlier, provides color photographs of numerous nutcrackers produced by the Steinbach Company, including traditional and more contemporary pieces. Detailed descriptions of each model pictured are also provided.

Contemporary German-style nutcrackers are being made outside of Germany, particularly in China. These are lower priced, lesser quality imitations of German designs. The Lenox House Hotel in Chicago uses almost 2,000 Asian models each year as part of its *Nutcracker Suite* weekend promotions during the Christmas holidays. The nutcrackers are appealing enough in combination with hotel amenities to have produced a regular following of guests who return each year to add to their collections.

Others, including ones being made in Taiwan (Plate 84), ordinarily lack the detail of the authentic German pieces, but are usually less expensive as well. Wooden figural nutcrackers being produced today are usually lever operated, rather than screw activated, and free-standing on a base instead of hand-held models. Two inexpensive but cute exceptions, shown in Plate 84, are a small nutcracker wearing a knitted red ski cap and a sailor with HMS on his cap for "His/Her majesty's service, ship, or steamer." Made in Taiwan for holiday gift-giving, these little fellows are both screw operated. Not only are wooden nutcrackers being made in Taiwan, but cast iron pieces as well (Plate 85). This one in the shape of a German soldier is brightly painted and mounted on a wooden base. It is imported from Taiwan by Midwest Importers of Cannon Falls, Minnesota.

PLATE 84
Left: Wooden screw-type sailor nutcracker. Paper label on bottom reads "Made in Taiwan." 6¼" high, 2⅛" across, 2" deep. Late 20th century.
Center: Wooden screw-type nutcracker, man with red knit hat. Paper label on bottom reads "Made in Taiwan for Dept. 56." 5¼" high, 3" deep, 3" across including hat. c. 1980s.
Right: Wooden bearded man nutcracker made in Taiwan. Wood burning decoration. 9⅞" high, 4½" across, 4" deep. c. 1990.

PLATE 85
Painted cast iron soldier nutcracker with paper label on bottom marked "Made in Taiwan" and "Midwest Importers." Wooden base - 7½" long, 2½" wide, ¾" high. Nutcracker - 5" high, 6½" long, 1¼" across. c. 1990.

CONTEMPORARY GERMAN NUTCRACKER MANUFACTURERS

A number of German companies are currently manufacturing nutcrackers. Some have been producing them for many years like the Steinbach Company, a fifth generation family-owned business. Other prominent names also in production still are Christian Ulbricht Holzkunst and Lothar Junghanel. Also important to the history of nutcracker manufacture were *Genossenschafts* like Dregeno which were associations of home workers. Each company has some distinctive features which distinguishes its nutcrackers from the others. Beech and birch woods are the popular choices for nutcracker construction, specifically with the Steinbach and Ulbricht Companies. Pine is also used along with a variety of imported woods.

The story of the Steinbach family began long ago. Originally expelled from Austria as exultants who practiced the Lutheran faith, the Steinbachs have been in Germany since at least the 1600s. Early on, this family became involved in the wood-working business in the Erzgebirge, purchasing a timber yard and sawmill. After World War II, they relocated to Hohenhameln in West Germany just north of the Harz Mountains.

The Steinbach Company manufactures nutcrackers from natural grained wood with glossily painted bodies, carved eyes and fake fur for hair and beards. Their nutcrackers were once labeled with paper stickers but are now marked with the company logo wood-burned into the bottom of each piece. Bases of the nutcrackers have been natural wood or sometimes painted green while the faces for years have been painted in flesh tones. The Steinbach nutcrackers are very detailed, and each one has many accessories to help identify the profession of the figure. (See Plate 86 for a highly accessorized model of Christopher Columbus.) The most expensive nutcrackers in this line are 11–15" in height while smaller pieces from the "Kings Court" are less detailed and less costly. A line of 4" miniature nutcracker ornaments has been made. They can be hung on Christmas trees or in a person's car to bring good luck. It has been reported that this line of mini-nutcrackers has been discontinued. In 1991, this company offered for the first time a limited edition model. The figure of Merlin, the sorcerer from the story of Camelot (Plate 87), was made in an issue of only 7,500 pieces. It quickly sold out and is rapidly appreciating in value. Steinbach plans to continue this practice by producing more figures from the story of King Arthur's court, including King Arthur himself, Lancelot, etc. Considering how rapidly the Merlin nutcracker was sold, the company purportedly plans the next character to be released in an edition of 10,500. Currently, the Steinbach company reports that the United States is the largest importer of nutcrackers with Japan second and England following with an ever-increasing demand.

Following World War II, Otto Ulbricht fled to West Germany and established his business, the Otto Ulbricht Company. As mentioned earlier, this manufacturer did not fare well during the early 1980s, eventually going bankrupt in November of 1985. The nutcrackers produced by this company were relatively simple in design. The body and head was one entity with a short arm and hand combination. The legs were straight, short, and thin. Instead of a base, the figure stood on oversized feet. The total effect was a comical and rather squat-looking figure with eyes painted as black dots and real rabbit fur for hair. These figures were 10½" in height.

The Holzkunst Christian Ulbricht Company was begun by Otto's son, Christian. It was started as a family-operated business with the help of 28 neighbors and now includes Christian's son and daughter. It gave Christian a long-awaited opportunity to display his design talent. His nutcrackers are similar to the Steinbach Company's figures. A wide variety of subjects is available and each is heavily accessorized. These nutcrackers are assembled from the feet up by stacking the individual parts on wooden dowels inserted into the base. They are colorfully painted and have a matte finish with flesh-tone painted faces. Fake fur is used for mustaches, beards and hair. Instead of the usual jaw opening and resultant fierce-looking face, a number of models have an open neck mechanism so they can have smiling faces. In particular, many of the female nutcrackers like the black and white

PLATE 86
Painted wooden Christopher Columbus nutcracker with fake fur hair and beard. Logo impressed or burned into bottom of base, "Original Steinbach Volkskunst Aus Hohenhameln - from Germany." Wooden base - 5⅞" long, 4⅛" across, ⅞" high. Nutcracker - 15¼" high, 7½" deep, 5½" across. c. 1991.

PLATE 87
Limited edition Steinbach wooden Merlin nutcracker with paper foil wrist band. Logo burned into the bottom of base, "Original STEINBACH Volkskunst aus Hohenhameln, from Germany." Paper label reads "Exclusive Distr. - USA Kurt S. Adler, New York, Limited Edition." Circular base - 4⅛" diameter, ¾" high. Nutcracker - 17" high, 5¼" across, 5½" deep. c. 1991.

cooks, the clown, and the witch are made this way. (The black cook has been discontinued.) The logo of the company is a circle with the company name and "Hand-made in Germany" printed around the perimeter and a Christmas tree with a nutcracker in its center in the middle. Prior to October 1, 1991, the label read "Hand-made in West Germany." This logo is burned into the bottom of the natural wood base of each piece. Each nutcracker also is accompanied by a gold foil wrist booklet which provides information on the history of the company. A delightful flower vendor with bouquet and scissors in hand is pictured in Plate 88. This company makes a variety of pieces ranging in size from 14" to 16" and from 10" to 12" in height. A 27" high Santa and Toymaker and a life-sized 5'8" high Toymaker are also produced.

Christian Ulbricht's brother, Otto, and sister, Finni, started their own nutcracker-manufacturing company

PLATE 88
Handpainted wooden flower vendor nutcracker with fake fur hair. Company logo of Holzkunst Christian Ulbricht burned into underside of base. Comes with wrist booklet with company information. 14½" high, 5½" across, 4⅞" deep. West German, c. 1991.

around the time Christian began his own, but they subsequently went bankrupt. Finni tried her hand at operating a business of her own, but that too was unsuccessful.

A company owned and operated by Lothar Junghanel has been in business since 1950. He first established his company by producing Hawaiian guitars and fine bass guitars and in 1975 decided to turn his efforts as a master woodcarver to making hand-carved nutcrackers. His models have rustic, yet realistic facial modeling achieved through hand-carving. There are 28 designs in his merchandise line with about 800 pieces produced annually. Each nutcracker is signed and dated and has the company trademark burned into the base. A certificate of purchase is also included. All the models are a little over 12" in height, and a few models like the Yankee, King, Santa and Confederate come with a Reuge music box in the base.

Lothar Junghanel's son, Hanno, was still in his twenties when he designed a series of 10 nutcrackers made of pine. Each piece was individually turned on a lathe with the grain of the wood centered and then polished and stained to enhance the wood grain. Limited to an edition of 1,500 pieces, each is signed, dated and has the trademark burned into the bottom of the base. Returning an enclosed registration card ensures a certificate of authenticity. These models are 11" in height, and like Lothar Junghanel's nutcrackers, they have natural rectangular wood bases with the tops painted green. Hanno Junghanel's series includes Davy Crockett, a Yankee, a Rebel, a Bavarian, a Musketeer, two Kings and two firefighters.

Another manufacturer is Gunter Ulbricht (no relation to Christian Ulbricht). He escaped from East Germany in 1975 under somewhat mysterious circumstances. When he first became involved in nutcracker-making is not certain, but he currently produces a line of six models which are shipped to the United States through a middleman. The nutcrackers in this merchandise line are a Bavarian Beer Drinker, a King, an English Guard, a Chimney Sweep, a French Guard, and a Hussar in red and blue. These models, strongly resembling traditional East German nutcrackers, have few accessories. Another group of his figures, including a Mushroom Hunter, an Innkeeper, a Bavarian, a Forester/Hunter, a Pilot and a Santa Claus, have more hair and accessories, showing a West German influence. The sizes of these pieces range from 13" to 15" in height.

Nutcrackers produced by the Holzkunst Zuber Company were initially quite similar in appearance to the hairy designs of Christian Ulbricht. (Zuber was a former employee of the Christian Ulbricht Company.) Zuber, a company in existence for about five years, is now producing a line of nutcrackers quite distinctive from the Ulbricht designs. Models which include a Pharmacist, a Firefighter, a Dentist, Robin Hood, a Postman, a Mountain Climber, a Cossack, Santa Claus and a Nightwatchman are made with several accessories appropriate to the character. Their bases are natural wood rectangles and each piece has a paper wrist identification tag. Models vary in size from 12" to 15" in height to a series of smaller models in the 10" to 11½" range. (A Zuber model of Geppetto with Pinocchio, is pictured in Plate 89.) Special editions like Paul Bunyan and William Tell have a 1,000 piece limit.

Volkmar Matthes is another nutcracker manufacturer. He and his family resettled in West Germany from Seiffen in the Erzgebirge in the early 1960s. His nutcrackers, which have a simple design, are popular with American servicemen stationed in Germany. He also produces some large and interesting variations of the nutcracker motif. One such item is a three-foot tall nutcracker bar stool, while more than 25 of his other nutcracker models are over 30" tall. Each are adorned with a double-sided paper trademark. Volkmar Matthes is also noteworthy for his creation of the world's largest nutcracker. It is nine feet in height and on exhibit in his retail store in Garmisch. (He owns five retail stores in Germany.) His factory in Affaltersbach-Wolfsoeden is open to visitors.

Difficult to find are nutcrackers produced by a manufacturer named Mrs. Petersen. For many years Petersen nutcrackers were produced by a husband and wife team. Mr. Petersen did the woodworking; his wife handled the painting. After his death, production was temporarily suspended, but now Mrs. Petersen continues the business alone. She hand paints two models – Ivan the Terrible and a King, and each is signed and dated. Unattractive by some standards because of their simple design, they are impressive nonetheless. Sizes for the two designs range from 10" to 12" and 14" to 15". Three-foot models are also produced and rumored to be sold at the exclusive Neiman Marcus department store during the holiday season.

The German-style nutcrackers of one Austrian manufacturer are rather distinctive because they are painted to resemble rosemaling. These models are apparently made and distributed through a Chamber of Commerce and bear no company name, but can be identified by the use of this special technique of painting. Also worthy of special mention is the Rhönholzschnitzerei, a German manufacturer which produced a variety of hand-held nutcrackers in addition to free-standing models over the years.

From time to time, the different models manufactured by these German companies are discontinued. This lack of availability increases the value of these pieces, making them very desirable and collectible. With that in mind, the prices for nutcrackers from the various German companies, as listed in the accompanying price guide, reflect their "for sale" costs around 1990 and not their "resale" prices as they become more difficult to find and more valuable in the years ahead.

SHOPPING FOR NUTCRACKERS IN GERMANY TODAY

On the main street in Seiffen called Hauptstrasse, small workshops still stand where wood-workers make and sell their wares. The Geschenkehaus im Museum on the Hauptstrasse exhibits products from various village workshops and is in the same building is the folk art museum. In Schneeberg (Snow Mountain), an old silver mining and carving center, a folk art cooperative produces traditional crafts, many of which are sent abroad for sale. To adjust to the new competitive business world, this co-op is renovating its workshop to include a showroom and demonstration area where buyers see the goods actually being made. In Chemnitz, there is a shop which carries a broad assortment of products from Erzgebirge villages.

Examples of German folk art, including nutcrackers, can also be purchased in other sections of Germany at major department stores and at open-air Christmas markets held in December each year. Items purchased from either of these two sources will usually be more costly than if purchased directly from craftsmen in their local villages.

PLATE 89
Geppetto and Pinocchio nutcracker, painted, with fake fur hair. Logo burned into bottom of base, "Made in West Germany - Zuber." Wooden base - 5" long, 3¾" across, ⅝" high. Nutcracker - 12¾" high, 5½" deep, 4½" across. c. 1991.

Chapter 6

OTHER INTERNATIONAL INFLUENCES

EAST INDIAN NUTCRACKERS

Nutcrackers are common in Eastern countries as well as European countries. Because of the importance of the areca nut in the East Indian diet and culture, it is not surprising that many beautiful examples of nutcrackers can be found of Indian origin. Brass nutcrackers have been produced in India for many centuries. Nutcrackers in both human and animal form have been found in Indian temples and as part of archeological excavations. Among the most common forms found are figures representing parrots, peacocks, swans, winged centaurs, horses, and human beings. Other designs include a ram, dragon,

sphinx, and lion. These nutcrackers often possess a "blade" for cracking the nuts and are sometimes referred to as "nut-slicers." I have seen this type of bladed nutcracker identified as an opium cutter, but whether this utensil ever served such a dual purpose is not clear. Most of these nutcrackers are forged or cast in iron or brass, although some are made of silver and others have ivory plaques covering their handles. Examples with inlaid copper or brass, sometimes repoussé or set with gems, also exist. (Repoussé work is shaped or ornamented with patterns in relief made by hammering or pressing on the reverse side of an object.)

Frequently, the handles of the brass and iron nutcrackers can be turned back to form a dagger which is used to cut out the meat from the nut. These nutcrackers are used to break open the hard areca nut, the fruit of the areca palm that grows in the vast coastal areas of India. The areca nut is mildly narcotic in nature and is often eaten with the betel leaf. As prolific as the areca palm is, thousands of tons of areca nuts are imported by India each year from Southeast Asia.

The horse-shaped nutcracker in Plate 90 is a fine reproduction produced for distribution by the Smithsonian Institution. The original of this nutcracker, made of heavy brass, came from Rajasthan. When the cutter operates, the rise and fall of the lever represents a horse in motion. The peacock-shaped nutcracker next to the horse is an original, dating back most likely to the late 18th or early 19th century. Close examination reveals a rough and uneven blade attesting to the heavy use this piece once endured.

As already mentioned, the eating of areca nuts is closely connected with the consumption of betel leaves (tàmbula). Betel leaf eating has considerable significance in the wedding rituals of most provinces of India. In addition, both betel leaves and areca nuts are thought to have medicinal properties, especially when used in specific proportions with lime, camphor, coconut, almond, nutmeg and other spices.

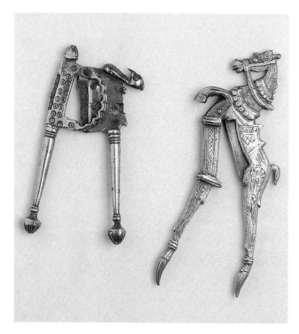

PLATE 90
Right: East Indian brass horse nutcracker. This reproduction is distributed by the Smithsonian Institution. 2¾" wide, 7½" across, ½" wide. c. 1980s.
Left: East Indian brass peacock nutcracker. 2¾" wide, 5⅞" long, ⅜" across. c. 1800.

Betel leaf cutters closely resemble the type of Indian nutcracker or nut slicer that incorporates a blade. Having a blade and two handles which are joined at one end, much like a hand-held direct action nutcracker, some of these betel cutters, are made of chased and damascened iron and are of Indo-Persian workmanship. Chasing is a form of raised decoration which is worked from the front with punches and chisels. Damascening, on the other hand, refers to a technique of inlaying metals into engraving. Undercut dovetailed grooves are made on the object to be decorated and then filled with gold, silver or copper wire. The inlay is hammered to cause it to spread and lock into place. The term is derived from the city of Damascus, a center for swordsmiths where the craft originated.

The betel leaf and areca nut culture in India can be traced back to the Gupta Period. The Gupta Period (320–467 AD) is considered to have been the greatest of all ages in India. A dynasty of kings called the Guptas ruled the northern part of the subcontinent bringing peace, prosperity and material well-being to a degree unmatched in that country before or since. Hindu literature, sculpture, architecture and painting reached creative peaks during the Guptas' reign.

In spite of the early origin of the betel leaf and areca nut culture, no recorded nor identifiable Sanskrit word for a nutcracking instrument exists. In modern Hindi, it is known as *sarota* which may have been derived from the word for sharp blade or *sarapatraka* (*sanskr*). In Gujarati, it is called *sudî*, which means female parrot and also refers to a small nutcracker. *Sûdo* is the word for male parrot and also means a big nutcracker. It has been hypothesized that these words are used to refer to nutcrackers because many nutcrackers in India are made in the form of a bird. A few peacock-shaped nutcrackers, when operated, suggest the rise and fall of wings making the bird's wings appear to flutter. In other dialects in India, different words are used to refer to nutcracking utensils. For instance, the common Marathi word for nutcracker is *âdkitta*, which appears to be a rough combination of two Kannada words, *adaki* (areca nut) and *ottu* (to cut, to crack). The word *pophalphodna* was used commonly for nutcracker in the Marathi language of the 13th century but has been replaced by the aforementioned word, *âdkitta*, in a later period.

A collection of four hundred nutcrackers was assembled by an Indian collector, Raja Dinkar Kelkar, who exhibited his collection in Pune in 1948. The collection

PLATE 91
Top: Brass nutcracker with wooden handles and brass finials, marked "India." 8½" long, 2" across, ⅝" deep. Mid-20th century.
Bottom: East Indian brass nutcracker depicting couple kissing. 6" long, 3" deep, ⅝" across. Late 19th to early 20th century.

contained nutcrackers from the 18th century to modern times. Most of these nutcrackers were forged in brass or iron with a few made of silver. In some nutcrackers, bunches of silver bells were attached to both levers to make rhythmic jingling sounds when in use. Ivory plaques covered the handles of at least one nutcracker in that collection. About 80% of this nutcracker collection came from Maharashtra with the remaining 20% from different provinces in Southern India, Gujarat and Rajasthan.

Some brass nutcrackers depict a family consisting of a man, a woman, and a child. These date back to the 19th century in Maharashtra. Other Maratha nutcrackers show various types of turbans. Another commonly found form, the *mithuna*, depicts an amorous couple embracing. In such forms, one of the levers is in the shape of a man and the other lever is in the shape of a woman. Moving the levers of these nutcrackers often suggests erotic acts. It has been hypothesized by some experts that these nutcrackers, along with those representing a lion or a ram, belong to a series of zodiac signs. Another theory connects the amorous nutcrackers to the Maharashtrian custom of biting off a betel leaf by the bridegroom from the mouth of the bride, as is suggested by the nutcrackers which depict a couple kissing when the nutcracker is opened (Plate 91). One fascinating nutcracker was made so that one side looks like a mother hugging a child while the other side depicts a man embracing a woman.

Also in Plate 91 is a more contemporary Indian nutcracker with carved wooden handles with small brass knobs. The brass triangular nut-cracking portion has two cavities for cracking nuts of different sizes.

NON-EASTERN
EROTIC NUTCRACKERS

Examples of eroticism also can be found in the nutcrackers of other cultures. Nutcrackers from the Phillippines, in the shape of women dressed in native costumes, are pictured in Plate 92. The shells of nuts are cracked by operating the legs of the figures, cracking the nuts between the upper legs or inner thighs. A wooden pin, just above the waist on the left side of the back, holds the leg in place and allows sideways movement. All three Filipino women have similar designs but exhibit different features. The one in the middle is painted black, has painted eyes, a short multi-colored sarong, and an actual beaded necklace. She appears to be the oldest of the three, probably from the early to mid-1900s. The one shown propped on her elbow is carved with considerable detail to the anatomical structure. The figure in the foreground is the simplest in form and is the most common. I have seen several like her, all of which exhibit no or very little evidence of wear, leading me to believe that this model was made within the last several years. A friend recently spotted this type of full-figure nutcracker being sold in Jamaica. It is likely that various island resorts have been producing them as souvenir items. The one seen in Jamaica involved a new twist on this familiar design. It had lights attached to its breasts that illuminated when the legs were moved – an amusing variation to some, while others would find it vulgar.

An interesting variation of this full figure nutcracker and one dated much earlier than the Filipino women is a

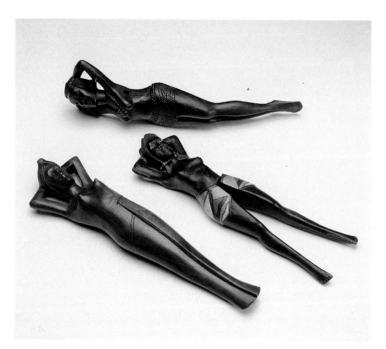

PLATE 92
Top: Wooden Filipino nutcracker of female with carved short sarong-type skirt and necklace. 12½" high, 2¼" across, 1¼" deep. Mid to late 20th century.
Middle: Wooden Filipino female nutcracker with painted sarong and beaded necklace. 12¼" high, 3⅜" across, 1½" deep. Early to mid-20th century.
Bottom: Wooden Filipino nutcracker of female with turban. 13¼" high, 3⅞" across, 1½" deep. c. 1970–1985.

truly beautiful silver-plated "Naughty Nellie" nutcracker, 8½" in length. It is similar in design to the "Naughty Nellie" boot jack, but much more refined, and most likely made in the late 19th century.

Other nutcrackers, made of a variety of substances, are in the shape of legs with no torso, operating under the same principle as the full-figure nutcrackers (Plate 93). The two wooden pairs of legs show little signs of age and are almost certainly mid-20th century creations. The nickel-plated aluminum piece, strengthened with magnesium, has high-heeled pumps and dates back to the 1940s or 1950s. The brass pieces are earlier, most likely English. Some similar 20th century pieces have been made with a detachable leather skirt with a wide center slit. The shapely female, a Victorian specimen, has an interesting leaf design on either side of the hips as if the figure were modestly wearing leaves in the manner of Eve after her expulsion from the Garden of Eden. The other brass nutcracker humorously sports high-heeled boots or shoes from its thin, bowed legs. The flesh-colored legs with cuffed ankles are probably American. Made of painted lead, a relatively soft substance, it is impractical as a nutcracker and was designed, no doubt, to amuse rather than use. The two brass legs and the flesh-toned model are probably from the late 1800s or early 1900s. Obviously, the legs design is a popular theme which has been repeated, with minor stylistic modifications, over a period of many years.

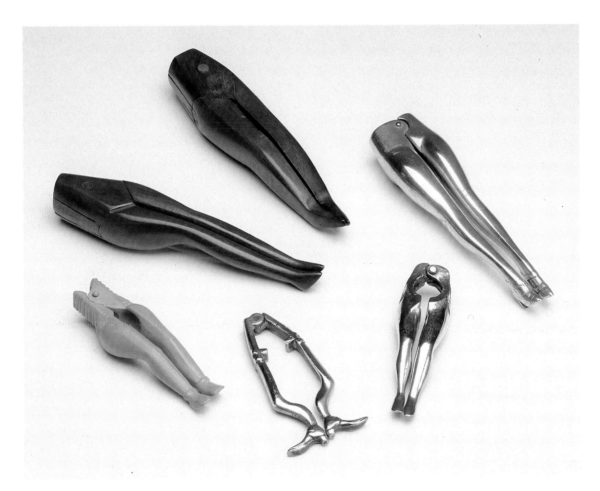

PLATE 93
Pair of wooden nutcrackers shaped like legs. (One set is slightly thicker and less curvaceous than the other set.) 7¼" high, 1½" across, 1⅛" deep. Mid-20th century.
Chromium-plated aluminum nutcracker shaped like legs with high heels. Aluminum hardened with magnesium. 7⅛" long, 1¾" across, 1¼" deep. Probably American, c. 1940-1950s.
Brass legs nutcracker with leaf design on sides. 4½" long, ¾" deep, 1¼" across. Probably English, late 19th to early 20th century.
Brass legs with boots nutcracker. 4¼" long, 2⅛" across, ⅜" deep. Probably English, late 19th to early 20th century.
Flesh-colored lead nutcracker shaped like legs with ankle cuff. 1⅝" long, 1¼" across, ⅝" deep. Probably American, early 1900s.

GREEK NUTCRACKERS

Apart from East Indian nutcrackers discussed previously, it is difficult to find nutcrackers with particular geographic or national origins apart from the wooden and brass European pieces and the cast iron and brass American examples. Greek nutcrackers, however, are identifiable for having a specific look. Good examples of Greek wood-carving are not plentiful because, over the years, the Greeks have apparently let this craft decline. One explanation is that wood is scarce in Greece, but this is true of Israel as well, and yet, there is a great deal of carving in that country.

In any case, the Greek tradition of wood-carving has diminished. Examples of wood-carving found, however, appear to be Thessalonian, from the rural northern and mountainous areas, made of olive or other local woods and decorated by peasants with chip carving and its variations. One such nutcracker in the shape of a fish (Plate 94) was sawed to shape, finished and jointed with a dowel before the decoration to simulate scales was added. The wood used was olive, which is relatively soft. Therefore the scales were formed by merely stamping with a small gouge permitting the lines to show quite distinctly against the polished wood without actually cutting. Dark stains have sometimes been applied to figures like this one and quickly wiped away to leave a residue of color in the depressions. This fish, a mid-20th century creation, is made to crack nuts in two circular or oval recesses carved into the interior of the jaw-handles. It is questionable how sturdy a nutcracker made of olive wood can be since this type of wood tends to split and splinter.

CHIP CARVING

Chip carving is a technique used by many cultures. The wood carving of Rumania, in particular, is characterized by incising, chip carving and chiselling. All three methods use geometrical patterns.

The chips in chip carving are triangular pieces of wood removed from the surface with stick and slicing knives. By arranging the patterns of these chips, overall designs are achieved.

Although incising, chiselling, chip carving, and the use of geometric designs are by no means unique to Rumanian wood carving, Rumania has produced many fine examples of this technique. Some patterns have a uniformity that can be traced back to primeval traditions. Among the most artistic and beautiful objects made over the years by Rumanian wood carvers are musical instruments, distaffs, cheese forms, and nutcrackers.

It should be noted that chip-carved items were produced in America as early as the 1700s and frequently thought to be of European origin. The geometric designs, often laid out with a compass first and then chipped with a chisel, included pinwheels and combinations of circles and swastikas. This form of chip carving has been found on various boxes used to store personal and household articles. This carving technique may have been employed in the United States to create nutcrackers as well.

The wood best suited for chip carving is widely used and is known by a variety of names. Fairly soft with a relatively tight grain and light color, it is called basswood or linden in America. In England, it is named lime or lime wood, and in German-speaking countries, it is called Lindenholz. Poplar and pine are also used for chip carving, but basswood is truly the best for this type of carving.

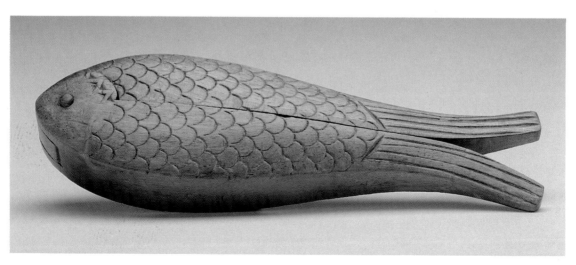

PLATE 94
Fish nutcracker made of olive wood. 8" long, 2¼" wide, 1" deep. Greek, mid-20th century.

Plate 95 shows two chip-carved nutcrackers. The one on the left exhibits a relatively simple chip-carved pattern. This piece is not particularly old, having been made within the last thirty years or so. It is, nonetheless, an attractive piece, nicely carved on both sides and a good example of the triangular chip-carving technique. The nutcracker on the left is abstract rather than figural, but may represent a stylized bird. I have seen this particular chip-carved design identified as Scandinavian, although the wood closely resembles the type used in the Greek fish (Plate 94). If Scandinavian, it shows almost no signs of age, which would suggest that it was made in the last half of the 20th century. However, I have seen the identical model dated as early as 1880 which could mean that the same design has been a popular form for nutcracker construction for many years.

NUTCRACKERS FROM OTHER COUNTRIES

A nutcracker obtained from a country not ordinarily associated with nutcracker manufacture is extremely exciting. The brass nutcracker in the shape of a bald man's head is marked "Made In Belgium" and was probably produced in the 1920s or 1930s (Plate 96). Nutcrackers are also coming into the United States from China. I have seen a brass alligator very similar to the small one in Plate 22 marked "China" that appeared to be a recent vintage. As stated earlier, the wooden soldier-style nutcrackers in Plate 41 were also made in the last few years in that country. The brass nut bowl on a pedestal with etched animal and foliage designs came from Israel, probably made in the last fifteen years (Plate 96). The green enameled brass piece is also a contemporary product of Israel. During 18th and 19th centuries, Spain produced some exceptional nutcrackers specifically made to crack pine nuts. Considering that nuts have been eaten throughout the world, an intensive search for nutcrackers identified with unusual national origins should produce results.

PLATE 95
Left: Stylized chip carved bird nutcracker. 8" long, 3" across, 7/8" deep. Possibly Scandinavian, mid to late 20th century.
Right: Wooden chip-carved nutcracker. 8" long, 2" deep, 1" across. Mid to late 20th century.

PLATE 96
Left: Brass and green enamel nutcracker, marked "Made in Israel" on bottom and "Israel" on top. Marked "DES 3317–7–" on bottom. 5¾" long including handle, 1¾" deep, 2¾" high. Late 20th century.
Center: Brass double-sided bald man nutcracker, marked "Made in Belgium." 5½" long, 1¼" across, 2¾" deep. c. 1930.
Right: Brass nutcracker and bowl, marked "TAMAR" and "Made in Israel" on bottom. 7¾" diameter, 5" high. Late 20th century.

Chapter 7

NUTCRACKER IDENTIFICATION AND PRICING

INFORMED PURCHASING

As in all antique collecting, several factors must be considered in evaluating whether or not to add a particular piece to a collection. Those factors that apply most to antique nutcrackers are age, rarity, condition, quality, and beauty or aesthetic appeal. In the higher price ranges, factors could include origin, source, attribution, and historical interest. Contained in this chapter is helpful information for the next time you contemplate a purchase. This material, at the very least, should better prepare you in determining what you are actually getting when buying a particular nutcracker and that the price is basically fair.

For me, collecting has been primarily emotional – I see it, I love it, and if at all affordable, I have to have it! This was especially true of my early collecting adventures. As my collection grew, however, I was forced to be more selective because of financial and space limitations. As I became more knowledgeable, I also became more discriminating – saving my money for the opportunity to buy one or two really special nutcrackers rather than half a dozen more common ones. I scrutinize my prospective purchases more carefully before deciding whether or not to buy. Although it often has been the emotional, not the rational, aspect of collecting that has made it so enjoyable, being armed with a little knowledge has helped me, and hopefully you, to have fun without suffering from painful and costly buying experiences.

AVAILABILITY AND PRICING

Most "antique" nutcrackers for sale today are of 19th and early 20th century origin with occasional pieces surfacing from the 18th century. Only very rarely do nutcrackers from the 16th and 17th centuries become available on the open market unless a collector or museum is liquidating a collection. It is worthwhile to keep your eyes open because early pieces do turn up from time to time. Assuming the seller is aware of their age and rarity,

they will most likely be priced well over $500.00 for the most beautiful and unusual examples.

Interestingly, nutcracker availability and cost in Europe, especially in France, seem to be comparable to the United States. In fact, an article on nutcrackers in the French publication, *Connaissance des Arts* in June, 1984 suggests that 16th and 17th century nutcrackers have become rarities and that 18th century pieces, when found, are usually priced at $350.00 to $375.00. Furthermore, more commonly available examples from the 19th and early 20th centuries normally sell for between $75.00 and $220.00, comparable with prices in this country.

Beware of clever fakes! Several years ago, Edward Pinto alluded to the existence of forgeries. Probably made in the early 1900s and based upon the early king types, these nutcrackers were made to deliberately duplicate earlier, more costly pieces. The use of unsuitable softer wood is an immediate tip-off that they are forgeries.

Because nutcrackers are so varied, it is extremely difficult to place a value on all examples or even to categorize some for the purpose of pricing. Seemingly subtle variations among nutcrackers can sometimes account for fairly significant differences in price. Such variations may be obvious and important only to experienced dealers and ardent collectors. Pieces which are very old, rare, or unique could at auctions or through specialized dealers cost the most avid collectors $1,000.00–$2,000.00 and above to obtain.

To further complicate the pricing structure, some nutcrackers, because of their style or subject matter, are desirable to those other than nutcracker collectors. For instance, the frog in Plate 26, with its hand-wrought quality and simple lines, could be appealing to devotees of the Arts and Crafts movement. The primitive head in Plate 14 is a striking piece of American folk art and has value apart from its intended function as a nutcracker. The painted cast iron head of a black man in Plate 97 would be a desirable item to an ever-broadening group of collectors specializing in Black collectibles. Factors such as these can escalate the cost of a piece which would otherwise be more moderately priced.

In the value guide at the back of this book, a price range is given to account for regional variations. These prices are based upon my own purchasing experiences and observations, together with a close examination of prices found in other currently available price guides which cover nutcrackers along with a wide variety of other antiques. (Generally speaking, I have found the prices set in many price guides to be on the low side for nutcrackers– at least low in regard to the prices I have seen being asked over the years for the same or similar pieces.) This price list is provided as a guide to the cost of unique – in some cases, specific– nutcrackers. In other instances, categories of nutcrackers are priced. A price list has not been provided for the illustrations because they represent such unique and/or early nutcrackers that are rarely available on the market. Accurate values for them are almost impossible to set.

As is prudent when purchasing all fine antiques, buying from reputable dealers who will provide a written authorization of the estimated age and/or origin of the piece in question is strongly recommended. This is particularly important where the cost of the nutcracker is especially high and the value is based on the age or unusual history of that particular piece.

In any case, one thing is certain concerning the pricing of nutcrackers: prices over the years have steadily risen. Although some have stabilized, prices show no signs of declining in the near future. Rather amusing, but also disconcerting for those of us who entered the collecting arena relatively recently, is an excerpt from John Mebane's book, *Treasure at Home*, published in 1964.

A popular type of nutcracker was made in the shape of an alligator in whose jaws the nuts were cracked. These may be found occasionally today for $3.50 to $4.50. A scarcer one in the shape of a man who cracked the nuts in his mouth is listed now at $17.50. There was one in the shape of a dog whose tail lifted to open its mouth in which the nuts were placed for cracking. One of these has recently been offered at $18. A similar one - a cast-iron elephant whose trunk was pressed to open its mouth, in which the nuts were cracked - is valued at $12.50. Other metal ones were made in the form of animals and birds. One dealer offers a hand-carved mahogany nutcracker depicting the head of a woman wearing a turban for $5.

As you can see from Mr. Mebane's book, nutcrackers could be purchased for considerably less in the 1960s even accounting for the fact that the dollar was worth a lot more in those days. In fact, prices for comparable nutcrackers would be, in many instances, ten to fifteen times as expensive today. Too bad I wasn't collecting back then!

PLATE 97
Head of black man nutcracker with old paint. Made of cast iron with wooden base.
Nutcracker - 5⅝" tall, 8½" long including lever, 1" deep. Base - 3⅛" across, 6½" long,
¾" high. c. 1884.

PROBLEMS WITH NATIONAL ORIGIN AND AGE IDENTIFICATION

Collecting is an ongoing process of discovery. Pieces in my collection are constantly being re-examined and re-evaluated in light of new information. Being open-minded to new data and not being afraid to apply it, even if it means retracking a previously held opinion about the age or origin of a particular piece, is crucial to the learning process. Correctly identifying the age and origin of specific nutcrackers can be very difficult. Especially where wooden specimens are concerned, there is no substitute for the experience which comes from examining numerous similar examples over a long period of time and becoming familiar with their different characteristics. Handling – actually touching pieces – can be very enlightening. Since most of us do not have access to a large variety of nutcrackers, the following discussion of "what to look for" will be accompanied by numerous photographs and illustrations which compare and distinguish nutcrackers in particular categories.

As far as wooden nutcrackers are concerned, it is not easy to conclusively identify the nationality of a particular piece because figures represented are often international, and the methods and styles of carving have transcended national borders. Some clues, however, do exist. For instance, according to English authorities, Owen Evan-Thomas and Edward Pinto, most wooden nutcrackers of fine quality from the 17th and 18th centuries were of French workmanship, regardless of whether or not those depicting humans were dressed in French costume. I have been unable to determine why nutcracker production flourished in France during the 1600s and 1700s, but I place a good amount of faith in Evan-Thomas's and Pinto's conclusions due to their considerable expertise in the area of early woodenware. (Mr. Evan-Thomas wrote *Domestic Utensils of Wood from the Sixteenth to the Nineteenth Century* in 1932, and Mr. Pinto wrote *Treen or Small Woodware Throughout the Ages* in 1949.)

Exemplary of the beautiful workmanship of early French wood-carvers is the Frenchman in Illustration 10 on page 66. Apparently intended to represent a member of the French Royal House, possibly a king, this late 16th century example is ornately carved with an interesting costume which is worth examining in detail.

The head-covering of this nutcracker has a close-fitting pleated crown. On its left side a knotted scarf is draped over the shoulder. Around the edge of the crown, a rolled embroidered chaplet alternates with a fleur-de-lis and a waved scroll pattern. A large disc-shaped earring is worn in the right ear. The generously proportioned mantle has long deep sleeves, braced by loops which are suspended from the collar. The collar is turned down and extensively embroidered. Another embroidered narrower collar is beneath this one, tapering from the back of the neck downwards. The hands emerge from the multi-folded sleeves, holding a crowned escutcheon with three fleurs-de-lis between them. The base of the shield held by the figure rests upon a head supported on a base of foliage. This truly exceptional nutcracker, unmistakably French, helps to illustrate the extraordinary skill of French wood-carvers of several hundred years ago.

As mentioned earlier, the fact that a nutcracker is dressed in a costume from a particular country does not guarantee that it was made by a wood-carver from that land. The existence of a symbol or form of adornment closely identified with a particular ethnic group is, however, a clue to where the piece may have been made. In the absence of any other conclusive information as to national origin, it is sometimes one of the only bits of information available. For example, the typically French garb on the aforementioned nutcracker, particularly the French fleur-de-lis, together with the knowledge that the majority of early finely-crafted wooden nutcrackers were from France, all but confirms a French origin.

Similarly, the fabulous walnut nutcracker in Illustration 15 has been identified as Italian. (The Tyrol, a former province of Austria, was divided in 1919 between Austria (modern Tyrol) and Italy (Trentino-Alto Adige). This section of Italy was responsible for a fair amount of nutcracker production.) Extremely unique, it represents two images of a Roman civilian dignitary. Both faces, it has been said, bear a striking resemblance to a once notorious Russian premier. Again, pointing almost definitely to an

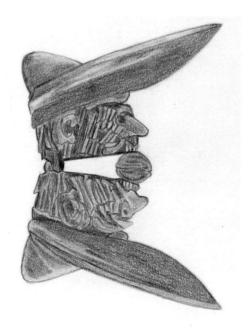

ILLUSTRATION 15
Carved wooden Italian nutcracker depicting two images of Roman dignitaries.

Italian maker, the dignitary dons a style of hat associated with the University of Rome, the hat serving as the handles of the nutcracker.

Some subjects common to a particular country have been utilized by other nationalities as well. The bear, for instance, is extremely popular with Russian carvers, but by no means exclusive to them. The unusual nutcracker in Plate 98 is almost definitely Russian, identifiable more by the style of carving and the use of interacting bears in the overall design than the subject itself. In contrast, the bears in Plate 3 and in Plate 99 are probably German, Swiss or Austrian, rather than Russian, because of the carving style and the dark staining of the wood.

Most European hand-held double-lever figural nutcrackers appear to have been made in the alpine regions of Switzerland, France, in the Austrian Tyrol, or in Scandinavia in the 1800s. Although Germany, no doubt, produced some of these examples, German wood-working

PLATE 98
Wooden bears on see-saw nutcracker. Bears have glass eyes; made possibly of pine. 11" long, 5" high, 1½" deep. Probably Russian, early to mid-20th century.

PLATE 99
Left: Wooden bear head nutcracker marked "Rici" on handle. Snout has been repaired. 7½" tall, 3¾" deep, 2¼" across. Probably German, late 19th to early 20th century.
Right: Wooden bear head nutcracker with front legs and glass eyes. 8" long, 4½" high, 2⅛" across. Probably German, early 20th century.

is much more closely associated with production of the free-standing single lever type in the form of a soldier or other authority figure.

Not only can it be tricky identifying the national origin of specific pieces, but age identification can be difficult to the untrained eye as well. Complicating age identification is the fact that some nutcrackers made as recently as the 19th and early 20th centuries repeat designs and motifs from earlier periods. Although many wooden nutcrackers produced in Europe today are made in factories, with the aid of various machinery, completely and partially hand-carved examples have been created in recent years by amateur carvers and have been made in quantity in Europe as a cottage industry during long winter months when agricultural activity was limited.

Metal nutcrackers may be found ridden with dirt or made sparkling bright through polishing, bronzing, washing in acid or lacquering, making examples from the late 1600s to the late 1800s look similar in appearance. Some signs of wear are usually evident and will be discussed later in this chapter. As metals often look much the same

PLATE 100
Brass Punch and Judy nutcracker. 5" long, 1" across, 1½" deep. Probably English, late 19th to early 20th century.

regardless of age, however, clues to age in subject matter and sometimes in design must be closely examined.

For example, the brass nutcracker in Plate 100 depicts Punch and Judy with one face on either side of the piece. It is probably mid to late 19th century English, but certainly no earlier than late 18th century. The story of Punch and Judy from a farcical puppet show originating in a popular Italian comedy did not gain widespread popularity in England and France until the 1700s. It is, therefore, unlikely that it would have been used as a nutcracker subject until the characters were well-known in these European countries.

The brass Punch and Judy nutcracker brings to mind a pair of wooden nutcrackers I once encountered, one Punch, the other Judy. This pair of nutcrackers represented a Victorian tradition reflecting status-conscious behavior which almost mandated that such implements be provided to dinner guests in twos. Over the years, of course, many of these pairs have become separated from each other. It is truly a special occasion when a pair of these matching or complementary nutcrackers are found still together.

Another example of how to determine age is found in the brass nutcracker with the Dickens character of Fagin on one side and Bill Sikes on the other in Plate 28. This example is probably late Victorian, but if made earlier, it could not have been before 1839, the year *Oliver Twist*, the book that introduced these characters, was first published.

Other clues to age, including the effects of oxidation, can sometimes be used in dating metal nutcrackers depending on what "clean-up" techniques have been employed on a particular piece. The formation of a patina from oxidation will be discussed at length later in this chapter. Because many reproductions are currently being made, especially of cast iron nutcrackers, a variety of criteria must be taken into consideration when identifying the age and origin. These criteria include identifying markings such as names, manufacturing symbols, dates, design characteristics, patent numbering, and the materials and techniques used in construction. The following is information in each of these areas which should be of assistance in the identification process.

Identifying Marks

Precise dating of wooden nutcrackers from the 16th to the 18th centuries is quite difficult. Wooden examples do not usually bear a signature or other identifying marks of the carver nor do they ordinarily show any reference to national origin. Likewise, they are rarely dated which is particularly true of wooden screw-type nutcrackers.

One important dated nutcracker, however, is at the Birmingham Museum and Art Gallery in England. Referred to earlier, it is the beautifully carved boxwood nutcracker, made in 1570, which represents Hercules astride and breaking the jaws of the Nemean Lion (Illustration 9 on pg. 65). Small nuts are cracked in the lion's jaws while larger nuts are cracked in a cavity between the levers. It depicts the story of Hercules who was the ancient Greek incarnation of man's ongoing struggle against death. As the son of Alcmena and Zeus, Hercules was half god and half man and the epitome of mortal strength. Hera (Juno) was always antagonistic to any offspring of Zeus born to mortal mothers. Even before he was born, she cheated Hercules of his kingdom. She sent two huge snakes to his crib which he strangled bare-handed. Hercules was then forced to submit to the master Eurystheus who assigned him twelve impossible labors, each of which was expected to cause his death. The first labor was to slay the monster lion which was terrorizing the Nemean valley. The lion was immune to Hercules' attacks with club and arrows so he ultimately threw the lion onto its back and strangled it. Thereafter, he wore the lion's pelt over his shoulders. This wonderfully detailed nutcracker is probably of Italian origin and was formerly in the Carnegie collection. It is a perfect example of a piece whose creation can be conclusively pinpointed in time. It must be emphasized, however, that this is a truly unique piece, and, although a product of the late 16th century, it is not really representative of the workmanship of most nutcrackers produced during this time.

Other handsome examples of marked wooden nutcrackers can be seen in Plate 99, where the word "RICI" appears on a handle of the bear's head nutcracker, and nut vendor in Plate 101 where "Mürre IV" is visible on the handle. What these words signify is not clear, but may be the name of a wood carver, a place, or a company. The word *Mürre* is German and we can assume that the nut vendor is probably of German origin, while the bear's head nutcracker could be German, Swiss or Austrian.

Unfortunately, the majority of identifying marks are not so telling. More often than not they are words or initials which mean nothing specific to us today. The nutcracker in Plate 102 has the letters "TS" carved in not one, but two places – on the handle and also on the back of the head. (The front view can be seen in Plate 71.) Obviously, these initials were very significant to the carver, but the letters "TS" by themselves have provided no real clues to identification. Other clues, namely the yew wood construction, the quality of the piece, and the early age (late 1600s), suggest it is most likely French.

The magnificent boxwood nutcracker in Plate 103, in addition to possessing extraordinary eyes and beautiful coloration, has the word "BERCHTESGADEN" meticulously carved into one of its handles. This is one of the

PLATE 101
Side view of wooden nut vendor nutcracker. 8⅛" high, 3¹/₁₆"
across, 4" deep. (Additional view and information in Plate 72.)

fairly rare instances when a nutcracker can be definitively identified as to origin, and an interesting origin at that.

Berchtesgaden is a town and resort area in southeastern Germany. The main industry of the town is the tourist trade, but other industries of the region have included salt mining, china painting and wood carving. The castle in Berchtesgaden was originally the home of the provosts of the town, later the summer residence of kings of Bavaria and eventually a museum. A basilica in the town dates back to the 12th century, making Berchtesgaden a very early and historical site in Germany. Adding to its historical significance is the fact that at Obersalzberg, 1640 feet above Berchtesgaden, were the chalets of Hitler, Göring, Bormann and other Nazi leaders during World War II. Hilter's private retreat was named the "Eagle's Nest." Air raid shelters, barracks and various miliary installations at Berchtesgaden were destroyed in an Allied air attack in April, 1945 and in 1952, the ruins were leveled to the ground and trees planted on the site.

Considering that Berchtesgaden has been such a popular resort area and that wood-carving one of its important industries, it is not surprising that a beautiful nutcracker such as this one was made there, possibly as a souvenir for a wealthy visitor in the early 1800s. Occasionally nutcrackers such as this one do have marks which aid in identification, so all pieces must be examined closely for special clues.

Generally speaking, one-of-a-kind nutcrackers which are made to commemorate a special occasion, to be given as a gift, or hold particular significance to the maker are more likely to be dated or signed than mass-produced pieces. (This refers to markings other than the fairly frequent patent numbering found on many manufactured metal pieces made during the last one hundred and fifty years or so.) The unique nutcracker in Illustration 5, obviously created with much pride by Dr. Hitchcock, was inscribed by him, making identification possible. On the other hand, contemporary, finely-made, mass-produced nutcrackers, especially the wooden German variety, are almost always marked with the manufacturer's name. This new interest in clearly labelling nutcrackers, however, merely reflects their current status as a collectible.

PLATE 102
Rear view of nutcracker with wooden head and torso and copper-coated metal plates. Note the carved initials "TS." (See Plate 71 for front view of nutcracker and additional information.)

PLATE 103
Side view of head with scarf nutcracker, made of boxwood. Marked on handle "BERCHTESGADEN." Face is stained and lacquered and has glass eyes. 8" high, 3" deep, 2" across. German, early 19th century.

Brass, bronze, and cast iron nutcrackers are more likely to bear some inscription referencing either the country of origin, the manufacturer, or more likely a patent number. A reference to the source will increase the value of an otherwise common design of nutcracker. An example of this is found in the numerous cast iron standing dog nutcrackers which, although very appealing to look at, are rather plentiful in comparison to some other forms of nutcrackers. A notation on the base of such a dog nutcracker, indicating its manufacturer, will set it apart from other similar models.

In the final analysis, some markings are obviously more helpful than others in identifying a particular nutcracker's origin, age, or maker. Some marks may not be immediately recognizable but, over time, through study or by accident, may be deciphered. To my mind, all marks, no matter how cryptic, are interesting. They enhance the appeal and sometimes the actual value and collectibility of a piece.

Dating Wooden Nutcrackers

The dating of wooden nutcrackers is especially difficult because wooden pieces are not patent numbered nor do they have touchmarks as found in pewter or hallmarks as are present in silver. Evidence of wear and the patina of the wood are two of the best age indicators of wooden nutcrackers because the figures and designs of some have been produced and reproduced over a period of many years. Any piece of wood that has been used over a period of time will show signs of wear and possibly nicks, scratches or other scarring. The amount of such evidence will depend upon the hardness of the wood, the type of use it has received, and the length of time it was used. As stated previously, many early nutcrackers were made of boxwood which is a very hard wood and will not scar as easily as other softer woods. The use of boxwood, if identifiable, is itself a clue to a fairly early origin. European commercially-produced wooden nutcrackers of the 19th and early 20th centuries were frequently made of fruitwood or walnut, which are not as strong as boxwood, and can more easily be damaged.

Although breaks, nicks and scratches can occur at any time, newer damage will be somewhat rough to the touch and will often expose a lighter-colored wood underneath. Sometimes a nutcracker will show signs of wear, but the damaged wood will have smoothed and darkened with time (Plate 104). The boar in this picture is quite unusual and very nicely carved, but it has suffered some breakage. The right ear in particular is battle-scarred, but the damage does not appear to be new, and in such an appealing piece, its value should not be affected. Older damage will usually be smoother to the touch than a chip which has just occurred, having "healed" naturally over a period of many years. This look can be duplicated to some extent with sandpaper and stain. (When chips or nicks do occur, they can be fairly well camouflaged with a little stain or a smidgen of matching shoe polish. Chapter 9 contains more information on the care of nutcrackers.)

PLATE 104
Wooden wild boar nutcracker with glass eyes. 9½" long, 3½" across, 3½" high.
German, Swiss, or Tyrolean, late 19th or early 20th century.

The smoothness which comes with age and wear will also provide clues to distinguishing between a nutcracker made by hand in the late 1800s as opposed to one that has survived from an earlier century. Of course, there is always the possibility that an earlier example will have received little handling and show little smoothing of the wood while a more recent piece that has been used frequently will exhibit wood smoothness suggestive of an earlier origin. For this reason, a combination of factors, rather than any one element alone, must be considered in dating nutcrackers, particularly wooden ones.

Another indicator of age is the fact that older wood is usually somewhat lighter in weight as a result of becoming dryer with age. Newer wood which contains more natural moisture will be slightly heavier. As soon as wood is exposed to light, air, and smoke, oxidation occurs and the wood begins to change color. This is particularly true of unfinished wood, but wood stains and paint will also discolor and fade to some degree over time. Keep in mind, different woods discolor differently.

Do not accept the presence of worm holes as a true indicator that a piece is old. These holes can occur at any time, in new as well as old nutcrackers. The insects and their larvae which cause the holes enter the wood and then turn and tunnel most often along the grain or occasionally across it. Always, however, the tunneling is done beneath the surface. This fact helps in determining real from fake worm holes and is also a good clue as to whether the holes were made before or after the piece was constructed. Only tiny roundish holes will be present if they were made after the nutcracker was created. If, instead, a series of channels covers the surface, the object was made from wood that was already infested. In this case, the wood may be much older than the workmanship. It is also possible that the piece was reworked or sanded down to such an extent that the worm channels are visible. This channel exposure through heavy sanding can occur with pieces of furniture but is highly unlikely where nutcrackers are concerned.

Plate 105 shows another angle of a nutcracker pictured in Plate 9. From the 1600s, note the exceptional smoothness of the wood, probably walnut. This nutcracker depicts a strange carved animal's head with a seated figure atop the second handle. The double figure is an example of unusual nutcracker construction. I feel especially fortunate to have this particular English nutcracker in my collection, not only because it is a very early and interesting specimen, but because it was pictured in Owen Evan-Thomas' book, *Domestic Utensils of Wood from the Sixteenth to the Nineteenth Century*, published in 1932. This book is credited with being among the first to call attention to the beauty, variety and historical significance of woodenware or treen. I understand Mr. Evan-Thomas' considerable collection of treen was sold upon his death. Although my nutcracker does not bear the little oval label which apparently adorned pieces from his collection at one time, it is unmistakably the same nutcracker represented in his book, not only because of the overall design, which could have been duplicated, but the specific scars and imperfections in the wood which have come about from age and use.

Screw-actuated wooden nutcrackers can be dated to some extent based upon the degree of design. Before the 19th century, most of them were relatively plain and simple, often Swiss or Tyrolean. The most common and least ornate screw-type nutcrackers are shaped like a ring. Made for many centuries, the ring is usually drilled right

PLATE 105
Rear view of wooden double figured nutcracker that was carved and turned on a lathe. (For front view and more information, see Plate 9.)

through. This type is virtually impossible to date accurately, although signs of age in the wood can help to some extent. Barrel-shaped versions are a variation on the same theme. A recent 20th century version of this simple design is shown in Plate 106. Acorn-shaped pieces are quite rare and most likely English. The 19th century examples, frequently English, are by contrast, more elaborately carved. The cavities of this type of nutcracker may be round, oval, only occasionally heart-shaped or square, but always with one wall of the cavity pierced with a hole which is threaded for a corresponding threaded screw.

According to Edward Pinto, decoratively carved screw nutcrackers with heart-shaped apertures, sometimes attributed to the 17th century, seem too plentiful and too well-preserved to be that early. They are more likely commercially produced examples from the 18th or early 19th centuries, most likely of Scandinavian design. Late 19th century screw-type nutcrackers are also frequently made of softer woods which results in usage problems due to the softness of the threads.

Studying some of the rare examples that are carved with original dates has provided valuable information which can be used to date other wooden nutcrackers. One such clue is that examples from the 16th and 17th centuries have smaller jaws than are found in later pieces. The smaller jaws are large enough to crack the cobs and filbert nuts popular during the 1500s to the 1700s. A secondary hollow or oval recess in the back of both levers was frequently added on many examples beginning in the early 1600s and was used for cracking walnuts. A number of examples from the 1500s which do exist also contain this secondary hollow. Brazil nuts were not introduced in Europe until the 16th and 17th centuries. While almonds were used extensively for flavoring in foods, they do not appear to have been used as a dessert in early times. Therefore, early wooden nutcrackers were usually required to crack only the filberts and cobs in their tiny jaws.

Numerous ornately decorated wooden lever-type nutcrackers were made in the 19th and early 20th centuries in the Austrian Tyrol, the Swiss and French Alps, and the Black Forest region of Germany. Although finely carved, these too are often made of relatively soft walnut or fruitwood instead of hardy boxwood or yew wood used extensively in earlier times. Consequently, they are more decorative than practical, often made as souvenirs. In fact, the bases of the front levers of these late 19th and early 20th century specimens are sometimes widened to form a kind of stand to facilitate their display (Plate 107). The dog and antelope were made around 1900. The practice of producing hand-held nutcrackers with bases which permit them to stand has been carried well into the 20th century.

The peasant woman in Plate 108 is a colorful, if somewhat crude, example of just such a piece. It was produced most likely in the 1930s or 1940s, probably in Germany. The wooden man with the red cap in the same photograph is not remarkable except for the base which was made to allow him to stand erect. It is doubtful that this base was created initially to accompany the nutcracker, but more likely that some clever owner of this piece fashioned it to match the nutcracker. I've never seen this done before, but it is an excellent idea which could be tailored to meet the dimensions of a variety of double-

PLATE 106
Wooden barrel-shaped screw-type nutcracker. 4½" long, 2½" across, 2¼" high. Late 20th century.

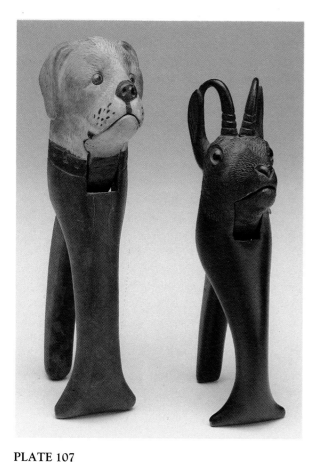

PLATE 107
Left: Painted wooden beagle nutcracker with glass eyes. 8½" high, 3¼" across, 3" deep. Swiss or Tyrolean, c. 1900.
Right: Small wooden antelope nutcracker with glass eyes. 7" tall, 2" across, 2½" deep. Swiss or Tyrolean, c. 1900.

PLATE 107

PLATE 108
Left: Wooden peasant woman nutcracker with original paint. 8½" high, 4½" across, 3" deep. Probably German, c. 1930s–1940s.
Right: Wooden man nutcracker with separate stand, painted and lacquered. Nutcracker - 8⅜" tall, 1½" across, 2" deep. Base - 5" long, 1⅝" across, ⅜" high. Swiss or Tyrolean, c. 1930s–1940s.

PLATE 108

levered nutcrackers, especially those with flattened handles like the figure pictured. Of course, Plexiglass stands are available for purchase at some craft supply stores and can be used as well. Other nutcrackers, like the boxer dog in Plate 109, have one handle with a flattened end and a screw hook attached so that they can be hung for display.

Wooden nutcrackers with glass eyes are usually the product of 19th and 20th century craftsmen despite the fact that the introduction of glass eyes in animal and human figural nutcrackers appears to be quite early. The yew wood piece in Plate 71 on pg. 68, which dates back to the late 1600s or early 1700s, has small, beady, white glass eyes with a black center. This is the earliest nutcracker, probably of French origin, that I have seen with glass eyes and the more widespread use of them seems to have taken place in the 1800s. In fact, they were probably not used to any great extent until the middle part of that century, but have continued to be used into the 1900s. The appearance

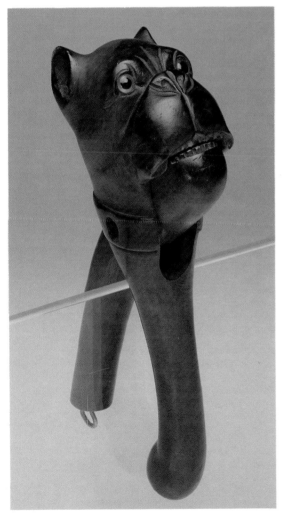

PLATE 109
Wooden boxer dog nutcracker, stained, with glass eyes. 7½" high, 2" across, 3½" deep. Swiss or Tyrolean, early 20th century.

of the glass eyes found in these specimens from the late 1800s and early 1900s have a distinctively different look than the ones which adorn the figure made 75 to 200 years earlier. The nutcracker in Plate 110 is exceptionally well-carved, and its interesting design allows it to sit flat with the face looking forward. The glass eyes, however, are what make this piece extra special. The highest quality eyes were obviously used, giving the face a very realistic appearance. This nutcracker was made around 1800 or possibly a little earlier. The type of extremely fine glass eye adorning this piece is not ordinarily found in later models. It should be remembered, however, that many fine nutcrackers were produced during this time period, and continue to be made today, with carved or painted eyes instead of glass ones.

Earlier nutcrackers are likely to be more original in design and often have greater detail than later examples. Those made in the late 19th century, although still interesting and imaginative in form and competently carved, sometimes exhibit signs of commercial duplication which are also prevalent in many 20th century examples.

Pictured in Plate 111 are three wooden dog-head nutcrackers – two have double levers and one is screw type. The large double-lever dog, possibly a beagle, on the left, is quite charming with his spots and his stud-like collar, but this is a much more common example than the dark, rather fierce looking canine on the bottom in the foreground. The wood on this one is almost silky in its smoothness and the detail is quite exceptional, even to the point of showing bared teeth in a rather predatory pose. Not only is this dog an earlier piece (c. 1800–1830), but it is the finer piece as well. Consequently, the dog on the left (c. 1890–1910) would be priced less than half of the cost of the older specimen. The small spaniel-type dog on the right is extremely likeable and well-carved but does not contain the detail of the other two. It was made around 1930 and would be priced accordingly.

Less clear, and in many ways highlighting the complex and often confusing nature of nutcracker identification, is the case of the wooden monkeys (Plate 112). The two larger monkeys are almost certainly of European origin, probably Swiss or Tyrolean from the late 19th or early 20th century. The style of the carving and the painted markings are representative of those produced during this period, more for display than for heavy use. In fact, the painted markings on the center monkey are quite remarkable for the extensive and realistic shading. The small monkey on the right, however, is somewhat of an anomaly, at least in my experience. The style is obviously quite primitive in comparison to the other two which would suggest an earlier European origin or more likely, the mark of American craftsmanship. As stated previously, American woodenware was not ordinarily as ornate

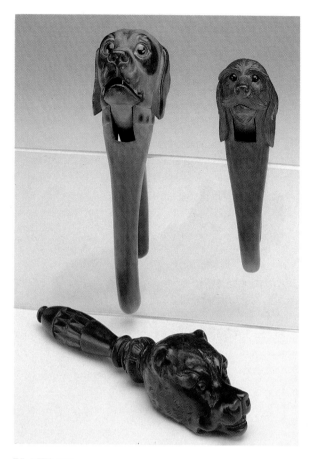

PLATE 110
Wooden head with ruffled hat nutcracker. Probably made of boxwood; has glass eyes. 8¼" long, 3¾" high, 1⅞" across. Probably French, c. 1800.

PLATE 111
Left: Wooden dog with collar nutcracker. Has glass eyes. 8½" high, 3" deep, 2¼" across. Swiss or Tyrolean, late 19th or early 20th century.
Right: Small wooden spaniel nutcracker with glass eyes. 6½" long, 2" across, 2¼" deep. Swiss or Tyrolean, c. 1930.
Below: Wooden screw-type dog nutcracker. 8½" long, 2" across, 1¾" high. Probably English, early 19th century.

PLATE 111

PLATE 112
Left: Large wooden monkey head nutcracker with glass eyes. 8½" long, 2¼" across, 3¾" deep. Swiss or Tyrolean, late 19th or early 20th century.
Middle: Stained and painted wooden monkey head nutcracker with glass eyes. 6¾" high, 2" across, 3" deep. Swiss or Tyrolean, early 20th century.
Below: Small primitive monkey nutcracker. 6" tall, 1½" across, 2" deep. Probably European, mid-19th century.

PLATE 112

as similar European creations. The dilemma, therefore, surrounds the eyes which surprisingly are glass. As mentioned, glass eyes do not appear to have been used extensively before the mid-1800s and were used primarily in mass-produced nutcrackers because of their availability to professional carvers. Apart from the glass eyes, this nutcracker has all the earmarks of a piece from the early 1800s, including a hand-made iron pin holding it together. It looks like the work of an individual rural American, and yet, the presence of the glass eyes strongly suggests that it was produced in Europe in the mid-1800s by a professional or semi-professional carver.

Luckily, the identification of most nutcrackers is more straight-forward as is true of the following example which compares three human form specimens – an Othello-type figure, a man in a tricorn hat and a black man with a scarf (Plate 113). Studying closely the pictures of these three human figural nutcrackers should help you to differentiate quality and age and their bearing on aesthetic value and price.

Shown in the center, "Othello" is fairly well detailed with brightly painted lips and teeth and finely carved features, including wavy hair and earrings. He was made between 1890 and 1920 and is probably of Swiss or Tyrolean origin. This figure was made at least in some quantity because I have seen a virtually identical piece in another collection.

The man in the tricorn hat is the only screw-type pictured but is not remarkable for that reason. He is distinctive because of the imagination of his carver. Note the broad smile and the glint in his eyes. He has personality and is almost definitely English. His price would reflect this appealing design and his early age, dating back to the early to mid-19th century. Pieces similar to him may have been made in the late 1700s because the tricorn hat that he dons was very popular in the late 1600s and 1700s. In the early 1800s, high-crowned beaver hats with shaped brims came into vogue.

The third man, a black man with a scarf, is truly a spectacular piece. Note the detailed carving of the muscles in the face, the staining of the wood, the curve of the eyebrows, and the waviness of the mustache and beard. Then look at the hypnotic glass eyes. They are very unusual and realistic glass eyes for use in a nutcracker. As

PLATE 113
Left: Front view of wooden head with scarf nutcracker. (See Plate 103 for additional information.)
Middle: Painted wooden Othello nutcracker. 8¼" long, 2" across, 4" deep. Swiss or Tyrolean, early 20th century.
Right: Wooden nutcracker of man with tricorn hat. 7½" long, 3" across, 2" deep. Probably English, early 19th century.

discussed earlier, this piece is quite unique and marked "BERCHTESGADEN" on one of its handles. The nutcracker was probably made between 1790 and 1820 by a master carver. If only this fellow could talk. One can only imagine his rich past and the fascinating journey which eventually brought him into my collection. Undoubtedly museum quality, the high price for this nutcracker would reflect a combination of rarity, quality, age, and origin.

Although each is nicely made and appealing in its own way, these three nutcrackers reflect the range in workmanship quality and design uniqueness which sets apart truly superior and often earlier nutcrackers from the more recent and run-of-the-mill examples.

Wood Identification

Identifying the type of wood used in wooden or treen nutcrackers is extremely difficult, even for experts in the field of wood and woodworking. There are 30,000 identified varieties of hardwoods and 75 varieties of softwoods, but only a small percentage were used for nutcrackers, with boxwood and yew wood being among the most common for early European pieces. Close-grained woods such as yew are technically softwoods, although they are much harder than many hardwoods and are often referred to as "hard woods." (The terms *hardwood* and *softwood* refer to whether the timber comes from a broad-leafed tree or from a coniferous tree. Balsa wood is very soft although it is classified as a hardwood since it is from a decidous tree. Evergreen yew is actually very hard although it is classified as a softwood.) Boxwood is close-grained and ivory-yellow to warm brown in color. Yew is also hard and close-grained, red brown in color with a light sapwood. It takes a high polish and is extremely durable. Walnut is an excellent wood for turning on a lathe and was used quite frequently in this type of construction. It has a gray to pink color with contrasting brown markings. Walnut achieves a good polish and is often mistaken for mahogany, a strong wood from the West Indies with a deep copper brown color.

Color, grain, and weight are significant indicators of wood type. Making wood identification difficult is the fact that nutcrackers are often coated with one or more decorative substances. Carvings frequently enhance the whole surface of a nutcracker and it may be stained, varnished, painted or highly polished in such a way as to cover the entire surface of the piece, concealing the true color of the wood. Also, in a small piece of wood, like a nutcracker (especially older pieces), the wood can be discolored by fats in foods, wines, or other stains and can be faded or darkened by age, making an examination difficult. Dirt and grease from handling nutcrackers will most often appear on the areas frequently grasped. Small remnants of

nutshells can also sometimes be found in the jaws or other recesses used for cracking. Previous owners or antique dealers may vigorously clean this surface dirt and thereby remove some of the clues to age. The only certain way of identifying a particular piece of wood is by performing a microscopic examination of a carefully prepared section of end grain, an examination which would have to be performed by someone with expertise in wood identification.

Cast Iron, Brass and Bronze Nutcrackers

Unfortunately, many metal artifacts, nutcrackers included, were lost to the "salvage drives" in England during World War II. During these drives, patriotic citizens contributed all kinds of metal objects, many old, to the war effort. However, a number of these objects did survive and are avidly collected today.

Reproductions

Both old and new examples of nutcrackers can be interesting and can enhance the variety of a collection. However, it is important that the price of a piece is appropriate to its age as well as its availability and condition. A number of the cast-iron nutcrackers have been duplicated in recent years, but they may not be identified as reproductions. Some have been made to sell as reproductions but may be offered as originals at some subsequent date by uninformed or unscrupulous sellers. Other pieces are made from the outset as fakes to be sold to unsuspecting buyers.

One factor in determining a reproduction is size. If you are already familiar with the size of an original example, it can be measured against a suspected duplicate. A reproduction will be smaller than the original. Cast iron shrinks about one-eighth of an inch per foot during casting.

Occasionally, nutcrackers have been reproduced in aluminum. Plate 114 pictures such a reproduction in the form of an aluminum lion nutcracker. The original piece is American, from an unknown maker. This nutcracker may be related to the Carlsen nutcracker patented in 1912 which, according to the patent specifications, was to take the form of a dog or a lion. (Discussed in detail in Chapter 2 under the "Cast Iron" section.) At first glance, painted aluminum can look like a similar cast-iron example. It can also be hardened with magnesium to provide added strength and/or plated with another substance such as nickel. Still, the one determining factor to identify aluminum is its light weight.

If the faker of cast objects uses an original mold, some of which still exist, it may be difficult to detect a recent casting except that detail is often lost on these later castings. In fact, slight detail is eradicated with each subsequent casting. However, cast-iron reproductions made from a new wooden pattern copied from an old

PLATE 114
This aluminum lion nutcracker is reproduction of an early 20th century American piece. Lion - 5⅝" high, 10" long including tail, 1½" across. Base - 6⅞" long, 2¾" across.

nutcracker will result in a piece which captures all of the detail of the original piece.

In general, recent pieces will not be finished as well as older ones because less time is spent working on individual pieces due to higher labor costs today. Also, modern casting sand tends to be coarser than the sand used a hundred or more years ago. This results in a much more pebbled surface that, even when painted, is not as smooth as older examples. If you can see the interior of an old cast iron nutcracker, it should be matte, not pebbled, and dull pewter in color, with perhaps some indications of slight rusting. It should not be bright and the insides should not be painted. The outer paint would normally show signs of use, be very hard, and worn off in spots with rusted iron frequently visible.

Although it is said that some reproductions are lighter in weight than the originals, the reverse may actually be true. Older cast iron pieces like doorstops and possibly nutcrackers were often made from scrap iron which has a lower density than the higher grade irons used today.

Patina and Corrosion

Considering that so many duplications have been made, it is important to become familiar with some of the basic age indicators like naturally-created patina and evidence of corrosion. These factors can help you distinguish the truly old iron, brass and bronze nutcrackers from convincing fakes and reproductions.

Metals offer almost as many signs of age as wood. Unlike wood, metals do not shrink with the passage of time, but even the hardest metals show marks and scars from use and abuse. Few older iron or steel nutcrackers have been kept consistently in a dry place and protected with oil or wax throughout the years. More likely, most have at some time experienced a slight oxidation which has left small blemishes and/or traces of rust in the original finish that even an early cleaning could not totally erase. Old corrosion on antique pieces should be dark brown in color, whereas new rust created to make a piece look old will often have an orange tone. Also, rust on an old nutcracker will usually have created some deep pitting, while corrosion created for purposes of deception, frequently accomplished by burying an object in the ground for a short period of time, is ordinarily more superficial. Furthermore, bronzes which were originally artificially oxidized will frequently show wear on high spots or on their bottoms as a sign of handling.

On iron and steel fakes made from scratch, a patina will often be produced to resemble a natural one by using acid. This can usually be detected because it is so uniform, whereas real rusting ordinarily develops patterns of more and less pitted areas. A distinct overall pattern is sometimes visible on acid-rusted surfaces where the acid has collected. Unlike normal moisture which creates rust slowly, acid acts quickly and can leave spots in the shape of droplets.

The oxidation of soft metals such as silver, brass, bronze, copper, and pewter is quite different. A false patina is produced on these metals usually by using sulphur, since it is sulphur in the air that causes genuine tarnish in most instances. For example, a piece of silver placed in a sealed container with a little amount of sulphur (or something similar) will develop a tarnish that is frequently impossible to distinguish from old patina. However, using this technique on brass, bronze or copper will produce an ugly black color rather than the greenish or brownish patina that forms naturally. (Plate 40 shows authentic greenish brown patina on a bronze dog.) Therefore, a black color should immediately raise suspicion.

The easiest method to duplicate a natural green-looking patina is to rub a green powder into the deep recesses in the object's surface. Such a substance can be quickly removed with a fingernail. Paint or pigment in oil is also occasionally used to falsify a patina, but these too are easily detected by looking closely. A fake patina can be removed with the point of a knife or pin. Real oxidation adheres tightly and has to be scoured or scraped off.

There are chemical techniques that produce convincing patinas, such as burying an object in manure for a long time. In such cases, you must look especially carefully for correct style, signs of manufacturing techniques, wear, and color uniformity of the oxidation.

Signs of wear in cast iron are in contrast to the rest of the surface which will almost always have a matte finish as a result of production by a sand mold. It takes hard abrasion or heavy pressure to produce evidence of wear on hard metals. You must look in areas where signs of wear are logical such as on pressure points. If the bottom or base of a nutcracker is uniformly smooth and free of scratches, or if the scratches are too regular, they may have been produced with some kind of sand paper in order to simulate wear. A magnifying glass or loupe is helpful in examining scratches. Scratches from real wear are random, are not exactly parallel, and do not have the same width or depth.

Other Age Factors

As you are probably aware, original paint is very desireable. In fact, the more original paint remaining on a piece, the better it is, and the higher the price will customarily be. Occasionally, an old nutcracker will have been repainted sometime along the way, making it less valuable. Usually, the more recent the re-painting, the more adversely it affects the value. Therefore, a piece repainted or "touched up" many years ago will have greater value than one repainted in the last several years.

Where brass is concerned, there are few ways to definitively determine the age or origin of a specific piece. Age or origin can only be confirmed when a nutcracker is marked with a name and/or date to commemorate an occasion or is marked with a patent or registration number which is engraved on its surface. One exception is in the case of non-figural nutcrackers made to resemble a popular silver pattern or motif. In such instances where a design was positively taken from a silver model, it would have been made with the intention to plate it. It is possible to be precise in such cases because there would be no reason to make a piece of high-fashion tableware once that style had been superseded by another. Therefore, the style of the brass piece would indicate the period in which it was made. New styles were slow to filter through the provinces and were popular for a while after they had fallen out of favor in the cities.

Early fine brass pieces are almost impossible to definitively identify as to origin. A piece could easily be English, Dutch, German, French or Flemish because identical items were made in all of these countries simultaneously. In fact, many brass pieces were made in England by foreign-born brass-makers who were duplicating designs being made at the same time in their own homelands.

The softer metals, such as silver, pewter and brass, wear away when polished, sometimes rounding edges, and almost obliterating engravings and patent numbers. Left behind is a silky finish of tiny scratches produced over a long history of polishing. Hard, sharp edges will indicate very little polishing on an older nutcracker or that the nutcracker is a newer piece. While old brass will usually have this silky texture as a result of polishing, and old

PLATE 115
Brass squirrel nutcracker with paper label on bottom marked "Made in Taiwan." It is a reproduction of an earlier design. 4¼" high, 5¾" long, 2" across. Late 20th century.

reproductions may also have it, new brass will not. Old brass should have a patina, unless wax or lacquer coatings were used to keep a normal patina from forming. (One of the more common methods of faking involves the addition of engraved names, dates and decorations. Close scrutiny of expensive nutcrackers whose value is derived mainly from such engravings is required.)

The brass squirrel in Plate 115 is virtually identical in size and design to the cast iron ones made much earlier in the United States. It is attractive and made from heavy brass. However, it is clearly a reproduction. It shows no signs of wear nor does it have the silky texture acquired through much use. This fact is confirmed by the paper sticker "Made in Taiwan" affixed to the bottom. Since homemakers and housekeepers traditionally kept their brass, pewter and silver gleaming, there ordinarily should be some signs of wear from polishing on very early nutcrackers, as well as an occasional nick or scratch from use. The closer you examine your brass pieces and the more familiar you become with these telltale signs of age, the more proficient you will become at dating them.

PATENT DATING

Checking the patent date is an excellent way of determining the age of brass, cast iron, or other metal nutcrackers. The first patent laws were adopted in the United States in 1790. The United States Constitution authorizes Congress to promote the progress of science and the useful arts by securing for limited times to authors and inventors the exclusive right to their respective writings and discoveries. (U. S. Constitution, Article I, Section 8, Clause 8).

The United States patent laws are provided to encourage inventors to disclose their inventions and share their knowledge with the rest of the scientific and engineering communities. In return, the patent holder can make and sell the patented item, thereby receiving the financial rewards from the invention during the patent time period. Once a patent has been granted, an inventor has the exclusive right to make, use, and sell the patented item for a period of seventeen years. (Originally, the patent time period was 14 years, but was changed to 17 years for utility patents in 1861. Design patents are for a shorter period of time, currently 14 years.) A patent cannot be renewed except by an Act of Congress.

Two separate categories of United States patents exist. One is the utility or invention patent, the other, the design patent. (Trademarks is a third and distinct category from these two types of patents.) According to the United States Patent Office, the utility patent is granted for an actual invention which has not previously existed and protects its appearance, function and performance for a longer period of time. On the other hand, a design patent can pertain to the modification of an existing design, relative to the appearance of the piece and nothing more. Design patent specifications are much less detailed than utility patents, offering no description of the component parts and their working relationship.

An item such as a nutcracker may be marked with the words "patent pending" or "patent applied for" to indicate that at the time of production, a patent application had been filed with the U. S. Patent Office but had not as yet been granted. Once the patent is granted, the item will most likely have the patent number, currently seven digits, or the patent date on it. Ordinarily it has taken between one and two years before a patent has been either granted or denied. When a patent has been denied, the mark "patent pending" or "patent applied for" can no longer be used. According to the U.S. Patent Office, this is at times a difficult prohibition to enforce.

The squirrel in Plate 116 was patented by Frank A. Humphrey of Worcester, Massachusetts on May 28, 1878. The patent date, shown in Plate 117, is cast into the base of the piece, between the back feet. Truly an exceptional example of iron casting, in detail and refinement, this model was probably a prototype for many squirrel-shaped nutcrackers made in subsequent years.

Among the other figural nutcrackers patented in the United States, circa 1900, which took the form of a squirrel, are a:

• Squirrel-shaped nutcracker perched upon a stump constructed so as to form a nutcracker, a receptacle for the cracked nuts and a match-safe. Squirrel's tail used as lever. Patent No. 660,806 by Charles C. Tombs of Johnstown, Pennsylvania on October 30, 1900.

• Squirrel-shaped nutcracker with attached bowl; Squirrel sits on stump which contains plunger. Nutcracker incorporates use of the tail as a lever and a plunger to crack nuts, exerting pressure appropriate to the cracking of different varieties of nuts. Patent No. 699,529 by John A. Hutchinson of Chicago, Illinois on May 6, 1902.

• Squirrel-shaped nutcracker using tail as lever perched on an attached branch. Patent No. 707,997 by August Wickstrom of Denver, Colorado on August 26, 1902. (Of special interest is the fact that Mr. Wickstrom patented the same nutcracker model with the British Patent Office in 1903 under Patent No. 1213.)

Patent Numbering

Numbering patents consecutively did not begin until July 13, 1836. The requirement to stamp an item as patented was not signed into law until 1842. From that time on, the owner of the patent would usually have the word "Patented" together with the date the patent was issued stamped on the article. Congress changed the law in 1927, requiring the patent number, rather than the

PLATE 116
Black painted cast iron squirrel nutcracker on wooden base. Base - 8" long, 3¾" across, ¾" high. Squirrel - 8½" high including tail, 8" deep, 2¾" across. American, c. 1878.

PLATE 117
Close-up of patent date on squirrel nutcracker in above photo. Patent dated May 28, 1878 (Patent No. 204,225).

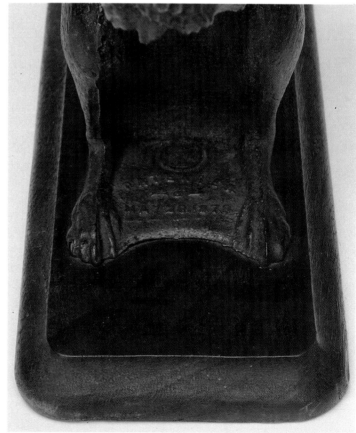

date, to be put on an article. With hundreds of patents issued each week by the year 1927, stamping the date alone made researching the patent on a particular item extremely difficult. Once a patent number, unique to a specific invention, was found on an article, gathering information on that patent would be easy.

Foreign Patents

The United States is not the only country with a patent system. In fact, patents for inventions have been available in England for over three centuries. British patents remain in force for 16 years from the issue date, providing that the required renewal fees are paid and the patent is not revoked. The date of filing the complete specifications is the date of the patent. In addition to a patent system, England also has a procedure for registering designs. Beginning in 1884 until January 1909, registered designs were numbered consecutively with the prefix "Rd" or "Rd No." Prior to this, the British Patent Office used a diamond-shaped registration mark, specifically between the years 1842 and 1883, inclusive. This mark showed the patent date (month and year) in letter coding on the bottom and right points of the diamond. The day of the month in actual numbers appeared on the top point. A parcel number appeared on the left point.

As mentioned previously, Appendix I contains a list of registered design numbers with corresponding issue years. When using the registered design list, it must be noted that an overlap occurred in 1884, when numbering began again at number one. According to the British Patent Office, there is no way to tell when an item was actually registered for the years 1839 to 1903. It could have occurred in either of two years according to which set of numbers one looks at, namely the list from 1839 to 1884 or the list from 1884 to 1903. Both include the same numerical series. The only way is to go through the patent records at a Federal depository in the United States which has foreign patent records or by calling direct to the Public Records Office in England. Other indicators of age may provide clues, which together with the registered design information, will allow one to date a particular piece without performing additional research.

World patent systems fall loosely into one of two categories. The first is a registration system like that in France whereby no or little attempt is made to establish whether an invention is contained in the filed claim and a patent is granted upon payment of a fee. The second, such as the German system, is a system of strict examination where an inventor must prove that his invention is an invention within the applicable regulations.

Patent Research

To aid in dating patented articles, lists are available which match patent numbers against the corresponding years in which the patents were granted. (See Appendix II for a list of utility and design patent numbers and trademark numbers and corresponding dates for United States patents from 1836 to 1964.) Appendix III contains a list of utility patents granted in the United States between 1853 and 1930 to inventors for nutcrackers and nutcracking devices. (Nutcracking machines are excluded from this list because they relate primarily to equipment used commercially.) This list is very complete but may not be entirely comprehensive. Searching through patent indices is not particularly straight-forward. Nutcrackers are listed under a number of different headings including Nutcracker, Nut-cracker, Nut-cracking Mechanism, Nut Sheller, Nut-cracking device, Nut Bowl and Cracker, etc. It is further complicated by class and sub-class distinctions within both Design and Invention (Utility) Patents. In the general index, nutcrackers are listed under the overall category of Utility Patents for Cutlery (30) with Shell Openers (120.1), a major heading, and nutcrackers under that (120.2). Additional categories then exist under nutcrackers. Within the Design Patent Classification system, nutcrackers can be found under "Equipment for Preparing or Serving Food or Drink Not Elsewhere Specified (D7 680 (72))." Curiously, the British index is even more circuitous with some nutcrackers listed under the heading "Machinery for cutting certain vegetable substances."

It is worth looking through patent records to gain more information about particular nutcrackers. It is especially helpful to peruse the invention specifications as they include drawings showing the inner components of the inventions and explain the workings of each piece. For a less detailed account, the *Patent Gazette* can be useful in providing an abstract of each patent granted.

The ingenuity of inventors is truly amazing as they constantly devise new ways to improve existing nutcracker designs. Each patented model exhibits a feature slightly different from those in existence. Take the "Harper" cracker as advertised in 1905. It was promoted as "the only cracker made that keeps the hulls from falling on the floor!" Instructions were given for its use as follows:

> *Place the nut between the jaws from the under side, press handles together, and crack the nut, letting the hulls and kernels drop in the receptacle or hand. The jaws of this cracker are much wider than any other, and the nut resting against the plate brings it on a line with the jaws, hence the nut is cracked all over evenly, while with other crackers only part of the nut is cracked.* (Excerpt from John Mebane's book, *What's New That's Old*, published in 1969.)

The "plate" mentioned refers to a metal ledge attached to the jaws of this crack. This crack together with six nickelplated picks wholesaled for only $.65 in a leatherette case. A similar silverplated set cost $1.70.

Each new nutcracker which is patented represents an innovation of sorts in the history of nutcracker-making. Some nutcracker models offer only subtle changes and/or improvements in their nutcracking mechanisms while others make more elaborate alterations. So taken are some inventors with the challenge of building "a better nutcracker" that they, like H. M. Quackenbush, design more than one nutcracker over the course of a career. Some inventors who have contributed to the development of nutcracking have been women. In fact, Helen Isabella Weed created a non-figural type called the Edible-Nut Cracker which was patented on May 3, 1910 (Patent No. 956,555).

IMPERFECTIONS:
THEIR EFFECT ON PRICE

As previously stated, boxwood and yew-wood were a favorite choice among early carvers of nutcrackers, but many fine examples, especially later ones, can be found which were made from other woods like pine, fruitwood, mahogany and walnut. However, these woods were not strong enough to crack some of the hardest nuts without being damaged. It is not unusual to find hairline fractures in human or animal-shaped nutcrackers, especially in animals with protruding snouts not reinforced with metal or brass. Two in my collection, a bear and an impala, have breaks below the eyes, along the top of their snouts. These fractures are barely discernible on the exterior, but are easily detected on the inside of the jaws where cracks are evident in the roofs of their mouths.

The lower jaw of this type of nutcracker, which is an integral part of the back lever, is sometimes chipped. Broken or chipped teeth in a nutcracker are also not that uncommon. In fact, in the E.T.A. Hoffman tale, *The Nutcracker and the Mouse King*, little Marie's Prussian soldier nutcracker breaks three teeth, much to her chagrin, while cracking a nut. In Tschaikovsky's *Nutcracker Suite*, Clara's nutcracker breaks its jaw during a scuffle with her brother, Fritz. Occasionally, levers and lower jaws have been replaced at some point over the years.

Before purchasing wooden nutcrackers, it is a good idea to examine them carefully for cracks, chips, or fractures in the wood or for replacement parts. Missing paint, reapplied paint (particularly of recent application), and missing or damaged parts can lower the value of a piece. In other words, anything which alters the original condition must be taken into consideration in pricing matters.

Although these imperfections may not detract from the aesthetic value of a nutcracker or from your enjoyment of it, they usually should be reflected in the purchase price relative to the extent of the "damage." However, many factors must be considered in evaluating the fairness of an asking price. The existence of such flaws in an otherwise beautiful, rare and/or old specimen will not ordinarily reduce the value significantly. After all, nutcrackers, particularly early specimens, were utilitarian objects and should show some signs of wear and use.

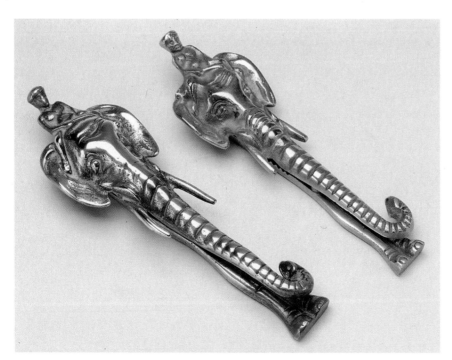

PLATE 118
Left: Brass African elephant and rider door knocker marked "Africa" on interior of back handle. 7¼" long, 2⅛" across, 1¼" deep. Early 20th century.
Right: Brass African elephant and rider nutcracker. 6⅝" long, 2" across, 1" deep. c. 1930s–1950s.

OBJECTS MISTAKEN FOR NUTCRACKERS

Occasionally a specimen will be found which at first glance appears to be a nutcracker but upon closer examination proves to be another utensil or hardware. A small to medium-sized brass or bronze door knocker can be mistaken for the type of nutcracker bolted to a wooden surface. Such an example appears to the left in Plate 118. This brass figure of a man seated on the back of an elephant is marked "Africa" and probably dates back to around 1900. It was sold to me as a nutcracker but appears to be a door knocker instead. It has two holes on the back "lever" so that it can be bolted to a door. Extremely curious are the roundish indentations in the interior of the piece which closely resemble the recesses found in nutcracking instruments. Just as obvious is its door-knocking capabilities evidenced by the sound achieved by working the elephant's trunk. Years after this door knocker was purchased, I did find a nutcracker of virtually identical design, pictured on the right in Plate 118. It contains no identifying marks with little evidence of wear and not as much attention to finishing detail but is also unmistakably a nutcracker. It appears to be a later creation than the doorknocker and probably was patterned after the doorknocker sometime between 1930 and 1950.

Another example of how much alike a door knocker and a nutcracker can be, can be seen in Plate 119. Pictured are examples of a nutcracker and a door knocker with the same theme. The two are similar in size and dimension, with the nutcracker slightly larger. The door knocker, however, has two holes at the top so that it can be bolted to a door and lacks a cavity into which a nut would be placed for cracking. Both specimens are English brass, representing the Dartmoor Pixie. Dartmoor is in Devon, England, and these brass pieces were probably souvenir items from the region. The design alludes to an English legend which states:

> *Below Dartmoor Bridge, if the river be followed on the right through a wood, the Pixy Holt is reached, a cave in which the little good folk are supposed to dwell. It is the correct thing to leave a pin or some other trifle in acknowledgment when visiting their habitation.* (Excerpt from *A Book of Dartmoor* by S. Baring-Gould written in 1900.)

On the other hand, nutcrackers do exist which resemble door knockers (Plate 76). One such nutcracker is a squirrel on a handle, which is marked "copyright 1916" on its under side. This handle became detached over the years from its original base, and now resembles a door knocker when held in an upright position. So similar, in fact, that it has two holes at the top which would suggest that it was made to be attached to a door. When you look closely, however, a coiled spring is evident under the handle, which, to my knowledge, is never found on door knockers. In the same plate is pictured another identical squirrel handle affixed to a wooden bowl as it was originally manufactured for sale.

Also, figural cork presses and tobacco and cigar cutters can he misidentified as the type of nutcracker which

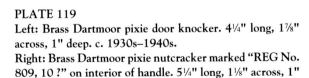

PLATE 119
Left: Brass Dartmoor pixie door knocker. 4¼" long, 1⅞" across, 1" deep. c. 1930s–1940s.
Right: Brass Dartmoor pixie nutcracker marked "REG No. 809, 10 ?" on interior of handle. 5¼" long, 1⅛" across, 1" deep. c. 1936.

is similar in appearance. (Cork presses were used to size corks for inserting into the necks of variously sized bottles. The corks were soaked in water and compressed before being used as stoppers in bottles.) See Plate 120 for such a nutcracker in the shape of an imp thumbing his nose. With holes in its base, this cast iron model was meant to be screwed to the top of a counter. Tobacco cutters found around 1880 and cork presses of the type that were used extensively before the advent of the screw-type cap around 1850 can look very much like nutcrackers, and examples exist which combine more than one of these functions.

NUTCRACKERS WITH MULTIPLE FUNCTIONS

There are even some pieces which combine three functions, including cracking nuts. Such an implement was made during the mid-1850s which could be used as a cork press, a tobacco cutter, and a nutcracker. The brass nutcracker in the leather pouch, which was referred to earlier in Plate 36, was marketed for use in cracking lobster claws as well as nuts. Furthermore, the heavy cast iron dog nutcrackers were advertised as doorstops and toys.

Fred Hildebrand of Cincinnati, Ohio, should be congratulated for his creation of a combination nutcracker and playing card press. On May 18, 1937, Mr. Hildebrand received a patent (No. 2,080,478) for his invention. As unusual as it was, it did resemble an earlier nutcracker pictured in Illustration 2, designed in the form of a letter press. Producing nutcrackers with additional functions apparently had early origins. Edward Pinto reported a rare carved combination nutcracker and apple scoop which was dated 1734. It was on exhibit at a museum in Cheltenham, England.

However, the prize for creating a device which incorporates the greatest number of functions, including nutcracking, must go to John Laurent Drouilly. Mr. Drouilly patented an invention in England in 1893 (Patent No. 18,460) in the shape of a hammer with a split handle hinged at a central point below the head. This implement was designed to operate, in addition to a nutcracker, as pincers or nippers, a hammer, hatchet, screwdriver, nail holder or vice, opening wrench, spanner, measuring rule, nail extractor and lever.

Another interesting nutcracker, similar in appearance to the reversible silver-plated English model in Plate 39, was patented in the United States on December 24, 1889 by Herbert Story of Kearney, New Jersey (Patent No. 417,951). The unique feature of Story's nutcracker is that it combined a nutcracker and a nut pick in its handle. The nut pick could be unscrewed, withdrawn from the handle and used separately from the nutcracker, or could remain in the handle of the nutcracker when not in use.

PLATE 120
Cast iron imp nutcracker. 4¼" tall, 6½" long, 1¼" across. Late 19th to early 20th century.

An extremely clever device which incorporated a nutcracker within its design was created by Edward Pinto. Described in his book, *Treen or Small Woodware Throughout the Ages*, it was composed of a "modern combination table centre, 'turned' from African mahogany…(made) for a Georgian octagonal table, the sections (of which) unscrew and may be used separately or in different combinations. The plateau revolves on ball bearings and saves passing small items which can be grouped on it." The interesting feature of this "lazy-susan" was that the bowl could be used as such or detached from the plateau, the vase removed and a nut-cracking anvil and nut shell ring screwed in its place. A mallet was then used with the anvil to crack nuts.

I have also come across at least one "mystery" piece. I purchased it impulsively because the price was right and then later doubted it was a nutcracker at all. (Plate 121). I was convinced at first that it was a nutcracker because it so closely resembled my other crocodiles. However, upon closer examination, I realized that it does not operate like the others because it does not have a lever. Rather, the top lifts directly up to reveal three divided compartments in the interior section. When the top lifts up, the jaws close and could presumably crack small nuts. This leads me to believe that this was not a nutcracker at all, or possibly it was made with a dual purpose – to crack nuts and to perform some other function. In questioning other antiques dealers about similar pieces that they have had in stock, these crocodiles were described as nutcrackers, ash trays, or ink wells. The one authentic ink well that I saw which looked very much like my crocodile opened from side to side, however, rather than from back to front. The side hinge gave better access to the ink. My crocodile must be held or supported open and cannot stay open by itself. Another very similar piece, labeled as an ash tray, had no hinge at all. The top of the crocodile merely lifted directly off to gain access to the inside compartments. A recent and imaginative suggestion was that it might have served as a cigar holder and extinguisher. A cigar could be held in the crocodile's mouth when not being smoked and could be quickly extinguished between "smokes" by resting it within the interior of the crocodile where an indentation like on an ashtray is present. In any case, this piece makes for interesting speculation, and I am sure that some day I will come across a dealer or collector who will solve this puzzle, once and for all. Perhaps you have an idea of your own!

Then there are items whose intended function may not be apparent at first glance but may turn out to be nutcrackers because of certain characteristics. One such item, given to me by a friend who is always searching for nutcrackers for my collection, it is a very unusual shoe or ship depending upon how you look at it (Plate 122). It is

PLATE 121
Cast iron crocodile with old paint. 11⅜" long, 3¼" across, 2½" high. Late 19th century.

marked on the bottom with the words "PAMIQTKA ZTODYGOWIC" which appears to be a name, probably Greek. It is also marked with a combination of numbers and Roman numerals (37 XII) and the date "1974." It is not antique and not truly vintage, yet it is a good example of a collectible. The removable mallet in its handle and the cracking surface provided by the "inner sole of the shoe" may classify it as a nutcracker. If so, it is a very unique handmade specimen.

One thing is certain, I have found collecting to be a great opportunity for learning. Having a collection of *any one thing* will invariably open your eyes to other varieties of collectibles which intersect or overlap with your area of specialization. Ultimately, you acquire a good deal of knowledge not only about your own field but about many other subjects as well.

PLATE 122
Wooden shoe. 7" long, 6" high, 2" across. Greek, dated 1974.

Chapter 8

NUTCRACKER COLLECTIONS

NUTCRACKER COLLECTORS

Nutcracker collecting has been going on for quite some time and in many parts of the world. Reference has been made to the collection of Raja Dinkar Kelkar, an East Indian collector, and to the former collections of such British notables as Owen Evan-Thomas and Edward and Eva Pinto, whose vast acquisitions of treenware contained many rare and beautiful wooden nutcrackers.

Each nutcracker collector approaches his collection differently. Some collect all varieties of nutcrackers while, just as I have limited my collecting to figural and ornamental pieces, others have narrowed their area of interest even further. I recently learned of a collector who only acquires carved nutcrackers of human "freestanding" figures.

No book on the subject would be complete without mention of Hal Davis, owner of the world's largest nutcracker collection, a collection with apparently no limitations, which took over 35 years to amass. All nutcrackers were appealing to this avid collector. Mr. Davis, a realtor from Santa Ana, California, unfortunately passed away recently. His extensive collection began with his first purchase in 1953 and contains approximately 5,000 nutcrackers. The collection is now owned by his daughter, Claudia Davis. Mr. Davis assembled his collection through a variety of sources, including buying through classified ads and making purchases on many trips to places like Belgium, Bavaria, Hong Kong, and many of the states within our own country.

Not only is the Davis collection the largest of its kind, it also contains the largest individual nutcracker in a private collection. (Nutcracker manufacturer Volkmar Matthes produced what is thought to be the world's largest nutcracker. It is nine feet tall and is on exhibit in his Garmisch retail store.) In the early 1970s, Mr. Davis commissioned Carl Rappl, a successor to the famous woodcarver, the late Anton Lang, to carve a life-sized nutcracker in the figure of a clown. This friendly looking clown, affectionately nicknamed "Nutty Nat," stands almost six feet tall and weighs 110 pounds (Illustration

16). Mr. Davis made a pilgrimage to Oberammergau, Germany to place the order for this unusual carving. Made from one flawless piece of pine and taking over a year to complete, the clown wears a scarlet striped shirt with a green and pink tie. His big toe protrudes from his tattered brown shoes, and he holds a white hat in front of him which stores the nuts. A pump handle lever in his back manipulates his jaw, which is strong enough to crack even the hardest Brazil nut.

Over the years, Mr. Davis shared his collection with many interested people through illustrated lectures which he conducted for groups including the Boy Scouts and senior citizen organizations. He was also the subject of a number of magazine and newspaper articles and appeared on television to talk about his fascinating collection.

Another nutcracker collector with a relatively small but impressive collection was Sam Cousley of Englewood, New Jersey. Mr. Cousley was among the first in the United States to appreciate the collectability of nutcrackers and to write about it, having penned an article in a 1974 book entitled *Spinning Wheel's Antiques for Men*, published by Castle Books. His daughter, Mrs. Bishay, has inherited his collection of nutcrackers along with several other interesting collections. Many have been displayed at various times over the years at banks in New York City. According to Mrs. Bishay, the nutcracker exhibit was always a favorite, especially during the Christmas holidays.

MUSEUM COLLECTIONS

Surprisingly, many of the foremost museums in the United States, including the Metropolitan Museum of Art in New York and the Philadelphia Museum in Pennsylvania have few, if any, nutcrackers in their collections. The Smithsonian Institution's National Museum of American History in Washington, D.C. has only a few utilitarian non-figural nutcrackers on exhibit. Its seasonal catalogue, however, occasionally features one or two fine-quality figural nutcrackers for sale, some as reproductions of antique designs such as the East Indian horse nut slicer in

Plate 90. The Museum of Fine Arts in Boston also has included a reproduction figural nutcracker from its collection in a past catalogue. This appealing man-in-the-moon is polymer with a hand-painted finish. The original, which is in the museum's collection, is made of wood (Plate 123).

The Birmingham Museum in England has a fabulous collection of treen, including some early and truly wonderful nutcrackers. This is due to the fact that Edward and Eva Pinto, the world reknowned collectors and authors on this subject, sold practically their entire collection of 6,000 items made in Europe, the United States, and the British Dominions to the Birmingham Museum several years ago. Prior to that, it had been on exhibit at their home, Oxhey Woods House in Northwood, Middlesex, about 15 miles outside of London. According to a current representative of the Birmingham Museum, because of the vastness of the Pinto collection, it is impossible to have it all on display at one time. Some of the nutcrackers are always on exhibit in the food and drink section of the woodenware collection.

Examples of treen for the table are found in many museums throughout the United Kingdom. Noteworthy collections of nutcrackers are said to be in the National Museum of Wales at Cardiff and the Rev. C. J. Sharp's Museum at Shepreth. Texas pecan grower and pecan candymaker Haywood Rigano opened a nutcracker museum in Mt. Pleasant, Texas on November 11, 1985. This museum, possibly the only one in existence devoted solely to the display of nutcrackers, is located adjacent to Rigano's pecan store and contains over 1,000 examples.

ILLUSTRATION 16
"Nutty Nat" nutcracker from collection of the late Mr. Hal Davis. The clown stand almost six feet tall and weighs 110 lbs.

PLATE 123
Polymer moon nutcracker with matching stand. It is a reproduction of a late 19th century wooden nutcracker. 5¼" high, 4½" across, 1⅝" deep. 1980s.

NUTCRACKER CLUBS

For those interested in sharing information with other nutcracker enthusiasts, the Nutcracker Collectors Association, organized by Mr. Rigano of the mentioned nutcracker museum, may be a good place to start. Rigano's group collects all types of nutcrackers – wood, brass, iron, mechanical, etc. Membership is free of charge; the only donations appreciated being one's time, interest and enthusiasm. The address is: Nutcracker Collectors Association, Route 3, P.O. Box 395, Mt. Pleasant, Texas, 75455.

I am certain nutcracker clubs exist in many other countries, but the only one that I have heard of outside the United States is in England. It was started by David Styles from Malvern, Worchestershire.

NUTCRACKER SHOPS

I am not aware of any shops which specifically carry antique nutcrackers on a regular basis although, as stated in my introduction, various antiques dealers may have a selection of nutcrackers for sale from time to time. However, there are a number of stores throughout this country which carry a large selection of contemporary nutcrackers, and most so-called "Christmas shops" have at least some on hand.

PLATE 124, 125
Collectors especially prize unusual nutcrackers like the wooden peasant adorned with a pair of carved spectacles and the little brass black boy with wide open mouth. Wooden peasant nutcracker - 8¼" high, 2⅛" across, 2½" deep. Swiss, Tyrolean or Scandinavian, 1920s–1930s. Brass caricature nutcracker, stained and lacquered, marked with indecipherable numbers on handle, ca. 1920s. 5¼" high, 1½" across, 1½" deep.

Chapter 9

CARE OF NUTCRACKERS

When caring for all types of nutcrackers, I ordinarily ascribe to the philosophy that apart from a simple cleaning and polishing, if necessary, "leaving well enough alone" is the best policy. However, circumstances may occasionally arise when additional action is required. The following information provides instructions on how to approach special situations when other specific care is required.

WOODEN NUTCRACKERS

Before cleaning an antique wooden nutcracker, examine it carefully under a strong magnifying glass to see if there are any fine lines indicating repairs such as the replacement of a section of carving. If such repairs are visible, do not wash the piece with soap and water as the glue used in the repair may be soluble. Instead, clean sparingly with a natural wax polish.

A problem can also arise when a wooden nutcracker has been varnished, usually a darker color, to conceal a repair. If you remove the varnish, try first to flake the varnish off by rubbing it gently with the edge of a coin. If this method is successful, the original patina will be underneath the varnish. If the varnish does not succumb to this procedure, a gentle commercial varnish and paint stripper can be applied sparingly. Do not leave the stripper on for more than a few minutes before wiping it off. Use a second coat only if absolutely necessary. Wipe with a cloth dampened with methylated spirits or denatured alcohol and quickly apply a wax polish. If done rapidly, the original patina should not be harmed. In instances where a heavier application of stripper is necessary, apply a generous coating of wax, leave in a cool place for several days, then brush with a clean brush and polish with a soft cloth. A warm dust cloth will aid the polishing process considerably.

Many wooden nutcrackers have been allowed to become dry and dirty over the years. Unfortunately, the dryness can lead to cracking in the wood while the dirt, especially surface dirt on a hard wood, detracts from the beauty of the piece by obscuring the fine grain and color of the wood. Excessive cleaning should always be avoided.

Clean the surface of an umpainted wooden nutcracker by gently rubbing with a damp cloth. A little mild soap can be used to remove surface dirt. Extra care may be obtained by using dry lather foam made from pure soap flakes. Particular care should be taken with painted or pigmented surfaces (i.e., scrimshaw) which will loose their brightness with too frequent cleanings. Rinse with another cloth moistened in clear water and wrung out until almost dry. Then rub with a soft polishing cloth or your bare hands to bring up the wood's natural gleam and decorative grain. A white wax composition can be used in lieu of soap and water in many instances to both clean and polish. Vigorous cleaning is never recommended as it can remove some of the beautiful patina which helps to set apart old nutcrackers from newer reproductions.

For very dry wood, a soft, clean cloth moistened lightly in lemon oil may be applied, allowing a small amount of oil to seep into all recesses. The oil may be left on the nutcracker for a period of 24 hours. Lay the nutcracker on newspaper to absorb the excess. Very dry wood ordinarily will absorb most of the oil in that time. If any oil remains after the 24 hours, it should be removed with a clean, dry, soft cloth and the surface of the nutcracker should be gently polished. The excess oil must be removed from the surface because it will otherwise leave a greasy film which attracts dust particles. It should be noted that lemon oil tends to darken wood and for that reason may not be suitable for use on nutcrackers made of light-colored woods. The use of lemon oil on painted surfaces is not recommended nor would it be advised for other forms of wooden tableware such as platters, drinking vessels, and the like from which food and beverages may be directly consumed.

For nutcrackers that are dusty, rather than dirty, a small semi-soft brush is recommended. Rags may smear dirt into the wood. Wooden nutcrackers should not be submerged in water. The wood will act as a blotter, absorbing water in unpainted areas. For painted nutcrackers (Plate 126), this can be especially damaging. Water absorbed into the wood, as from an unpainted base, will cause the paint to peel from the inside out. (This peasant woman nutcracker is especially well painted right down to the white carved teeth in her mouth. Carved teeth can be found in a number of carved head models but are often not as visible because they are either not painted or have been worn down or broken from cracking nuts.)

The climate of the room where your wooden nutcrackers are stored should not be too dry or too moist. Bright sunlight and excessive dampness are both harmful to fine wooden objects. During dry winter months, a humidifier can add a little moisture to the air, benefiting all wooden objects in your home, nutcrackers included.

The threads on screw-type nutcrackers are sometimes worn from frequent use and may have lost their grip. Fine sewing silk can be wrapped around the screw in a color matching the wood as closely as possible to add some grip in an inconspicuous manner.

Another occasional problem in older wooden nutcrackers is worm infestation. If worm holes are present, the insects responsible, such as post beetles, death-watch beetles or possibly termites may be long gone. However, if you see any sign of recent activity (as I did this past year upon discovering sawdust on the table around a newly purchased piece), immediate action must be taken to prevent additional damage. I have heard that products called wood dewormers are made, although worms are not really the culprits. Instead of a dewormer product, household insecticide may be sprayed directly into the holes. Any excess spray should be wiped off and the piece allowed to dry. Repeat the treatment as required. Insecticide spray should not be used on wooden bowls, spoons, forks and other cooking and eating utensils. Let the nutcracker stand for a day or two and then apply polish. If there are numerous worm holes, you can close them with pure beeswax. The beeswax can be colored with a pigment to

PLATE 126
Painted wooden nutcracker of peasant woman with red scarf. 7⅞" high, 3" deep, 2" across. Mid-20th century.

match the wood and then rubbed into the holes. The wax should be allowed to harden before polishing. I have only three nutcrackers with worm holes. The insects , now gone, left behind only a dozen or so tiny holes which I frankly do not mind and prefer not to fill.

BRASS NUTCRACKERS

Unless brass has been lacquered, washing alone will not restore the shine. Brass cleaner can be applied to brass nutcrackers to polish them to a more lustrous finish. A polish will last considerably longer if the item is washed clean first to remove all residual polish from previous cleanings. It should then be dried with a clean cloth and polished. An old toothbrush is an excellent tool for removing the dry polish from crevices and other indented areas.

The piece can be waxed or oiled very lightly to prohibit oxidation if frequent handling is not anticipated. The coating of wax or oil should prolong the intervals between required polishings by at least one-half.

I personally prefer to polish brass nutcrackers only to the extent that the detail on the pieces is clearly visible, detail which can be obscured on badly tarnished ones. Leaving a trace of the rich patina which has developed over the years often enhances an antique nutcracker and distinguishes it from recent examples and reproductions.

IRON NUTCRACKERS

Many old pieces of cast iron will have some evidence of rust resulting from exposure to water or dampness. Wrought iron is less likely to be rusted because it is tempered with oil during production. The vast majority of nutcrackers that I have seen have little rust. Therefore, most of the time, no work is required other than providing a climate in your home in which additional rust does not form. A dehumidifier may be needed if your home is excessively damp. If a piece is badly rusted, kerosene can be applied with rags and a wire brush to remove rust quite effectively. Stubborn rust may need to be chipped off with a small hammer. Once the process is completed and the surface of iron is wiped free of residual kerosene, the oily rags must be disposed of carefully to avoid spontaneous combustion. Painted cast iron nutcrackers should be treated with extra care and cleaned very gently. Removing original paint through over zealous cleaning will depreciate the value of the piece.

SILVERPLATED NUTCRACKERS

Wash tarnished silverplated nutcrackers one at a time in hot, soapy water, using a soft cloth to wipe the pieces. Then rinse in hot, clean water and dry completely to prevent stains. Buffing thoroughly with a dry soft cloth may be all that is required to give the silverplate a deep shine. If the piece is badly tarnished, however, a mild abrasive commercial polish may he needed to completely restore a brilliant shine.

BRONZE NUTCRACKERS

The rich patina which develops over the years on bronze pieces is not only beautiful to the eye but also enhances the value of the object. Consequently, abrasives and metal polishes should not be used on bronze. Instead, bronze nutcrackers should simply be washed in soapy water and dried thoroughly. If tiny spots of bright bluish efflorescence appear on your bronze nutcracker, it is showing signs of "bronze disease", a condition which develops from moisture. An expert should be consulted on the best course of treatment, but if you are unable to see one immediately, gently brush off the loose efflorescence and place the piece in a dry place.

PEWTER NUTCRACKERS

If you are fortunate enough to have an extremely rare pewter nutcracker, little care is ordinarily necessary. Pewter develops a gray patina which is attractive and should be left alone. As with bronze, removing the patina on a pewter item can reduce its value. If a slight dull oxide stain exists, however, this can be removed with a mild abrasive mixed with a small amount of kerosene to form a paste. Either rottenstone or ground chalk can be used as a base for the paste, which can then be applied gently with a rag. Afterwards, the piece should be wiped clean with denatured alcohol, washed in warm, soapy water, rinsed and dried.

One note of caution – do not display pewter near oak as this wood contains an acid which attacks this metal.

Let me emphasize that unless a nutcracker in need of a significant amount of repair and restoration is found at truly a bargain price, it is best to save your funds and purchase a piece that is in good condition already.

CONCLUSION

Over the centuries, nuts have been a staple in the diets of many people throughout the world. In bygone years, nuts formed part of the dessert course, and therefore, nutcrackers were needed in the dining room as well as in the kitchen. In today's world, a nutcracker is more likely to be found next to a bowl of nuts in a living room or den, as nuts are now ordinarily considered more of a snack than an actual dessert.

The readily available convenience packs of shelled nuts also have greatly reduced our reliance upon nutcrackers in modern households. However, even in a majority of contemporary homes, at least one nutcracker is kept on hand for its functional use, while others are still highly regarded for aesthetic, historical, and sentimental reasons. Nutcrackers are also likely to surface during the Christmas season as part of the holiday tradition and for decoration.

Nutcrackers continue to fascinate us as is evidenced by the ever-increasing number of collectors of antique and modern pieces. As previously mentioned, reproductions of early nutcrackers continue to be made. Some of these finely reproduced examples, based upon or inspired by exceptionally interesting older designs, have been featured in recent years in various museum catalogues. These reproductions, as well as the antique originals, still have great appeal as part of nutcracker collections and as decorative and functional objects in 20th century homes.

Hopefully, in the years ahead, nutcrackers will begin to receive the recognition that has, for the most part, eluded this area of collecting. The diversity and ingenuity exhibited in many of these utensils make them worthy of greater study and appreciation.

APPENDICES

APPENDIX I

BRITISH REGISTERED DESIGN NUMBERS AND CORRESPONDING YEARS OF ISSUE
(1839 – 1989)

1	Aug.	1839	119225	Apr.	1859	271200	Mar.	1873
300	Apr.	1840	133300	Sep.	1860	280600	Feb.	1874
700	Jun.	1841	144400	Oct.	1861	288700	Jan.	1875
1000	Jan.	1842	154600	Sep.	1862	299000	Mar.	1876
8500	Jul.	1843	163400	Jun.	1863	308300	Mar.	1877
21500	Apr.	1844	183000	Jan.	1865	322500	Jun.	1878
30000	Aug.	1845	198000	Jun.	1866	331500	Jan.	1879
43500	Jun.	1847	205850	Feb.	1867	350400	Jun.	1880
58800	Mar.	1849	217400	Mar.	1868	362000	Feb.	1881
72300	Oct.	1850	227800	Mar.	1869	376100	Jan.	1882
87800	Nov.	1852	240500	Apr.	1870	393100	Jan.	1883
102900	Dec.	1855	248450	May	1871	408900	Jun.	1884
111600	Oct.	1857	261800	Apr.	1872			

A slight overlap occurred in 1884, when numbering began again at No.:

1	Jan.	1884	206100		1893	385180		1902
20000		1885	225000		1894	403200		1903
40800		1886	248200		1895	424400		1904
64700		1887	268800		1896	447800		1905
91800		1888	291400		1897	471860		1906
117800		1889	311677	Jan.	1898	493900		1907
142300		1890	332200		1899	518640		1908
164000		1891	351600		1900	535170		1909
186400		1892	368186		1901	548919	Sep.	1909

(The last number held at Kew)

Some Textile numbers run concurrently as follows:			Numbers were also given to Non-ornamental (Useful) designs between 1843 & 1884 as follows:				
1		1908	1		1843	4000	1857
8400		1909	1000		1847	5000	1869
15000		1910	2000		1849	6000	1878
26000	Dec.	1910	3000		1851	6740	1884

BRITISH REGISTERED DESIGN NUMBERS AND CORRESPONDING YEARS OF ISSUE
(1839 – 1989)

548920	Oct.	1909	817293		1937	914536		1964
575817	Jan.	1911	825231		1938	919607		1965
594195		1912	832610		1939	924510		1966
612431		1913	837520		1940	929335		1967
630190		1914	838590		1941	934515		1968
644935		1915	839230		1942	939875		1969
653521		1916	839980		1943	944932		1970
658988		1917	841040		1944	950046		1971
662872		1918	842670		1945	955342		1972
666128		1919	845550	Jan.	1946	960708		1973
673750		1920	849730		1947	965185		1974
680147		1921	853260		1948	969249		1975
687144		1922	856999		1949	973838		1976
694999		1923	860854		1950	978426		1977
702671		1924	863970		1951	982815		1978
710165		1925	866280		1952	987910		1979
718057		1926	869300		1953	993012		1980
726330		1927	872531		1954	998302		1981
734370		1928	876067		1955	1004456		1982
742725		1929	879282		1956	1010583		1983
751160		1930	882949		1957	1017131		1984
760583		1931	887079		1958	1024174		1985
769670		1932	891665		1959	1031358		1986
779292		1933	895000		1960	1039055		1987
789019		1934	899914		1961	1047478		1988
799097		1935	904638		1962	1056076		1989
808794		1936	909364		1963			

APPENDIX II

UNITED STATES PATENT NUMBERS AND CORRESPONDING YEARS OF ISSUE
(1836 – 1964)

YEAR	PATENTS	DESIGNS	TRADE MARKS	YEAR	PATENTS	DESIGNS	TRADE MARKS
1836 July 13	1	—	—	1885	310,163	15,678	11,843
1837	110	—	—	1886	333,494	16,451	12,910
1838	516	—	—	1887	355,291	17,046	13,939
1839	1,061	—	—	1888	375,720	17,995	15,072
1840	1,465	—	—	1889	395,305	18,830	16,131
1841	1,923	—	—	1890	418,665	19,553	17,360
1842	2,413	—	—	1891	443,987	20,439	18,775
1843	2,901	1	—	1892	466,315	21,275	20,537
1844	3,395	15	—	1893	488,976	22,092	22,274
1845	3,873	27	—	1894	511,744	11,397	23,951
1846	4,348	44	—	1895	531,619	23,922	25,757
1847	4,914	103	—	1896	552,502	25,037	27,586
1848	5,409	163	—	1897	574,369	26,482	29,399
1849	5,993	209	—	1898	596,467	28,113	31,070
1850	6,981	258	—	1899	616,871	29,916	32,308
1851	7,865	341	—	1900	640,167	32,055	33,957
1852	8,622	431	—	1901	664,827	33,813	35,678
1853	9,512	540	—	1902	690,385	35,547	37,606
1854	10,358	626	—	1903	717,521	36,187	39,612
1855	12,117	683	—	1904	748,567	36,723	41,798
1856	14,009	753	—	1905	778,834	37,280	43,956
1857	16,324	860	—	1906	808,618	37,766	48,446
1858	19,010	973	—	1907	839,799	38,391	59,014
1859	22,477	1,075	—	1908	875,679	38,980	66,892
1860	26,642	1,183	—	1909	908,436	39,737	72,083
1861	31,005	1,366	—	1910	945,010	40,424	76,267
1862	34,045	1,508	—	1911	980,178	41,063	80,506
1863	37,266	1,703	—	1912	1,013,095	42,073	84,711
1864	41,047	1,879	—	1913	1,049,326	43,415	89,731
1865	45,685	2,018	—	1914	1,083,267	45,098	94,796
1866	51,784	2,239	—	1915	1,123,212	46,813	101,613
1867	60,658	2,533	—	1916	1,166,419	48,358	107,875
1868	72,959	2,858	—	1917	1,210,389	50,117	114,666
1869	85,505	3,301	—	1918	1,251,458	51,629	120,005
1870	98,460	3,810	1	1919	1,290,027	52,836	124,066
1871	110,617	4,547	122	1920	1,326,899	54,359	128,274
1872	122,304	5,452	608	1921	1,364,063	56,844	138,556
1873	134,504	6,336	1,099	1922	1,401,948	60,121	150,210
1874	146,120	7,083	1,591	1923	1,440,362	61,748	163,003
1875	158,350	7,969	2,150	1924	1,478,996	63,675	177,848
1876	171,641	8,884	3,288	1925	1,521,590	66,346	193,597
1877	185,813	9,686	4,247	1926	1,568,040	69,170	207,437
1878	198,733	10,385	5,463	1927	1,612,790	71,772	222,401
1879	211,078	10,975	6,981	1928	1,654,521	74,159	236,987
1880	223,211	11,567	7,790	1929	1,696,897	77,347	251,129
1881	236,137	12,082	8,139	1930	1,742,181	80,254	265,655
1882	251,685	12,647	8,973	1931	1,787,424	82,966	278,906
1883	269,820	13,508	9,920	1932	1,839,190	85,903	290,313
1884	291,016	14,528	10,822	1933	1,892,663	88,847	299,926

UNITED STATES PATENT NUMBERS AND CORRESPONDING YEARS OF ISSUE
(1836 – 1964)

YEAR	PATENTS	DESIGNS	TRADE MARKS	TRADEMARKS ACT OF 1946
1934	1,944,449	91,258	309,066	
1935	1,985,878	94,179	320,441	
1936	2,026,510	98,045	331,338	
1937	2,066,309	102,601	342,070	
1938	2,101,004	107,738	353,324	
1939	2,142,080	112,765	363,536	
1940	2,185,170	118,358	374,062	
1941	2,227,418	124,503	384,047	
1942	2,268,540	130,989	392,581	
1943	2,307,007	134,717	399,378	
1944	2,338,081	136,946	404,974	
1945	2,366,154	139,862	411,001	
1946	2,391,856	143,386	418,494	—
1947	2,413,675	146,165	426,610	500,001
1948	2,433,824	148,267	435,590	500,002
1949	2,457,797	152,235	441,742	505,324
1950	2,492,944	156,686	443,654	519,384
1951	2,536,016	161,404	444,377	535,490
1952	2,580,379	165,568	444,623	552,624
1953	2,624,016	168,527	444,746	568,680
1954	2,664,562	171,211	444,794	581,249
1955	2,698,431	173,777	444,807	600,188
1956	2,728,913	176,490	444,811	618,396
1957	2,775,762	179,467	639,154	
1958	2,818,567	181,829	656,643	
1959	2,866,973	184,204	671,998	
1960	2,919,443	186,973	690,716	
1961	2,986,681	189,516	709,163	
1962	3,015,103	192,004	723,702	
1963	3,070,801	194,304	742,786	
1964	3,116,487	197,269	762,526	

APPENDIX III

UNITED STATES INVENTION (UTILITY) PATENTS FOR NUTCRACKERS*
(1853 – 1930)

PATENT NO.	DATE ISSUED	INVENTOR	ADDRESS	INVENTION
9,985	Sept. 06, 1853**	P.E.W. & J.A. Blake	New Haven, CT	Nut-cracker
24,018	May 17, 1859	R. Frisbie	Middletown, CT	Nut-cracker
24,238	May 31, 1859	E. Ripley	Troy, NY	Nut-cracker
26,885	Jan. 24, 1860	L. A. Clark	Bridgeport, CT	Nut-cracker
28,311	May 15, 1860	S. J. Smith	New York, NY	Nut-cracker
40,825	Dec. 08, 1863	T. Earle	Providence, RI	Nut-cracker
Des. 1920	Mar. 15, 1864	E. W. Blake for		
		E. F. Blake	New Haven, CT	Nut-cracker
76,247	Mar. 31, 1868	E. L. Pratt	Boston, MA	Nut-cracker
83,959	Nov. 10, 1868	C. Hayden	Collinsville, CT	Nut-cracker
109,495	Nov. 22, 1870	P. Ceredo	Dusseldorf, Prussia	Nut-cracker
119,144	Nov. 08, 1870	J. Pusey	Philadelphia, PA	Nut-cracker

PATENT NO.	DATE ISSUED	INVENTOR	INVENTION
174,142	Feb. 29, 1876	C.B. Martin	Nutcracker
198,678	Dec. 25, 1877	S. Poole	Nutcracker & Pick
204,225	May 28, 1878	F.H. Humphrey	Nutcracker
207,897	Sept. 10, 1878	C.F. Ritchell	Nutcracker
215,243	May 13, 1879	C.F. Ritchell	Nutcracker
244,145	July 12, 1881	M. Renz	Nutcracker
246,034	Aug. 23, 1881	M. Renz	Nutcracker
343,351	June 08, 1886	C.R. Watrous	Nutcracker
Des. 17,446	July 12, 1887	A.D. Judd	Nut-cracker
397,023	Jan. 29, 1889	F. J. Rabbeth	Nutcracker
Des. 18,888	Jan. 29, 1889	H.M. Quackenbush	Nut-cracker
404,016	May 28, 1889	H.M. Quackenbush	Nutcracker
417,951	Dec. 24, 1889	H. Story	Nutcracker & Pick
425,428	April 15, 1890	T. Holmes	Nutcracker
483,334	Sept. 27, 1892	D.C. Wheeler & W.W. Sperry	Nutcracker
484,049	Oct. 11, 1892	O.H. Robertson	Nutcracker
508,355	Nov. 07, 1893	N.R. Streeter & C. P. Mosher	Nutcracker & Picker
512,818	Jan. 16, 1894	R.C. Hall	Nut-cracker & Pick
522,846	July 10, 1894	S. Moore	Nutcracker
538,717	May 07, 1895	Clark H. Williams	Nutcracking Anvil
Des. 27,093	May 25, 1897	C. Collins	Nutcracker
622,262	April 04, 1899	J. Prode	Nut-cracking Device
627,401	June 20, 1899	W. H. Edwards	Nut-cracker Adjustable
634,518	Oct. 10, 1899	A. Baumgarten	Nut-cracker
641,581	Jan. 16, 1900	L. L. J. Currence	Nut-cracker
660,033	Oct. 16, 1900	E. P. Sedgwick	Nut-cracker
660,762	Oct. 30, 1900	G. L. Thompson	Nut-cracker
660,763	Oct. 30, 1900	G. L. Thompson	Nut-cracker

The above patents exclude nut-cracking machines.

(*) A few design patents also are included, preceded by Des.

(**) No patents were found for nutcrackers between 1790 and 1853; 1790 being the year that patents were first issued in the United States.

UNITED STATES INVENTION (UTILITY) PATENTS FOR NUTCRACKERS
(1853 – 1930)

PATENT NO.	DATE ISSUED	INVENTOR	INVENTION
660,806	Oct. 30, 1900	C.C. Tombs	Nut-cracker
687,896	Dec. 03, 1901	E.W. Murphy	Nut-cracker
696,805	April 01, 1902	W.V. Dickey	Nut-cracker
698,734	April 29, 1902	H.M. Quackenbush	Nut-cracker
699,529	May 06, 1902	J.A. Hutchinson	Nut-cracker
706,179	Aug. 05, 1902	K. Hordish	Nut-cracker
707,997	Aug. 26, 1902	A. Wickstrom	Nut-cracker
718,977	Jan. 27, 1903	H. Budesheim	Nut-cracker
759,033	May 03, 1904	C.E. Smith	Nut-cracker
768,062	Aug. 23, 1904	H.W. Mather	Nut-cracker
788,599	May 02, 1905	D.L.R. Rochlitz	Nut-cracker
827,648	July 31, 1906	J.B.P. Miller	Nut-cracker
851,210	April 23, 1907	M.A. Wheaton	Nut-cracker
888,738	May 26, 1908	F.E. Proctor	Nutcracker
896,044	Aug. 11, 1908	P.H. Quackenbush	Nutcracker
928,958	July 27, 1909	H.R. Gilson	Nut-cracking Mechanism
930,796	Aug. 10, 1909	H.M. Quackenbush	Nut-cracker
931,562	Aug. 17, 1909	W.M. Burkle	
947,932	Feb. 01, 1910	S.C. Peckham	Nutcracker
951,016	Mar. 01, 1910	A. Loock	Nut-cutter
956,555	May 03, 1910	H. I. Weed	Nut-cracker, Edible
964,259	July 12, 1910	A. Huberth	Nutcracker
964,414	July 12, 1910	F.W. Fort & H.T. Cruger	Nutcracker
1,003,917	Sept. 19, 1911	A. Konarski	Nutcracker
1,005,692	Oct. 10, 1911	K. Chmurowicz	Nutcracking Device
1,013,168	Jan. 02, 1912	T. Jankosky	Nut-cracking Device
Des. 42,143	Feb. 06, 1912	A.L. Mordt	Nutcracker
Des. 42,144	Feb. 06, 1912	A.L. Mordt	Nutcracker
1,017,424	Feb. 13, 1912	W. Kwiatkosky	Nutcracker
1,030,805	June 25, 1912	A.M. Carlsen	Nutcracker
1,033,487	July 23, 1912	J. Stugner	Nutcracker
1,037,966	Sept. 10, 1912	F.W. Moser	Nutcracker
1,038,873	Sept. 17, 1912	M. Golek	Nut-cracking Device
1,041,531	Oct. 15, 1912	J. Wackowiez	Nut-cracking Device
1,044,448	Nov. 12, 1912	S. Flis	Nutcracker
1,049,183	Dec. 31, 1912	H.C. White	Nut-cracking Device
1,052,663	Feb. 11, 1913	I.F. Harris	Nutcracker
1,052,926	Feb. 11, 1913	F. Kogut	Nut-cracking Device
1,061,470	May 13, 1913	W.N. Gradick	Nutcracker
1,073,694	Sept. 23, 1913	M. Love	Nut-cracking Mechanism
1,087,617	Feb. 17, 1914	R.A.K. Traber	Nutcracker
1,093,549	April 14, 1914	M. Dolerga	Nutcracker
1,094,698	April 28, 1914	E.A. Bostrom	Nutcracker
1,097,773	May 26, 1914	L.M. Sawin	Nutcracker
1,099,996	June 16, 1914	R.A. Parsons	Nut-cracking Device
1,107,288	Aug. 18, 1914	M.M. Gillam	Nut-cracking Device
1,108,920	Sept. 01, 1914	F.B. May	Nutcracker
1,110,747	Sept. 15, 1914	E. Dato	Nutcracker
1,117,726	Nov. 17, 1914	J. Varga	Nutcracker
1,117,945	Nov. 17, 1914	F.W. Fort	Nutcracker
1,123,852	Jan. 05, 1915	L. Costa	Nutcracker
1,129,213	Feb. 23, 1915	G.K. McEwen	Nutcracker
1,134,265	April 06, 1915	J. M. Harper	Nutcracker
1,146,683	July 13, 1915	W. H. Bagby	Nutcracker

UNITED STATES INVENTION (UTILITY) PATENTS FOR NUTCRACKERS
(1853 – 1930)

PATENT NO.	DATE ISSUED	INVENTOR	INVENTION
1,148,893	Aug. 03, 1915	E.D. Ekstedt	Nutcracker
1,151,110	Aug. 24, 1915	W.O. McDaniel	Nutcracker
1,153,433	Sept. 14, 1915	J. Kittrell	Nutcracker
1,176,639	Mar. 21, 1916	W.H. Bagby	Nutcracker
1,192,846	Aug. 01, 1916	C.T. Boyer	Nutcracker
1,194,318	Aug. 08, 1916	J. Power	Nutcracker
1,194,592	Aug. 15, 1916	W.E. Blair	Nutcracker
1,194,837	Aug. 15, 1916	T. Hachmann	Nutcracker
1,201,953	Oct. 17, 1916	F.W. Fort	Nutcracker
1,202,830	Oct. 31, 1916	A. Goldsmith	Nutcracker
1,202,992	Oct. 31, 1916	F.C. Goff	Nut-cracking Device
1,203,086	Oct. 31, 1916	C.J.E. Watson	Nutcracker
1,210,414	Jan. 02, 1917	F.J. Burkhardt	Nut-cracking Device
1,219,830	Mar. 20, 1917	C. Marsh	Nutcracker
1,219,859	Mar. 20, 1917	A.G. Paxton	Nutcracker
1,222,330	April 10, 1917	H.J. Sauvage	Nutcracker
1,225,484	May 08, 1917	W.J. Payne	Nutcracker
Des. 51,071	July 24, 1917	A.H. Kolker	Nut-Bowl
1,235,246	July 31, 1917	F.K. Russell	Nut-cracking Mechanism
1,242,436	Oct. 09, 1917	T.P. Greenshaw	Nutcracker
1,243,121	Oct. 16, 1917	G. A. Willis	Nutcracker
1,246,397	Nov. 13, 1917	F. B. Deming	Nutcracker
1,248,313	Nov. 27, 1917	W. Gradick, Sr.	Nutcracker
1,254,119	Jan. 22, 1918	Z. J. Chamberlain & F. Low	Nutcracker
1,255,808	Feb. 05, 1918	J.H. Spencer	Nutcracker
1,268,484	June 04, 1918	J. Olasz	Nutcracker
1,272,803	July 16, 1918	F. Hayes & C. Rupp	Nutcracker
1,274,856	Aug. 06, 1918	F.B. Cook	Nutcracker
1,282,278	Oct. 22, 1918	F.A. Neumann	Nutcracker
1,289,351	Dec. 31, 1918	R.C. Abt	Nutcracker
1,312,149	Aug. 05, 1919	F. Zaljs	Nutcracker
Des. 53,711	Aug. 19, 1919	J.S. Kepler & M.O. Kepler	Combination Nut Bowl & Cracker
Des. 53,712	Aug. 19, 1919	J.S. Kepler & M.O. Kepler	Combination Nut Bowl & Cracker
Des. 53,713	Aug. 19, 1919	J.S. Kepler & M.O. Kepler	Nutcracker
1,315,557	Sept. 09, 1919	J.S. & M.O. Kepler	Nutcracker
1,318,182	Oct. 07, 1919	C.J. Schiemer	Nutcracker
1,322,393	Nov. 18, 1919	W.H. Bagby	Nutcracker
1,331,351	Feb. 17, 1920	M.L. Minor	Nutcracker
Des. 55,460	June 15, 1920	A. W. Geigand, J. J. Geigand	Nutcracker
1,344,731	June 29, 1920	C. Smith	Nutcracker
1,351,983	Sept. 07, 1920	S.L. Allen, Dec'd.	Nutcracker
1,357,472	Nov. 02, 1920	M.R. Randall	Nutcracker
1,367,384	Feb. 01, 1921	T. Harrison	Nutcracker
1,370,137	Mar. 01, 1921	A. Lopes	Nutcracker
1,388,071	Aug. 16, 1921	S.G. Simons	Nutcracker
1,391,751	Sept. 27, 1921	H. C. Atwood	Nutcracker, Hand
1,400,099	Dec. 13, 1921	G. A. Pueppke	Nut-cracking Device
Des. 60,394	Feb. 14, 1922	F. C. Baker	Combined Nutcracker & Bowl
1,412,249	April 11, 1922	H. W. McClung	Nutcracker
1,415,338	May 09, 1922	A. C. Guhl	Nutcracker
1,417,272	May 23, 1922	A. R. Maness	Nutcracker
1,420,263	June 20, 1922	I. Isaachsen	Nutcracker
1,429,444	Sept. 19, 1922	B. L. Mallory	Nut Bowl & Cracker
1,436,571	Nov. 21, 1922	G. Bokor	Nutcracker

UNITED STATES INVENTION (UTILITY) PATENTS FOR NUTCRACKERS
(1853 – 1930)

PATENT NO.	DATE ISSUED	INVENTOR	INVENTION
1,437,860	Dec. 05, 1922	H. M. Pitman	Nutcracker
Des. 61,801	Jan. 16, 1923	J. L. Emery	Nutcracker
1,445,532	Feb. 13, 1923	L. B. Merriam	Nutcracker
1,526,593	Feb. 17, 1925	M. French	Nutcracker
1,526,656	Feb. 17, 1925	V. G. Apple	Nutcracker
1,543,797	June 30, 1925	J. Sciortino	Nutcracker
1,555,518	Sept. 29, 1925	B. S. Romey	Nutcracker
1,556,424	Oct. 06, 1925	F. B. Cook	Nutcracker
1,560,349	Nov. 03, 1925	J. W. Schweitzer	Nutcracker
1,567,884	Dec. 29, 1925	A. Woldert	Nutcracker
1,591,251	July 06, 1926	R. E. Vaughn	Nutcracker, Hand
1,598,490	Aug. 31, 1926	K. M. Miller	Nutcracker
1,626,905	May 03, 1927	L. R. Zifferer	Nutcracker
1,647,029	Oct. 25, 1927	W. T. Williams	Nutcracker
1,649,468	Nov. 15, 1927	I. H. Greene	Nutcracker
1,650,681	Nov. 29, 1927	W. T. Anderson	Nutcracker
1,665,557	April 10, 1928	J. F. Miller	Nut Cracker
1,682,681	Aug. 28, 1928	F. E. Modlin	Nutcracker
1,698,620	Jan. 08, 1929	C. D. Clark	Nutcracker
Des. 77,734	Feb. 19, 1929	L. Bemelmans	Nutcracker
1,710,629	April 23, 1929	W. M. S. Lindsey	Nutcracker
1,720,575	July 09, 1929	John W. Smith	Nut Sheller
1,724,049	Aug. 13, 1929	B. D. Smith	Nutcracker
1,743,449	Jan. 14, 1930	R. C. Goodell	Nutcracker
1,762,573	June 10, 1930	R. E. DeGolyer	Nutcracker
1,764,238	June 17, 1930	A. E. Ashlemon	Nutcracker
1,767,917	June 24, 1930	A. Demek	Nutcracker
1,785,328	Dec. 16, 1930	C. B. Repp	Nut Cracker

Annual Report Of The Commission Of Patents For The Year _____
  Washington, Goverment Printing Office

Compiled and published under the direction of M. D. Leggett, Commissioner of Patents,
  Washington, GPO, 1874, Reprint 1976 by Arno Press Inc.

Subject - Matter Index of Patents for Inventions,
  Issued By The United States Patent Office from 1790 to 1873, Inclusive, Volume II.

BIBLIOGRAPHY

Adburgham, Alison, introduced by
Very Best English Goods.
New York and Washington: Frederick A. Praeger, Pub., 1969.

Althoff, K.W.
The Legend of the Nutcracker and Traditions of the Erzgebirge.
Cannon Falls, Minnesota: Midwest Importers, Inc., 1989.

Ames, Alex.
Collecting Cast Iron.
Ashbourne, Derbyshire, England: Moorland Publishing, 1980.

Annual Reports of the Commission of Patents.
Washington: Government Printing Office, 1874–1930.

Arthur, Eric and Thomas Ritchie.
Iron: Cast and Wrought Iron in Canada from the Seventeenth Century to the Present.
Toronto, Buffalo and London: University of Toronto Press, 1982.

Ayres, James.
British Folk Art.
Woodstock, New York: The Overlook Press, 1977.

Baring-Gould, S.
A Book of Dartmoor.
New York: New Amsterdam Book Co., 1990.

Barton, Wayne.
Chip Carving Techniques and Patterns.
New York: Sterling Publishing Co., Inc., 1984.

Bishop, Robert.
American Folk Sculpture.
New York: E. P. Dutton & Co., Inc., 1974.
The Knopf Collectors Guide to American Antiques. New York: Alfred A. Knopf, 1983.

Boehm, Klaus and Aubrey Silberston.
The British Patent System.
Cambridge: The University Press, 1967.

Bridgewater, Alan and Gill.
The Craft of Wood Carving.
New York: Arco Publishing, Inc., 1981.

Burgess, Fred W.
Chats on Old Copper and Brass.
New York: Frederick A. Stokes Company, 1914.

Butturini, Paula.
"A German Tradition of Fun with Wood."
The New York Times, Sunday, December 1, 1991.

Card, Devere A.
The Use of Burl in America.
Utica, New York: Munson-Williams – Proctor Institute, 1971.

Carter, Michael, ed.
The Encyclopedia of Popular Antiques.
London: Octopus Books Limited, 1980.

Celehar, Jane H.
Kitchens and Gadgets – 1920 to 1950.
Des Moines, Iowa: Wallace Homestead, 1982.
Kitchens and Kitchenware.
Lombard, Illinois: Wallace Homestead, 1985.

Chappell, Warren.
The Nutcracker, adapted and illustrated.
New York: Alfred A. Knopf, 1958.

Christensen, Erwin O.
Index of American Design. New York: MacMillan, 1950.
Early American Wood Carving.
New York: Dover Publications, Inc., 1952.

Clayton, Michael.
The Collector's Dictionary of the Silver and Gold of Great Britain and North America.
New York: The World Publishing Company, 1971.

Colliers Encyclopedia. William D. Halsey, Ed. Dir.
New York: MacMillan Educational Company, 1986.

Comstock, Helen.
The Concise Encyclopedia of American Antiques, Vol. II, 1st Ed.
New York: Hawthorne Books, Inc.

Coomaraswamy, Amandak.
Arts and Crafts of India and Ceylon.
London and Edinburgh: T. N. Foulis, 1913.

Coysh, A. W.
  Don't Throw It Away.
    Newton Abbot London: David & Charles, 1977.

" 'Crackin' ' Good Nutcrackers!"
  D. Branch, Ill. *Organic Gardening* 27:117– 23 D 80.

*The Culture of Tambula: Betel Boxes, Lime Containers
  and Nut-crackers (in the Kelkar Museum, Poona, India).*
    J. Jain. bibl. f il Marg 31: 84– 92 Je 78.

Curtis, Anthony.
  The Lyle Price Guide to Collectibles and Memorabilia.
    Glenmayne, Galashiels, Scotland: Lyle Publications, 1988.

Curtis, Tony, ed.
  Kitchen Equipment, Antiques and Their Values.
    Lyle Publications, 1977.

D'Allemagne, Henry René.
  Decorative Antique Ironwork.
    New York: Dover Publications, Inc., 1968.

de Jonge, Eric (Ed.)
  Country Things From the Pages of the Magazine Antiques.
    New York: Weathervane Books.

"Des casse-noisettes figuratifs"
  F. Duret-Robert, il (pt. col.) *Connaisssance des Arts*, no.
    388:60 Je 84.

De Sanctis, Paolo and Maurizio Fantoni.
  Schiaccianoci (Nutcrackers), Milan: Be-Ma Editrice, 1990.

Dible, Donald M.
  *What Everybody Should Know About Patents, Trademarks
  and Copyrights.*
    The Entrepreneur Press, 1978.

"Discovering Antiques"
  The Story of World Antiques.
    New York: Greystone Press, Vol. 4, 1973.

Dorn, Sylvia O'Neill.
  The Insiders Guide To Antiques, Art and Collectibles.
    Garden City, New York: Doubleday & Company, Inc., 1974.

Drepperd, Carl W. and Marjorie Matthews Smith.
  Handbook of Tomorrow's Antiques.
    New York: Thomas Y. Crowell Company, 1953.

Drepperd, Carl W.
  Victorian, The Cinderella of Antiques.
    Garden City, New York: Doubleday & Company, Inc., 1950.
  Pioneer America, Its First Three Centuries.
    Garden City, New York: Doubleday & Company, Inc., 1949.

Eberlein, Harold Donaldson and Abbot McClure.
  The Practical Book of American Antiques.
    Philadelphia: J. B. Lippincott, 1927.

Encyclopedia Americana.
  Danbury, Connecticut: Grolier Incorporated, 1988.

Encyclopedia Britannica.
  Chicago: William Benton, Pub., 1970.

Evan-Thomas, Owen.
  *Domestic Utensils of Wood from the Sixteenth to the
  Nineteenth Century.*
    London: Owen Evan-Thomas Ltd., 1932.

Forty, Anne.
  Treen and Earthenware.
    Tunbridge Wells, Kent: Midas Books, 1979.

Franklin, Linda Campbell.
  *America in the Kitchen, from Hearth to Cookstove,
    An American Domestic History of Gadgets and Utensils
    Made or Used in America From 1790 to 1930.*
      Florence, Alabama: House of Collectibles, Inc. 1974 &
      Rev. 1976.
  300 Years of Kitchen Collectibles, 2nd Ed.
    Florence, Alabama: Books Americana, Inc., 1984.

Franks, T. Q.
  "The Quest of the Knocker."
    Country Life in America, 1911.

Gentle, Rupert and Rachel Feild.
  English Domestic Brass.
    New York: E. P. Dutton & Co., Inc., 1975.

Gould, Mary Earle.
  Early American Wooden Ware and Other Kitchen Utensils.
    Springfield, Massachusetts: The Pond-Ekberg Company,
    1942.

Grober, Karl.
  Alte Oberammergauer Hauskunst.
    Augsburg: Dr. Benno Filser Verlag G.M.B.H., 1930.

"Grotesque Figures Crack Nuts."
  K. Keith, *Popular Mechanics,* Dec. 1930.

"Hal Davis' Nutcracker Suite"
  G. Ziemer. *American Collector,* 7– 9 Dec 75.

Hamburg, Marilyn G. and Beverly S. Lloyd.
  Collecting Figural Doorstops.
    New York: A. S. Barnes and Company, 1978.

Hansen, H. J., ed.
  European Folk Art in Europe and the Americas.
    New York: McGraw Hill Book Company, 1967.

Heynold-Graefe, Blida.
  Oberammergauer Schnitzkunst.
    München: Deutsches Verlagshaus Bong, 1950.

Hillier, Bevis.
  The Simon and Schuster Pocket Guide to Antiques.
    New York: Simon and Schuster, 1981.

Hoppe, H.
  Whittling and Wood Carving.
    New York: Sterling Publishing Co., Inc., 1969.
Hornung, Clarence P.
  A Source Book of Antiques and Jewelry Designs.
    New York: George Braziller, 1968.
  Treasury of American Design.
    New York: Harry N. Abrams, Inc.

Hudgeons, Thomas E. III, ed.
  *The Official 1983 Price Guide to American Silver and
  Silver Plate,* 3rd Ed.
    Orlando, Florida: The House of Collectibles, Inc., 1982.
  *The Official 1984 Price Guide to American Silver and
  Silver Plate,* 3rd Ed.
    Orlando, Florida: The House of Collectibles, Inc., 1983.

Hughes, G. Bernard.
  Sheffield Silver Plate.
    New York: Praeger Publishers, 1970.

Hughes, Therle.
  Cottage Antiques.
    New York: Frederick A. Praeger, 1967.

Huxford, Sharon and Bob.
  Schroeder's Antiques Price Guide.
    Paducah, Kentucky: Collector Books, 1991.

Ickis, Marguerite.
  Pastimes for the Patient. rev.ed.
    New York: A. S. Barnes and Co., Inc., 1945 and 1966.

Jackson, Albert and David Day.
  The Antiques Care and Repair Handbook.
    New York: Alfred A. Knopf, 1984.

James, E. O.
  Seasonal Feasts and Festivals.
    New York: Barnes & Noble, Inc., 1961.

Johnson, Hugh, foreword by
  The International Book of Wood.
    New York: Crescent Books, 1984 and 1987.

Kauffman, Henry.
  Pennsvlvania Dutch American Folk Art.
    New York: Dover Publications, Inc., 1946 and 1964.

Ketchum, William C., Jr.
  Collecting American Craft Antiques.
    New York: E. P. Dutton, 1980.
  The New York and Revised Catalog of American Antiques.
    New York: Gallery Books, 1980.
  American Basketry and Woodenware.
    New York: Macmillan Publishing Co., Inc., 1974.

Kinard, Epsie.
  The Care and Keeping of Antiques.
    New York: Hawthorn Books, Inc., 1971.

Klamkin, Marian and Charles Klamkin.
  Wood Carving, North American Folk Sculpture.
    New York: Hawthorn Books, Inc., 1974.

Kovel, Ralph and Terry.
  Know Your Antiques.
    New York: Crown Publishers, Inc., 1967 and 1973.
  The Kovel's Antiques Price List, 14th Ed.
    New York: Crown Publishers, Inc., 1981.
  The Kovel's Antiques Price List, 15th Ed.
    New York: Crown Publishers, Inc., 1982.
  The Kovel's Antiques and Collectibles Price List 1989, 21st Ed.
    New York: Crown Publishers, Inc., 1988.

Knopf, Alfred A.
  The Knopf Collector's Guide to American Antiques.
    New York: Alfred A. Knopf, 1983.

Lantz, Louise K.
  Old American Kitchenware 1725–1925.
    Camden, New York: Thomas Nelson Inc. and
    Hanover, Pennsylvania: Everybody's Press, 1971.

Leggett, M.D., Comp.
  *Subject-Matter Index of Patents For Inventions Issued By The
  United States Patent Office from 1790 to 1873 Inclusive.*
    Washington, D.C.: Government Printing Office, 1874. Vol
    II., Reprint Edition. New York: Arnce Press Inc., 1976.

Lichten, Frances.
  Folk Art of Rural Pennsylvania.
    New York: Charles Scribner's Sons, and London:
    Charles Scribner's Sons, Ltd., 1946.

Lindsay, J. Seymour.
  Iron and Brass Implements of the English and American House.
    Deer River, Connecticut: Carl Jacobs, 1964.

Lipman, Jean and Alice Winchester.
  The Flowering of American Folk Art (1776–1876).
    New York: The Viking Press, 1974.

Little, Nina Fletcher.
  Country Arts In Early American Homes.
    New York: E. P. Dutton & Co., Inc., 1975.

Marion, John L., ed.
  Sotheby's International Price Guide, 1986–1987 Ed.
    New York: The Vendome Press, 1986.

Marshall, Jo.
  Collecting For Tomorrow - Kitchenware.
    Radnor, Pennsylvania: Chilton Book Company, 1976.

McClinton, Katharine Morrison.
  Antiques Past and Present.
    New York: Clarkson, N. Potter, Inc., 1971.

McNerney, Kathryn.
  Antique Iron Identification and Values.
    Paducah, Kentucky: Collector Books, 1984.

Mebane, John.
  Treasure At Home.
    New York: A. S. Barnes & Company, Inc., 1964.
  The Poor Man's Guide To Antiques Collecting.
    Garden City, New York: Doubleday & Company, Inc., 1969.
  What's New That's Old.
    South Brunswick and New York: A. S. Barnes & Company,
    Inc., 1969.

Michaelis, Ronald F.
  Antique Pewter of the British Isles.
    New York: Dover Publications, Inc., 1971.

Mills, John Fitzmaurice.
  The Care of Antiques.
    New York: Hastings House, Publishers, 1964.

Miniter, Edith.
  "When treen ware was The Ware." *Antiques,* 18:504-7 D'30.

Montgomery, Charles F.
  A History of American Pewter.
    New York: E. P. Dutton, 1973.

The New Lexicon Webster's Dictionary of the English Language.
  Encyclopedia Edition.
    New York: Lexicon Publications, Inc., 1989.

Newby, Frank.
  How to Find Out About Patents.
    Oxford: Pergamon Press, 1967.

Newman, Harold.
  An Illustrated Dictionary of Silverware.
    London: Thames and Hudson, Ltd., 1987.

Norwak, Mary.
  Kitchen Antiques.
    New York: Praeger Publishers, 1975.

"Nutcracker and Pick."
  B. Betensley. *Illustrated Hobbies,* 86:102 J 82.

"Nutcrackers."
  Early American Life, M. Handler. Dec. 1990.

Osburn, Burl N. and Gordon O. Wilber.
  Pewter Spun, Wrought and Cast.
    Scranton, Pennsylvania: International Textbook Company:
    1938.

Oughton, Frederick.
  The History and Practice of Woodcarving.
    London: Allman & Son, Ltd., 1969.

Owen, Francis C.
  Nuts and Their Uses.
    Dansville, New York: F. A. Owen Publishing Company, 1928.

"Patent Penning: Changing patent laws can make research
  difficult."
    G. McAndrews. *Antique Week,* Eastern Edition. Vol. 23, No.
    14 (Whole 1113), 1990.

Perry, Evan.
  Collecting Antique Metalware.
    Garden City, New York: Doubleday & Company, Inc., 1974.

Peters, Geoff.
  Woodturning.
    New York: ARC Books, Inc., 1961.

Peterson, Harold L.
  How Do You Know It's Old.
    New York: Charles Scribner's Sons, 1975.

Pfeiffer, Christine.
  Germany – Two Nations, One Heritage.
    Minneapolis, Minnesota: Dillon, Press, Inc., 1987.

Phipps, Frances.
  The Collector's Complete Dictionary of American Antiques.
    Garden City, New York: Doubleday & Company, Inc., 1974.

Pile, John.
  Dictionary of 20th Century Design.
    New York: A Roundtable Press Book, 1990.

"The Pinto collection of wooden bygones."
  E. H. and E. R. Pinto. *Antiques,* M. 57, P.458.

Pinto, Edward H.
  Treen or Small Woodenware Throughout the Ages.
    London: B. T. Batsford, Ltd., 1949.
  Treen and Other Wooden Bygones.
    London: G. Bell & Sons, 1969.

"Nutcrackers for a Tough Nut to Crack."
  Poese, Bill. Dubuque, Iowa: *The Antique Trader Weekly,
    Annual of Articles on Antiques.* Babka Publishing Co., Inc. 1973.

Raycraft, Don and Carol.
  The Collector's Guide to Kitchen Antiques.
    Paducah, Kentucky: Collector Books.

Revi, Albert Christian, ed.
  The Spinning Wheel's Complete Book of Antiques.
    New York: Grosset and Dunlap, 1949.
  Spinning Wheel's Antiques for Men.
    Castle Books and Hanover, Pennsylvania: Everybody's Press,
    1974.

Rinker, Harry L., ed.
  Warman's, 16th Ed.
    Elkins Park, Pennsylvania: Warman Publishing Co., Inc., 1982.
  Warman's Americana & Collectibles, 4th Ed.
    Radnor, Pennyslvania: Wallace-Homestead Book Company, 1990.

Riotte, Louise.
  Nuts for the Food Gardener.
    Garden Way Publishing: 1975.

Root, Waverly.
Food.
New York: Simon & Schuster, 1980.

Saylor, Henry H., ed.
Collecting Antiques for the Home.
New York: Robert M. McBride and Company, 1938.

Schiffer, Peter, Nancy & Herbert.
The Brass Book: American, English and European Fifteenth Century through 1850.
Exton, Pennsylvania: Schiffer Publishing, 1978.

Schroeder, Joseph J., ed.
Sears, Roebuck and Co. Consumers Guide Fall 1900.
Northfield, Ill.: DBI Books, Inc., 1970.

Schubach, Manfred.
The Nutcracker Collector's Guide.
1987.

Schulberg, Lucille and The Editors of Time-Life Books.
Historic India.
New York: Time-Life Books, 1968.

"The Scope of Wooden Ware and the Part It Played in History."
M. E. Gould. *Old Time New England* V. 35, p. 21–27.

"Serving As An Art."
Victoria, Oct. 1988.

Sprackling, Helen.
Customs On the Table Top.
Sturbridge, Mass: Old Sturbridge Village, 1958.

Steinbach, Christian.
Steinbach GMBH.
Hohenhameln, W. Germany: Vertrantes und Neues, 1990.

Strong, Roy, introduced by
The Random House Collector's Encyclopedia - Victoriana to Art Deco.
New York: Random House, 1974.

Switzer, Ellen.
The Nutcracker, A Story and A Ballet.
New York: Atheneum, 1985.

Tangerman, E. J.
Carving Flora and Fables In Wood.
New York: Sterling Publishing Co., Inc., 1981.
Carving Wooden Animals.
New York: Sterling Publishing Co., Inc., 1980.
The Modern Book of Whittling and Woodcarving.
New York: McGraw-Hill Book Company, 1973.
Whittling and Woodcarving.
New York: Dover Publications, Inc., 1962.

Tannahill, Reay.
Food in History.
New York: Crown Publishers, Inc., 1988.

Thuro, Catherine.
Primitives and Folk Art, Our Handmade Heritage.
Paducah, Kentucky: Collector Books, 1979.

Toller, Jane.
Turned Woodware For Collectors, Treen and Other Objects.
South Brunswick and New York: A. S. Barnes and Company, 1975.
Discovering Antiques – Where to Look, What to Look For, How to Restore.
New York: A. S. Barnes and Company, 1975.

Tunis, Edwin.
Colonial Craftsmen And the Beginnings of American Industry.
New York: Thomas Y. Crowell Company, 1965.

Turner, Noel D.
American Silver Flatware 1837–1910.
New York: A. S. Barnes and Company, 1972.

Turner, Pearl.
Collector's Index.
Westwood, Mass.: F. W. Faxon Company, Inc., 1980.

Vaughn, Floyd L.
The United States Patent System.
Norman, Oklahoma: University of Oklahoma Press, 1956.

Walther, K. Dr., and Zwonitz/M Biechschmidt,
Aue Erzgebirgische Volkskunst.
Das Erzgebirge und seine Volkskunst produktion.
Olbernhau: R. Steinert.

Warman, P. J.
Antiques and Their Prices, 15th Ed.
Uniontown, Pennsylvania:
E. G. Warman Publishing Co., Inc., 1980.

"Wooden Nutcrackers – Not Just for Christmas and Not Just for Nuts."
P. Derus, *The Antique Trader Weekly,* Babka Publishing, Nov. 28, 1990.

"Wooden Soldiers Called Out of Step With the Holidays."
T. Aeppel, *The Wall Street Journal.*
Dow Jones & Company, Inc., Dec. 24, 1991.

"Five Million Non-Ivory Buttons,"
World Monitor, April 1991.

VALUE GUIDE

PAGE 6
PLATE 1
Black cast iron dog $65.00–85.00
Black cast iron squirrel .... reproduction $15.00–20.00
                                                original $30.00-40.00

PAGE 7
PLATE 2
Wooden squirrel w/reddish stain $45.00–55.00
Black cast iron squirrel $35.00–45.00
Gold-painted cast iron squirrel $300.00–350.00
Brown-painted cast iron squirrel $35.00–45.00
Brass-plated cast iron squirrel $250.00–300.00
Brass squirrel seated on branch $35.00–40.00
Brass squirrel on branch $45.00–55.00

PAGE 8
PLATE 3
Wooden sitting bear $175.00–200.00

PAGE 9
PLATE 4
Non-figural steel nutcracker, small $8.00–10.00
Non-figural steel nutcracker, large $12.00–15.00

PAGE 11
PLATE 5
Brazil nut pods..each $10.00–20.00
PLATE 6
"The Nuts," grouping of nuts $10.00–20.00

PAGE 12
PLATE 7
Quackenbush screw-type nutcracker,
        reproduction $4.00–6.00
        original $15.00–20.00

PAGE 13
PLATE 8
Nickel-plated, cast iron squirrel hammer $30.00–40.00
Silverplated brass hammer
        w/walnut-shaped base $125.00–150.00

PAGE 18
PLATE 9
Wooden double-figure nutcracker $1,200.00–1,500.00

PAGE 21
PLATE 11
Wooden eagle nutcracker.............................$125.00–150.00
PLATE 12
Wooden nutcracker, bearded man w/hat $150.00–175.00
Wooden nutcracker, man w/stocking cap ...$150.00–175.00

PAGE 22
PLATE 13
Wooden lion...$150.00–175.00
Wooden antelope $175.00–200.00
Wooden ram $200.00–225.00
PLATE 14
Wooden folk art head $1,200.00–1,500.00

PAGE 24
PLATE 15
Milford Saint Nicholas nutcracker $175.00–225.00

PAGE 25
PLATE 16
Standing peasant nutcracker w/tray $200.00–225.00

PAGE 26
PLATE 18
Wood carving, squirrel w/nutcracker $30.00–40.00

PAGE 28
PLATE 19
Painted cast iron nutcracker,
        man in red coat $400.00–450.00
Painted cast iron nutcracker, elf w/beard $400.00–425.00
Painted cast iron nutcracker, black man $400.00–450.00
PLATE 20
Wooden dog, knotty pine............................$175.00–200.00
Cast iron dog, painted green $90.00–110.00
Copper-plated cast iron dog $150.00–200.00
Brass dog face nutcracker $70.00–90.00

PAGE 29
PLATE 21
Porcelain enamel-plated cast iron dog $250.00–275.00

PAGE 30
PLATE 22
Painted cast iron alligator, small, marked w/"T" ..$40.00–50.00
Copper-plated brass crocodile, large $125.00–150.00

Painted cast iron alligator, large $100.00–125.00
Aluminum crocodile $40.00–50.00
Nickel-plated alligator, small $30.00–35.00
Brass alligator, small $20.00–35.00

PAGE 31
PLATE 23
Cast iron dragon nutcracker........................$275.00–350.00
Nickel-plated cast iron fish nutcracker $150.00–175.00
PLATE 24
Cast iron horse nutcracker, copper-plated ..$150.00–175.00

PAGE 32
PLATE 25
Skull & cross bones nutcracker $80.00–100.00
Cast iron painted clown nutcracker $40.00–50.00
PLATE 26
Wrought iron frog nutcracker $250.00–300.00
PLATE 27
Hand-finished cast steel bird $150.00–165.00

PAGE 34
PLATE 28
Brass Shakespeare nutcracker.........................$85.00–110.00
Brass Fagin/Bill Sikes nutcracker $50.00–75.00

PAGE 35
PLATE 29
Brass full-length cat nutcracker.......................$65.00–75.00
Brass grandfather's clock nutcracker $65.00–75.00
Brass cat w/bow nutcracker $70.00–80.00
PLATE 30
Brass double-faced clown nutcracker $75.00–85.00
Brass lion w/crown nutcracker $65.00–70.00
Brass devil or horned monkey nutcracker $65.00–75.00

PAGE 36
PLATE 31
Hand-wrought brass whale nutcracker $110.00–125.00

PAGE 37
PLATE 32
Pair of brass eagle nutcrackers, each $30.00–35.00
Pair of brass rooster nutcrackers, each $30.00–35.00
PLATE 33
Copper-plated cast iron elf $75.00–85.00
Painted wooden elf w/red stocking cap $50.00–75.00
Brass elf w/stocking cap $60.00–80.00

PAGE 38
PLATE 34
Rhodium-plated cast iron dog, small...............$65.00–85.00
Cast iron dog w/red paint traces, small $60.00–75.00
Brass dog, small..$60.00–75.00

PAGE 39
PLATE 35
Double-faced brass jester, large $80.00–100.00
Double-faced brass jester, small $65.00–85.00
PLATE 36
Brass figural nutcracker in leather case $100.00–125.00

PAGE 40
PLATE 37
Brass standing horse nutcracker $50.00–70.00
Brass running horse & jockey nutcracker........$50.00–70.00
PLATE 38
Brass monkey caricature nutcracker $70.00–80.00

PAGE 42
PLATE 39
Silverplated non-figural nutcracker $20.00–25.00
Silverplated non-figural nutcracker
    w/decorative handles $35.00–40.00

PAGE 44
PLATE 40
Copper-plated bronze striding dog $200.00–225.00
Bronze squirrel nutcracker $175.00–200.00

PAGE 47
PLATE 41
Wooden soldier nutcracker $10.00–15.00
Wooden soldier/king $15.00–20.00
PLATE 42
Silhouette, young girl & nutcracker $35.00–45.00
PLATE 43
Toy soldier ornaments $5.00–10.00
Football player ornament $10.00–12.00

PAGE 49
PLATE 44
Aluminum Miller Cracker $25.00–35.00

PAGE 50
PLATE 45
Wooden nut bowl w/mallet $35.00–45.00
Wooden nut bowl & metal cracker................$35.00–50.00

PAGE 51
PLATE 46
Brass mermaid nutcracker $100.00–125.00

PAGE 52
PLATE 47
Wooden orange-beaked bird $250.00–300.00
PLATE 48
Brass-plated, cast iron kangaroo $150.00–175.00

PAGE 53
PLATE 49
Painted cast iron elephant nutcracker $275.00–325.00
PLATE 50
Aluminum nut-shaped cracker......................$20.00–35.00

PAGE 54
PLATE 51
"Tough Nut" sailor $650.00–800.00

PAGE 55
PLATE 52
Wooden rabbit head nutcracker $125.00–135.00
Wooden cat head nutcracker $125.00–135.00
PLATE 53
Man w/bowler hat nutcracker, wooden.......$250.00–275.00

Miscellaneous Prices

PAGE	ITEM	DESCRIPTION AND/OR PRICE
28	Intermountain Nutcrackers	General line of nutcrackers (American) – $75.00
28	Christmas Village Nutcrackers	Models 14" tall (American) – $75.00
28	Milford Nutcrackers	Models 12" to 15" tall (American) – $165.00–200.00
45	Recent reproduction, Cockerel Nutcracker	Brass model – $20.00
61	Horchow Toy Soldier Nutcracker	Model 59" tall – $550.00 plus shipping
90	Squirrel Nutcracker on Attached Leaf	Reproduction – $17.00 plus $3.00 postage & handling
101	East German Nutcrackers produced under Communist rule	Sold far below West German prices – $25.00–50.00 (Some as low as $6.50)
107	Silverplated Naughty Nellie Nutcracker	Sold at auction in the 1980s for $357.00

Contemporary German Nutcrackers Manufacturers and Prices

PAGE	ITEM	DESCRIPTION AND/OR PRICE
108	Steinbach	Models 11–15" tall – $110.00–185.00 Smaller King's Court models – $20.00 Limited Edition "Merlin" – $165.00–170.00
109	Otto Ulbricht (no longer in business)	Models 10½" tall – $90.00–100.00
109	Holzkunst – Christian Ulbricht	Models 14–16" tall – $100.00–165.00 10–12" tall – $80.00–95.00 27" tall (e.g. Santa & Toymaker) – $500.00 5'8" tall Toy Maker – $5,000.00
110	Lothar Junghanel	Models are approximately 12" tall – $165.00–185.00
111	Hanno Junghanel	Models 11" tall – $65.00–85.00
111	Günter Ulbricht	Models 13–15" tall – $70.00–80.00
111	Holzkunst Zuber	Models 12–15" – $125.00–135.00 10–11½" tall – $75.00–80.00
112	Volkmar Matthes	Model 30" tall – $500.00 and up
112	Peterson	Model 36" tall – $135.00–200.00

Schroeder's ANTIQUES Price Guide

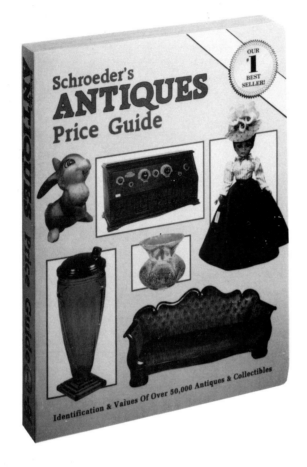

Schroeder's Antiques Price Guide is the #1 best-selling antiques & collectibles value guide on the market today, and here's why . . . More than 300 authors, well-known dealers, and top-notch collectors work together with our editors to bring you accurate information regarding pricing and identification. More than 45,000 items in almost 500 categories are listed along with hundreds of sharp original photos that illustrate not only the rare and unusual, but the common, popular collectibles as well. Each large close-up shot shows important details clearly. Every subject is represented with histories and background information, a feature not found in any of our competitors' publications. Our editors keep abreast of newly-developing trends, often adding several new categories a year as the need arises. If it merits the interest of today's collector, you'll find it in Schroeder's. And you can feel confident that the information we publish is up to date and accurate. Our advisors thoroughly check each category to spot inconsistencies, listings that may not be entirely reflective of market dealings, and lines too vague to be of merit. Only the best of the lot remains for publication. Without doubt, you'll find Schroeder's Antiques Price Guide the only one to buy for reliable information and values.

8½ x 11", 608 Pages   **$12.95**

COLLECTOR BOOKS

A Division of Schroeder Publishing Co., Inc.